Common SENse for the
Inclusive Classroom

of related interest

Count Me In!
Ideas for Actively Engaging Students in Inclusive Classrooms
Richard Rose and Michael Shevlin
Foreword by Paul Cooper
Part of the Innovative Learning for All series
ISBN 978 1 84310 955 6

Asperger Syndrome in the Inclusive Classroom
Advice and Strategies for Teachers
Stacey W. Betts, Dion E. Betts and Lisa N. Gerber-Eckard
Foreword by Peter Riffle
ISBN 978 1 84310 840 5

Addressing the Unproductive Classroom Behaviours
of Students with Special Needs
Steve Chinn
ISBN 978 1 84905 050 0

Making it a Success
Practical Strategies and Worksheets for Teaching
Students with Autism Spectrum Disorder
Sue Larkey
Foreword by Tony Attwood
ISBN 978 1 84310 204 5

Quick, Easy and Effective Behaviour
Management Ideas for the Classroom
Nicola S. Morgan
ISBN 978 1 84310 951 8

Common SENse for the Inclusive Classroom

How Teachers Can Maximise Existing Skills to Support Special Educational Needs

RICHARD HANKS

Jessica Kingsley *Publishers*
London and Philadelphia

First published in 2011
by Jessica Kingsley Publishers
116 Pentonville Road
London N1 9JB, UK
and
400 Market Street, Suite 400
Philadelphia, PA 19106, USA
www.jkp.com

Library of Congress Cataloging in Publication Data
A CIP catalog record for this book is available from the Library of Congress

British Library Cataloguing in Publication Data
A CIP catalogue record for this book is available from the British Library

ISBN 978 1 84905 057 9

Printed and bound in Great Britain by
MPG Books Group

Contents

Author's note

Say it a second time — say it louder — and say it slower.

This was how a teacher colleague summed up her 'special needs' method recently. She said it with half a smile, and half wistfully. Of course, she knew this was not sufficient, but she did not know what else to do. She is actually approaching retirement, but had travelled her whole career with this uncertainty.

As a sincere and committed teacher, undoubtedly she would have tried to support certain of her students in special ways, and no doubt she would have had some success, but always with that underlying feeling of inadequacy, of not feeling she understood the problem, and not knowing how to solve it. Furthermore, her dilemma is getting much worse, as 'inclusion' (which she does not oppose) comes ever more to the fore.

My colleague is a mainstream teacher who loves school life, and contributes mightily to the corporate life of a vibrant school. She loves the hustle and bustle of the many aspects of everyday schooling. She has had no wish to become a special needs specialist, but always there has been that underlying regret that for some students all she can do is, 'Say it again, say it louder, and say it slower.'

This book is written for this colleague — and thousands of others like her.

Preface

In these days of inclusion, whether it be by design, philosophy, accident of timetabling, or staff shortage, virtually all teachers in every school will regularly find in one, some, or all of their classes students (of either sex) who – it becomes apparent sooner or later – are somewhat different from the majority of the class. This may be with regard to either their learning and ability to produce work, their conduct, or their general demeanour.

These students will puzzle and perplex the majority of teachers. Yet, the vast majority of this majority will want to cope with, care for, and provide for these exceptional students, this significant (and, quite possibly, not so silent) minority, in as positive a way as they can. What these teachers will not be, and will probably not want to be, are special needs specialists.

They need something to which they can turn that is really hands-on, not too cumbersome (either physically or intellectually) and is useful to the busy teacher in everyday working life. They need something which will give them the opportunity to handpick and cherrypick some strategies they can optimistically adopt. (The *optimistic* point is an important one: strategies adopted as a belated counsel of despair are probably doomed to failure anyway.) If, as they adopt these strategies, these teachers can be given a framework which will inform their choices (although the choices remain *theirs*) and, also, have a handy reference book explaining in accurate, but jargon-free, terms what might be making these children tick, they will be more than happy to do their best, in ways which are pragmatic and practical, to support these children – and enhance inclusion and differentiation.

This book will help such teachers in the following ways:

- It reverses the usual order of presentation of the contents of books on education. In this book, the practical sections are in the front, and the theoretical part comes after the practical, so that teachers are given something they can see as being of immediate use in their classrooms as soon as they open the book.

- It introduces teachers to the *A La Carte* approach: this is both a concept and a practical way of empowering teachers. It gives them a positive framework in which to think – and something to think about, so that they can quickly arrive at worthwhile strategies.

- The book is to the point (without sacrificing intellectual rigour); it is written as if talking directly to an individual teacher.

- It makes sense to the non-specialist in special needs.

- It combines practical teaching strategies with factual information about the four (probably) most commonly found disabilities in the inclusive classroom.

- It respects teachers, values the skills they have, and encourages them to appreciate that they are more than able to utilise these skills to provide a measure of support to special educational needs (SEN) students.

- The non-specialist SEN teacher will gain in confidence and knowledge, and will be empowered to take positive measures to meet the varied special needs of the modern classroom. They will come to appreciate that they are not helpless, they are not inadequate, and they do not merely have to wait for an expert.

- Teachers will gain a greater understanding of their SEN students in the inclusive classroom, and find practical ways they can support those students without having totally to re-gear their work and organisation.

- In short, they will come to realise that they know more, and can do more, than they hitherto may have appreciated.

- Very importantly, teachers will come to be at ease with themselves about the decisions that they make about how to teach students with a range of special educational needs.

- Additionally, this book will be useful for the trainers of teachers and In-Set, while school governors or governors with responsibility for SEN will find it useful to benchmark the special provision their school is currently making. Parents will find it useful in that it will be comprehensible, and will be shown that measures that do not require rocket science can be put in place to help their children.

Introduction

Common SENse or teaching Granny to suck eggs

This is a practical book for committed teachers in classrooms which, for whatever reason, contain some students who may be regarded as having some degree of 'special needs'. Therefore, it is for thousands of teachers and classrooms across the land. The teachers do not have highly specialised qualifications in 'special education'; they may not have much experience of SEN students.

Not always, but typically, it seems that teachers feel unequal to the task of satisfactorily teaching their SEN students; it may be a characteristic of the profession that teachers lack confidence with such students, and feel inadequate because they think they lack the skills. This is something of a myth to be disproved. Teachers know more than they think they know; the problem is getting them to appreciate this.

A little later on this book, we shall begin to show in more detail how teachers really can at least try in positive and systematic ways to teach these students effectively, but let's just try to get into the right mind-set.

A very good starting principle is that good teaching is good teaching! Although practices may well need to be modified in order to fit the particular bill, good teachers are good teachers, whichever students they are teaching. This is not simplistic; it is true, and needs stating. If teachers grab hold of this notion, they immediately feel more confident in at least attempting to meet those special needs.

Teacher common sense now really comes into play. Clearly, what is needed is a teaching strategy, a method of working, an approach that, within this inclusive classroom, can particularly benefit the SEN students (and, incidentally, probably make life much easier for the teachers).

What is essential is that teaching strategies are 'Thoroughly Thought Through' (the three 'Ts'). Again, it sounds so simple, but thinking about SEN students does require some quality time, and this book will help with that. It does need to be said that working out a decent strategy is unlikely to be done in a hurry, or in a flustered or stressed state – and SEN students can bring those conditions about!

Start by considering the student in the round; the negatives are what teachers wish to change or eliminate, but it is to be hoped that these aspects are not the only facets of the student. That said, place the student as an individual at the heart of your thinking. Then, consider the problem, whether it be behavioural or learning; in fact, do more than 'consider' the problem – identify it precisely. Do this almost in tandem with identifying exactly what you want the outcome to be of whatever strategy you decide to adopt, and be very clear about what you expect as a result of your strategy.

At this point, if you have been having major difficulties in the classroom, either in managing behaviour, or with aspects of the student's learning, you may have to be realistic, and identify only some features, among several, that it will be feasible to change initially. You cannot necessarily do everything at once, at the first stage, and you may have to consider a phased or sequential approach, but be clear about your one or two initial targets.

It is helpful if schools have a culture of removing barriers to learning across the curriculum; if it is absent within the school as a whole, then teachers have to develop it within their own classrooms. In other words, a positive outlook is essential, and teachers must inculcate this into their classroom assistants and technicians, too, if they are lucky enough to have them. Although the going may be tough, and everyone gets 'down' from time to time, a belief that you can make things at least somewhat better (which you can) has to be the foundation for any work, whatever the particular approach, with SEN students.

In the literature, there is reference to the 'moving school' (Ainscow 2001) which is a school that is continually trying to develop and refine its approaches to SEN students; similarly, Ainscow refers to the 'collegiate' approach, and the efficacy of a whole-staff team approach. These factors do make for the ideal climate for teachers in ordinary schools to have the confidence to go about making provision for their SEN students. If these conditions do not exist, teachers have to keep their peckers up, and be 'moving teachers' if they can't be in moving schools.

If they are in the right frame of mind, or can use this book to engender that happy state, teachers will find they know more than enough to choose from the menu of choices that will be laid before them here, and these will go some way to ensure they are providing for their SEN students.

So, we have established that as a class or subject teacher, it is almost inevitable that you will have several students who give you particular cause for concern, either in terms of their poor educational progress or their unwillingness or inability to settle to classroom tasks or routines.

The first step towards supporting these students is to recognise that all teachers experience this (whether or not they are prepared to acknowledge it). However, let us be more positive. In what constructive way can every teacher begin to resolve these situations, particularly without greatly increasing personal stress levels? Take the following analogy:

You are in a favourite restaurant: before you lies the utterly pleasurable experience of choosing a meal from an *A La Carte* menu, which you know from previous experience, will not disappoint. How do you feel? You are relaxed, confident, and away from the hurly-burly. You are in your own time. You have prepared yourself for the evening out. Most important of all, you know that on this menu you will find a selection of dishes that will suit your mood and be exactly what you, and only you, are feeling you would like on this particular occasion.

In this book, there follows a range of menus of different types offering possible options that you may choose from, but, just like choosing from a restaurant menu, the secret of success lies largely in the actual choosing. You do not select from a menu when you are knotted up with problems, or other tasks need completing or require your immediate attention. You take your time, you consider, you reflect, you weigh this dish against that. You may very well discuss the options with the others sitting around the table. You are interested to hear their choices and preferences, and they are interested to hear yours. You may change your mind in the light of what they say; they may change theirs in the light of what you say. You do not rush. You enjoy the experience.

You know that at the end of it you will feel satisfied and contented. That is the way to choose from the educational *A La Carte* in this book.

Do not choose from it immediately after Ryan has got all his spellings wrong yet again, or after Sophie has again refused to do any work, and again muttered about what a waste of time your lessons are. Reflect on the student, the problem, the situation, and what you consider a significant improvement would consist of. Do this later, at leisure, when it suits you.

Relate the menu items to what it is you want to achieve. Choose from it. Choose sparingly: you are not a gannet, but a gourmet. Be happy to discuss with colleagues; encourage them to share their views and experiences. Be happy to talk to the SENCo (the head waiter), but choose what you think will suit you.

Put these measures into operation. Be consistent with the ones you have chosen; use only those. Give them time to work; you cannot enjoy a course of a meal if you do not actually eat it, nor if you rush it.

Bonne appétit!

Chapter 1

&

The *A La Carte* of Classroom Management

Tasters

A little later in following chapters we shall come to specific strategies that have a good chance of being successful with particular students who are showing signs of particular difficulties, and we will relate strategy to student and vice versa, but before we reach those, let's reiterate some good tips that apply to all successful teaching, but which have particular relevance across a range of SENs.

These are our first two *A La Carte* menus. They are samples: items to whet your appetite, and give you a flavour of what's to come. They are not the menus for those rather special occasions but, nonetheless, they contain individual items that teachers may wish to select personally on a regular basis as they think their own teacher metabolism requires, so that they remain healthy practitioners.

The first one relates to teaching and learning, and the second to general classroom management, but with special regard to those times, which we all have, when behaviour problems seem to be developing.

How to read a menu

Starting here, and in considerably more detail later, we begin to peruse menus. Reading is an umbrella term, under which there is a range of sub-skills, such as skimming and scanning. Reading is situation specific, and different types or styles of reading are required for different tasks, such as reading a comic, a novel, a legal document, or an Education

Act. How does one read a menu; what does one bear in mind while doing so?

- Always choose carefully and sparingly (avoid at all costs strategy-obesity), and choose what suits your own palate. There are many dishes or courses throughout this book; no one requires all of them – and certainly not at one time.

- Different teachers, in different situations, will find different strategies useful at different times. We do not expect everybody in our party to choose the same items from a menu.

- The art, and the enjoyment, lies in choosing the items that suit you.

But how does one go about this?

- Calmly!

- Not immediately after a bad lesson (if you ever have such a thing!). The bad lesson may persuade you that you need to do something; it does not mean that you have to do it at that very moment.

- Leave it for a bit. When you are able to consider rationally, possibly when reclining in a favourite armchair, with a G&T or glass of wine to hand, ponder upon what you would like the guy in question (let's call him Alistair) to do that he is currently not doing.

- When the image of a slightly changed Alistair is clear in your mind, scan the menu(s) to see which items might bring this about.

- Select – just one, or two, or three items (strategies).

- Select what suits your own situation.

- Try them. Stick with them. Give them a chance. Be consistent with them. Miracles do happen, but they may not be instantaneous.

- In due time, review the situation (quite possibly again with a G&T or glass of wine close by). Cautiously add to the strategies, or delete some, or replace with some new ones.

Your enjoyment of a great meal in a fine restaurant lies partly in the chef's brilliant cooking, but it lies at least equally in your choosing from the menu exactly what is right for you on this particular occasion. Ditto the meeting of special needs.

Teaching and learning

- Give instructions in very clear, unambiguous language.

- Provide very clear directions for tasks (pay particular note to establishing the sequence in which instructions need to be followed).

- Use active language. 'What did Henry VIII think of the Pope?' Not, 'Bearing in mind what he had read in the Bible, the inability of Catherine of Aragon to give him a son, his love affair with Anne Boleyn, his growing political might, and his personal vanity, describe Henry's relationship with the Pope.'

- Summarise at the start of the lesson key points you intend to cover (so that students are clear about what to expect).

- Summarise towards the end of the lesson the points you actually have covered.

- Break down large tasks into very 'bite-size' pieces.

- Consider use of some group work to support and involve 'weak' students.

- Allow extra time for some tasks for certain students, such as for the below average readers to read a chapter.

- Provide frequent deadline reminders. It helps students to know how much longer they have.

- Provide support with regard to time management/organisation of books and equipment (before the student gets into a muddle).

- Display lists of essential new vocabulary, meanings, and concepts.

- Have a small supply of extra pens and pencils available, and allow access to them without undue comment.

- Do not overload students at any one time. Introduce work in phases.

- Check regularly that the student is understanding. Provide support as soon as you can tell he or she is not understanding.

- Check regularly the students are 'on task'. As soon as they are not, tell them what they should be doing; no need to refer to what they are actually doing but should not be doing!

- Prepare the student for any change of routine, or change in type(s) of activity.

- Expect/allow for some student inconsistency from lesson to lesson.

- Be positive whenever and wherever possible. Do not underrate the effects of simple praise.

Reading for information, use of textbooks and other resources

- Be aware of the 'readability' level (see Chapter 6, 'Marking, Spelling Correction and Readability') of texts you are asking students to read/learn from.

- Keep reading load to a minimum for some students (consider alternative texts; abridged texts; reading of crucial sections only; reading of previews, summaries, overviews only).

- Be cautious about asking some students to read aloud.

- Use different colours for different points on whiteboard/ PowerPoint.

Notemaking and notetaking

- Encourage/demonstrate use of highlighters; Post-It notes; different colours for different points or sections; to emphasise different points, use asterisks, capital letters, underlinings, etc.

- Keep the copying of notes from the board to a minimum.

- Make your own board work very clear and totally unambiguous.

- Consider allowing/encouraging the student access to a fellow student's notes.

- Consider enlarged diagrams for the sake of clarity.

Handouts

- Have handouts ready for early distribution.

- Number paragraphs – and refer to the numerals if going through handout with class.

- Take care over choice of font (size and variety).

- Take care over colour of font.

- Consider judicious use of colour, underlinings, bold, asterisks, capitals, italics, etc. to emphasise key points, or to distinguish points from each other.

- Consider vocabulary, and complexity of language.

Written work and its presentation

- Consider providing an ideal model for page layout (date, underlined headings, margin, etc.).

- Consider providing ideal, model essays/answers.

- Consider encouraging use of computer for word processing.

Ask the students what would be helpful

Briefly discuss with them how things might be made better for them. There is a process known as Metacognition, which is the understanding of one's own learning processes. This is what one is aiming at here. It may be a little ambitious, but that is not to say it is not to be borne in mind, and tried with the right students. At an appropriate level it can be tried as part of the package.

Classroom management and behaviour

This menu is for the rather large number of students who are being a definite nuisance in the class, but whose disruptive activities, although serious in a cumulative sense, may still be described as low-level. Other strategies would be required for the students who are seriously disruptive, and may themselves be disturbed individuals.

- Make explicit what the ground rules are, but keep them to a minimum; do not 'fuss' over students.

- It is very helpful indeed if these rules are consistent from classroom to classroom, teacher to teacher – and essential that this is the case within any one classroom.

- That said, do not be afraid to have slightly different personal regimes from one student to another, depending upon the different problems they are showing. However, so far as each individual is concerned, be consistent.

- Make explicit what happens when the ground rules are broken. If they are broken, make sure that what you said would happen, does happen.

- Express the rules in a positive way. Rules are about what we *will do* and what we *do do* in this room (as opposed to a list of 'do nots').

- Involve the students if possible in the formation of the rules. At the least, explain the reasons for the rules.

- Classroom rules are very likely to include the matters of: calling out; asking questions; talking to other students; active listening; turn taking; noise level; and the rights of students to work without distraction.

- Amicably agree seating arrangements, probably with certain students at the front of the class. Designate this arrangement as a regular plan at the beginning of lessons/term (this is much better than resorting to it after confrontation).

- Consider having a 'good influence' student always sitting next to a student who is something of a behaviour problem.

- Keep re-establishing eye contact.

- Set individual behaviour targets. Make these targets simple and explicit.

- Be consistent.

- Be positive whenever and wherever possible. Do not underrate the effect of simple praise. Be very careful with the use of sarcasm, irony or even what, to you, may be friendly teasing.

- Agree a non-verbal 'stop doing that' sign which you can use without interrupting the lesson, for example, a thumbs down.

- Agree a time-out system. Time-out properly applied is a relatively neutral and even positive act whereby the student can collect him/herself; it is not just throwing a student out of the class.

- Pre-empt confrontational situations as far as possible. De-fuse issues in advance in a low-key fashion. Take the heat out of situations before a flare-up.

- Try to keep calm. Keep your own feelings under control. In fact, keep your own feelings out of it.

- Prepare students for any change of routine.

- Give instructions in unambiguous language, adopting a tone of expectation.

- Give active, direct instructions – but keep volume to the minimum practical.

- Couch instructions as if they are (firm) requests.

- Break down large tasks.

- Provide frequent deadline reminders.

- Give support with regard to time management/personal organisation.

- Check regularly that the student is in task.

- Consider having spare equipment (pens, rulers, etc.) available to avoid time wasting distractions over getting started.

- Consider providing breaks in lessons to aid concentration; even the chance to move around.

- Check regularly that the student is understanding.

- Expect/allow for some inconsistency in behaviour from lesson to lesson.

- If a particular student or group of students is/are becoming an increasing behaviour problem, be prepared to analyse the situation over a period of time (before taking drastic action!). In particular, consider the following:

o Frequency of the behaviour problem.

o During which activities does it occur (which lesson/subject; extended task; oral/written/physical task; group/individual task; specific activity at moment of disruption)?

o At which time(s) of day?

o What is the teacher reaction to the particular problem at the time?

o What is the student reaction to the teacher reaction?

o What is the class reaction if the 'incident' is in a class situation?

o Are any explanations emerging, for example, is the student avoiding a difficult task; hungry/tired; gaining peer kudos; seeking attention; or exploiting vague rules?

o Which teacher strategies have been used in the past? Were they successful?

o Formulation of future strategy (possibly shared with student).

Work with the student

Discuss what might improve the situation.

Individual Education Plans (IEPs)

It is likely that many of the students who teachers think about as they read this book will have an IEP. Certainly, all students with a degree of special educational needs deserve that there should be a specific individual plan in place.

Throughout this book there are points about how teachers can best consider their students: what it is they want to change, to remove, to improve, to develop, and sometimes to maintain. This process will lead to the foundation of essential IEP targets. Then, the strategies chosen become the means by which these targets can be hit.

The construction of a formal IEP or a teacher's personal in-class plan becomes a naturally arising result of using this book.

Chapter 2

&

A Menu for Supporting the Student with Dyslexia in the Inclusive Classroom

First concerns

What a great day out we had had. It was a privilege to be able to take a group of the less literate secondary school students to spend a day on an army camp with a crack regiment at Aldershot. And how they had enjoyed it – the soldiers and us, I believe! We participated in any number of activities: assault courses; abseiling; map reading; weapon cleaning, and so on. The only tricky bit – so far – was at lunchtime, when we were allowed to join with the soldiers in their canteen, and this was a bit overwhelming and daunting for some (including the matter of handling money and paying for your meal at the end of the queue). Of course, their behaviour was impeccable, and they impressed and charmed the soldiers. The afternoon was to end with something of a wind-down with a visit to the regiment's library cum museum. This was fine; the group was ready for a less active session by now. The books they did not gravitate towards, but they were very interested by the exhibits: the models of armoured vehicles; the weaponry; the scale models of battlefields. They were fascinated by everything, and interested chatter bubbled away.

'Can't you read?' A voice of the soldier in charge (sorry, can't remember his rank) cracked the length of the room, and all the students froze. After a moment, they dared to glance in the direction of the voice, and saw an apoplectic soldier pointing with ramrod arm at the wall. 'Silence must be observed in this room at all times,' said a large notice in bold, black letters on a white background.

No one dared to give him the answer to his question. Incidentally, there was nobody else apart from us in the room.

Introduction

There has been much debate over the years about the nature and causes of dyslexia (although it is more than likely that not all the students above were actually dyslexic) and, to a degree, this continues. Indeed, even the discussion of the very existence of dyslexia is not entirely over.

It can happen at a national level in the political forum: in January 2009 Graham Stringer, MP, wrote a highly contentious, well-publicised piece not only claiming that dyslexia did not exist, but that it was invented by educationalists to cover up poor teaching and wrong teaching methods (Stringer 2009). He also referred to the 'dyslexia industry' that has grown up around the assessment and teaching of children with dyslexia, and his belief that it should be killed off. (But it is only fair to point out that Mr Stringer wrote very sympathetically about problems faced by children who are illiterate.)

Incidentally, on the subject of illiteracy (although not dyslexia as such), it was also in January 2009 that Edward Leigh, MP, said that the current seriously poor levels of adult literacy (and numeracy) were largely attributable to there being something wrong with our teaching in England (House of Commons Public Accounts Committee 2009).

But as we know, 'seven days is a long time in politics', and so we should not be surprised that six months later, in June 2009, the Government accepted and adopted the recommendations of Sir Jim Rose's report, *Identifying and Teaching Children and Young People with Dyslexia and Literacy Difficulties* (note the 'bracketing' of dyslexia and literacy difficulties) (Department for Children, Schools and Families 2009a). This report not only accepts the existence of dyslexia in the UK, but goes on to give a definition of it, and proposes a variety of steps that should be taken to deal with it, by no means the least of which is the firm proposal to train 4000 specialist teachers, and a suggested system of grouping schools so that these teachers could be 'shared out'. It would certainly seem, therefore, that as a nation, the UK officially recognises dyslexia, but it may be true that echoes of Graham Stringer's vibrant opposition can be heard in other arenas, too. Somewhat earlier, in 2005, this was exemplified by a TV programme, *Dispatches: The Dyslexic Myth* (Channel 4 2005), which, arguably, brought academic and popular voices together in debating, or even debunking, the existence of dyslexia, with Professor Julian Elliott, of Durham University, being a main proponent of the 'dyslexia is a myth' argument (at least in the minds of some, although this is an oversimplified summary of his views), and achieving a degree of fame or notoriety, depending on how you see it, in the process. The heat may have been lowered by now, but it is doubtful if it has been extinguished.

Coming down to the chalkface, most teachers know when they come across a student who has significant difficulties in reading, spelling, writing and comprehension skills (either all of, some of, or one of). Sir Jim Rose is of this view, too, pointing out that the initial trigger for action is the child having noticeably more difficulty with reading than his or her peers. Actually, this is also a bit of an oversimplification, too, in that dyslexia can be much more than just reading difficulties, as has just been said and as Sir Jim's report thoroughly acknowledges in other parts, but it has the great merit of the application of common sense based on sound professional judgement on the part of teachers. Hurray!

At the first sign, the teacher needs to feel that something can be done to support the student; there is no room for throwing hands up in horror about how impossible it is to teach such a student in an ordinary classroom, or for counsels of despair. This book is about helping to enable teachers – all teachers – make some wise yet pragmatic choices with regard to how they can get on and attempt to support certain of their students. To a considerable degree, backing for this approach can be found in Sir Jim's report:

> It is important to emphasise that it it is not necessary
> to wait for a child to be identified as having a special
> educational need (or, more specifically, as having dyslexic
> difficulties) before interventions are made... Children
> with proven and persistent difficulties should not be kept

waiting for intervention support until they reach Action Plus. (Department for Children, Schools and Families 2009a, p.46)

Unwittingly, Sir Jim's report has here summed up one of the themes, indeed, one of the pleas, of this book. A difference, though, might occur over what is meant by 'intervention', with Sir Jim looking for specialist dyslexia teachers, and with Brian Lamb, with Recommendation 7 of the Lamb Inquiry, likewise looking for the development of teachers with specialist SEN skills (Department for Children, Schools and Families 2009b). Without in any way decrying the usefulness and value of 'specialists' in schools and SEN services in LEAs, this book throughout focuses on what the classroom teacher can be getting on with in the almost immediate future if there is any possibility of a wait for, or an absence of, other support. So, having systematically noticed and noted the student(s) having that marked degree of extra difficulty, a teacher will be able to think in a positive way about how best to provide support.

The second thing that must be done is *not* to assume that such difficulties automatically mean dyslexia; therefore, do not start bandying the term around the staff room, or at this stage, to the parents, and certainly not to the student. Your concern should be communicated early to the Special Educational Needs Coordinator (SENCo). Do not be afraid to do this. Equally, do not merely refer the student to the SENCo, think your job is done and leave it all to him/her from there on. Most SENCos cannot know all the students who are mentioned to them and cannot cope single-handed by virtue of weight of numbers. While for you, although you seek, request, and welcome support, it is professionally and personally not satisfying to you just to hand over your concerns around this student to someone else.

Most important of all, whatever interventions, assessments, and remedial programmes do occur, two underlying features will almost inevitably be true in every such instance:

1. If any formal/formalised, and possibly statutory, developments and plans do occur, time will probably still elapse; precious time, when at least something specific to that student could be being thoughtfully tried by you in your classroom.

2. Second, the strong possibility is that the student will, when all is said and done, remain in your classroom, and be your responsibility. Although further advice might become available to you later, for the student's sake, and for your own professional pride, it will be better to consider carefully employing some of the strategies in this book, rather than do little more than let the situation drift and go on in the same old way.

The next step

Literacy and language deficits could be attributable to any one of a number of factors or, quite possibly, a combination of factors (which, it must be admitted, can complicate the issue). The more technical term for these factors is *variables*, so let's use it. Variables can cause or exacerbate difficulties in reading, spelling, writing, comprehension and language skills. These variables include:

- Poor hearing or eyesight.
- Lack of schooling through illness.
- Adverse or deprived social conditions.
- English as a second language.
- Behavioural factors; poor adjustment to classroom situation.
- General developmental/intellectual delay.
- Poor teaching.
- Dyslexia.

By a process of elimination, you and/or the SENCo may arrive at the conclusion that the likelihood is that the student is a student with dyslexia. Working your way through the variables will take a certain amount of time as you have to go through the student files, notes and records, and make enquiries (perhaps this is where the SENCo does have the role, in which case communication between the SENCo and the class teacher is important). It may well be that variables can be ruled in or out because there will be evidence for or against their existence which is, mostly, not too difficult to discover and evaluate.

If dyslexia is, then, basically the only variable left, you are still not in a position by any means to say the student is dyslexic – but you are in a much better position to work with and for the student than you were when you were merely fretting over all the things the student could not do in your lessons.

You can say the student *may* be dyslexic. In any event, bear in mind that, as Sir Jim says: 'Dyslexia is best thought of as a continuum, not a distinct category, and there are no clear cut-off points' (Department for Children, Schools and Families 2009a, p.34). But you may well now request, through the SENCo, more formal assessment, with the SENCo then invoking the appropriate procedures. This, in itself, is something positive; equally, as already pointed out, do not over-anticipate any immediate solutions being handed to you on a plate.

You can now begin positively to think about choosing some particular strategies for (and possibly with) this student. In other words, you can consult the following menu. However, before you do so, you must think about the student; there are, in practical terms, as many aspects of dyslexic students as there are students with dyslexia. As with most terms, including all those in this book, the terminology is only an umbrella (and one only needs an umbrella occasionally and for specific purposes).

Just as you make your own considerations before choosing from a menu, and the choices you make are just for you, so you must take a little time to reflect on this particular student, and exactly what is it that, at this particular time, he or she cannot do very well, what is it that you would like him or her to be able to do much better, and why you feel that. Be specific, be focused; Rome wasn't built in a day, and you are not going to try to rectify everything at one fell swoop. This is the beginning of a process, and you will return to it and this particular student, and develop it little by little.

When you have got some clarity on these points in your mind, you can then proceed.

Some real action

Now we come to the enjoyable part, where you can get down to working with this student in a positive way, and begin really to feel that you are doing something constructive for him or her.

Look at the following *A La Carte*. There will be things there that take your fancy; things that suit you and, of course, which you think will suit your particular student. Remember one or two key points: choosing from a menu is an enjoyable experience, done in a pleasant, anticipatory fashion, with the prospect of good things to come. Scan it when you are in the right, relaxed, positive frame of mind. Do not rush it; there is no pressure here. Reflect, and make your choice(s). Pick out those which seem to you may be especially helpful to the student you have in mind, and concentrate on those.

A La Carte of dyslexia teaching strategies
Reading

- Be careful with your board work (an uncrossed 't' may be an 'l' to a dyslexic student). Good readers can use context and, particularly, extrapolation to make sense of unclear writing. This is much less of an option for students with dyslexia.

- On the board, whiteboard, or PowerPoint, use different colours to delineate points. So, when the colour changes (no matter how many of the previous paragraphs have been in the same colour), the student knows that a new aspect of the topic is about to be presented. The actual text may be in different colours, or it may be just enclosed in boxes of different colours or, possibly, just have appropriately coloured lines down the margins alongside the text.

- Be similarly careful with your *handouts*, so that they are clear and easily legible. As well as the above, consider:

  o Choice of font (size 12, Comic Sans is well worth starting with, but experiment and involve the student(s)).

  o 'Readability' (see Chapter 6). There is a delicate balance here: teachers will never want to patronise or 'talk down' to students, yet do not overestimate what students with dyslexia can cope with if they are, also, fully to understand what they are reading (which is, clearly, what the subject teacher will want).

  o Sentence length and construction. Even when orally very competent, which it is possible they are, students with dyslexia may be thrown by unnecessarily complicated or cumbersome sentences. Again, the balance referred to in the previous paragraph comes into play.

o Overall appearance and attractiveness. A clean, uncluttered page, possibly with some illustrations or diagrams, is more appealing to anyone, especially when engaged on a learning task, not just a student with dyslexia.

o Not having too much on one page (judicious use of spaces can do much to break up that impregnable wall of print). Resist the temptation to cram as much information as possible onto each page. The first impression students with dyslexia get in those initial moments when they first receive a handout and glance at it may be crucial in determining the frame of mind in which they approach it.

o Although it would be asking quite a lot of a student to make this worthwhile, providing handouts in advance in the hope that students would read them before you talk them through in the lesson is a possibility worth considering.

o Leaving spaces on handouts for the students' further annotations is good practice. The student with dyslexia can add brief supplements in his own way which will be self-supporting.

• Let them read in a quiet atmosphere. Students with dyslexia generally require maximum concentration if the reading task requires a high degree of reading accuracy and/or comprehension (not all do). This is probably better achieved without distractions going on round them. Depending on the general ethos of the classroom, it may be necessary to negotiate with the students with dyslexia a certain reading area within the room they go to at appropriate times, if there are distracting activities or noise levels in other parts of the room.

• Give them the time they require. Time is not a total panacea. If the reading is impossible, it is impossible. However, many students with dyslexia are slow readers, but will get there in the end, if given time to do so.

- Alternatively, differentiate the task. Give them less reading to do while still encompassing the main points, or show them parts of the reading it is safe for them to omit without losing the main points.

- Some students may find it easier to read on a writing slope. This is a physical thing, involving the angle of the book, position of the body, and alleviation of reading fatigue, and is a strategy that should, perhaps, be tried more often.

- Consider enlisting a certain amount of support from appropriate classmates (obviously, where this will have no undue effect on the work of the classmate). A more fluent reader may, for instance, be able to read a worksheet to a student with dyslexia before they both start work on it independently.

- Perhaps the text book(s) the class is using is available in two formats; the usual format with relatively complex and longer sentences and a sophisticated page layout, and an alternative format with less print, more illustrations, etc. (but with, essentially, the same or entirely adequate subject content).

- A good deal of reading nowadays is likely to be off a computer screen (as when researching a topic on the Internet), in which case consider text to speech software which lets them listen without having to read. Or they can scan in what they want to 'read' and, again, just listen to the computer (but really encourage them to try to read as they listen).

- Be very cautious over asking them to read aloud in front of the class; there are many tales of excruciating embarrassment and tension, recalled by older students or adults, being caused by having to do this in the past. Apart from the trauma, the student is, of course, further put off reading, when all the time one of the most important things teachers can do for their students with dyslexia is to keep them positive.

- Be empathetic when a student reads to you individually. This may be only marginally less stressful for them than reading in front of the class; in fact, depending on how it is or is not organised, reading to the teacher can be virtually reading in front of the class, with everyone in the room able either to hear the reader, or the teacher's responses and reactions, or both. There is a teaching skill and art in hearing students read, especially those with a reading difficulty. It involves:

o gauging how much support to give

o being clear about how it will be given (e.g. the teacher supplies the word, the teacher helps the student build the word phonically, etc.)

o how long to wait for the student to read the word

o how much praise to give

o what body language to use

o how long to allow the session to run

o how often to do it

o when to do it, etc.

A sensitivity to the teacher–student relationship is called for as it is almost a personal situation, and variations in approach, depending on the particular student, the level of difficulties, and the personality and attitude of the student, are also called for.

• Subject teachers may choose to consider a strategy of highlighting or in some other way drawing the student's attention to key words in a topic, ensuring that students can read and recognise these words, are clear as to their meaning or the concept they embody and, just possibly, can spell them. Such words might include: in Biology, *photosynthesis, respiration*; in History, *monarchy, Parliament*; in Maths, *quadrilateral, theorem*. In a sense, the list is endless, but to allow it to become too long defeats the object of the exercise, so the teacher needs to exercise judgement.

• In more general terms, the teacher may wish to decide if there is any enjoyment in reading for the students with dyslexia. Reading is such hard work for some students that there is little pleasure to be gained from it. Bringing back the enjoyment, and allowing the student to read in a stress-free atmosphere, is something teachers may choose to do. This might be done by allowing students to read for some of the time relatively easy books (if the content level is apt), and by allowing them free reading time, in which their reading is scarcely checked so they are free just to get on and enjoy the book.

- Teachers may wish to show their students that reading is something with a general application, that is, it is not really about working your way through a reading scheme, important though that is. Reading is a useful tool, and so teachers might make a special effort to bring the reading materials that students are generally expected to read as part of general classroom life and work into the specific teaching or improving of their reading. Thus, some subject words of the type listed previously, or a chapter from the Geography text book, could be studied alongside the reading scheme materials.

- Other material that students need to read is their own writing when they have finished it to check, and to look for mistakes (proofreading). It is probably not unfair to say that students with dyslexia are notoriously poor at this; they find it difficult to spot their errors (which, actually, is not really surprising), a fact which they come to realise deep down, and so are soon unmotivated to try. Again, systematic proofreading is a skill in its own right, which it may well be worth teaching, if time can be found.

A method worth considering is to get away from the one and only readthrough, look-for-all-mistakes-as-you-go approach. It is better to replace this with the idea that students should skim their work several times, looking only for specific categories of error with each skim.

1. The first, and most important, skim is 'relevance', that is, have I answered the question that was asked or done the task that was set, and have I included any irrelevant material?

2. The next is 'sense', that is, no jumbled sentences, no words missed out, etc.

3. Third might be punctuation.

4. The last one, the one that students with dyslexia find most difficult, is 'spelling'. A way to address this is to say that if you think you have spelt a word right, then you will continue to think you have spelt it right even if it's wrong, and there is nothing to be done about it. However, there are almost certainly a number of words which you suspect are not spelt

correctly; these you check in the dictionary if you can, and if you cannot (as in most exams) you look at them again and have a think, but do not agonise for too long. A group of spelling mistakes you really might spot are those where you have just been 'careless' (e.g. where you have left a syllable out – *beging* for *beginning*; left a letter out, or even put an extra one in – *leter*, *lettter*; made a reversal – *diary* for *dairy* – or vice versa).

To develop this approach does take time, as the student builds up the level of personal discipline to employ it. Actually, this style of proofreading, as opposed to 'read once, find everything', takes very little extra time, and is less mental effort, because only one thing has to be thought about at a time, but students may take time to accept this. The best way to come to this realisation is by actually doing it several times, of course. Teachers may consider introducing it by stages, and allow students to become reasonably competent at one stage (such as 'sense') before expecting them to move on to another.

Inculcating the notion that proofreading is virtually automatically part of any task set, and not just a bolt-on or optional activity, for which time needs to be allowed in the original planning of how the task is to be accomplished, is something teachers may wish to consider taking on board.

If proofreading really is a profound problem, then teachers might consider a commercial proofreading program for the computer, which will look for missing words, reversals, etc. for the student.

Writing

- Expect minimal copying from the board; for some students, the chore of constantly looking up from book to board and back again (and, for some, it will be 'constantly') is just too much – they will be slow, probably unable to finish in the time available, inaccurate, and may not understand the content because the mechanics of completing the copying get in the way.

- Copying from a textbook or a piece of paper by the side is generally rather easier, but it's still not likely to be a wonderful experience.

- Encourage planning and drafting of written work before expecting the final version.

- Teach specific techniques to these ends, for example use planning tables and writing frames so that in, for instance, having to describe the changing relationship between two characters throughout a play (such as Macbeth and Lady Macbeth) the student's page is divided down the middle, one side for each character, and the relevant scenes are listed down the left-hand side of the page. The page is then ruled up into a grid, and a brief note can be put into each box where something relevant happens between the two. (This is a method which can also be used in notemaking.)

- Be 'sympathetic' towards spelling mistakes (see Chapter 6).

- Do not over-emphasise use of a dictionary; for some students, the dictionary can itself become another obstacle, since it requires a certain level – higher than is sometimes appreciated – of reading and spelling skills in order to access the word in question.

- Dictionary use is to be *gently* encouraged, but for some students it is best thought of as a means of confirming something they almost know, but just need to check, or they nearly know but just to need to fine-tune. Very rarely indeed is the teacher justified in merely telling a student with dyslexia to 'Look it up!' or in responding to a question with the retort, 'Use a dictionary!'

- The spellchecker on a computer can certainly be utilised, and this is true when the student needs a spelling even when not word-processing a piece of work. But there is the obvious danger that in obtaining the correct spelling, the student is not in any way getting closer to learning the word for him/herself. (The same can be true of dictionary use, actually, although this pitfall is then slightly less obvious.) Please see the section in Chapter 6 on the teaching of spelling.

- Rather similarly, some students may well appreciate being introduced to handheld spellcheckers.

- Consider an aural dictionary, with which a word can be found by how it sounds, so lessening the amount that needs to be known about how the word is spelt before it can be looked for.

- Consider allowing or encouraging the use of a laptop or word processor in the production of at least some of their work for the students whose dyslexia shows itself in handwriting which is difficult to read, no matter how hard they try. However, there is not much point in arranging for a student to have the use of a laptop and then saying, in effect, 'There, now you get on with it', or even worse, 'Problem solved'. Laptops are not panaceas for all ills; a degree of keyboard skills and word processing proficiency is also needed.

- Another Information and Communication Technology (ICT) based option is a speech recognition program for the computer. With this, the student speaks to the computer, and the text of what is said appears on the screen. There is no physical writing on the student's part. (Obviously, this technology is also a consideration for students with dyspraxia: see Chapter 3.) Teachers will possibly only want to consider this approach with students whose needs are extreme in this regard. It is probably fair to say that such a program can take a while to acclimatise, and can run into technical problems at this stage of its development. It is, however, an exciting development, and may liberate students for whom there seems no point in persisting with trying to develop writing skills. That said, teachers may also wish to consider not viewing the situation as an 'either/or' one; that is to say, perhaps teachers may come to think of speech recognition programs as aids to encouraging writing among students, and as a supplement to handwritten work, rather than necessarily as a replacement for it.

Notetaking and notemaking

- If the students' own genuine efforts at making (writing) useful notes are consistently in vain, they may benefit from specific tuition in how to make and take notes, for example:

  o how to group topics

  o how to bullet point them

  o how to lay out a page of notes so that they are easy to read again when they are returned to.

- Beyond this sort of approach, consider allowing them to have a photocopy of a sample set. Or allow them to photocopy the notes of another student whose handwriting is neat and clear, which they can keep alongside the ones they have made.

- Consider using: visual notes (diagrams, even cartoons); spider diagrams; Mind Maps. Each of these may help them organise their thoughts into a written form which is logically set out.

- Allow (even encourage) the use of abbreviations, such as 'hyp' = 'hypotenuse'. (We're crossing subject boundaries again.) But make sure they know what they mean; students with dyslexia may be slower to take this onboard for themselves.

- Encourage them to leave out the 'unimportant' words, such as *to*, *is*, *the*.

- In fact, the above touches on the heart of notemaking, which is to be confident enough to summarise (itself another important concept and skill) and express concepts in your own words. It is the antithesis of copying out word for word from the book or source. It requires good comprehension of what has been read, the confidence to know you have got this right, and then to be able to express it and write it in what is essentially your own way. Notes are really for the individual's personal use, but are also useful for referring to in the future (e.g. for exam revision!).

- Notes for future reference and for organising subject matter are not things to be scribbled or jotted down higgledy-piggledy. They require a reasonable amount of attention being paid to their presentation; this is something it may be difficult to convince some students about!

- Notes are generally best when well spaced out, with generous use of paper. Cramped notes are likely to be difficult to discern and decipher in, say, six months' time.

- Use headings and sub-headings under which to group like-points. The mechanics of inserting headings and sub-headings forces the sensible sorting of the material, rather than just, metaphorically, piling it up in a heap, any old point on top of any old point.

- The use of colour (e.g. with highlighters or coloured pencils), underlinings, capital letters, asterisks and bullet points to make items stand out one from one another is usually a skill well worth developing. It must be systematic (e.g. all points in red relate to Macbeth, all points in green relate to Lady Macbeth) and not just multi-coloured for the sake of it. The idea is to appeal to the visual memory, but in a way which adds logic and order to the material.

- It is probably best to write on only one side of the paper. It has been known for students to forget that they had a second set of notes on the reverse side.

- If the written aspects of notetaking/notemaking really are very difficult indeed, consider allowing or encouraging illustrations which replace words, for example, in History, the word *battle* may be depicted by a gun; in Geography the word *mountain* or *mount* by a triangle. If students think up their own symbols, this in itself can help them remember the fact, although they should develop a consistent cartoon-vocabulary, or the whole thing just gets out of control and becomes meaningless.

- Number the pages.

- Date the notes on the front page, and also write there, always in the same place on the page, exactly where they came from.

- All the above applies whether the students are making handwritten notes, or are word processing them.

- If notemaking proves impossibly slow or inadequate, consider allowing the use of a dictaphone.

Instructions

- Be careful about how you give instructions. Even, 'Turn to Chapter 4, second page, third paragraph,' which is admirably clear and sequential, may actually be too much, too quickly, and have to be given as a three-step instruction, with the student having time to carry out the preceding step before going on to the next.

- Have certain students repeat the instructions to you; this does not, of itself, prove they understand them even if they repeat them correctly, but it is a help.

If you feel you need more choice than is contained in the above menu with regard to 'instructions', please see Chapter 3, 'A Menu for Supporting the Student with Dyspraxia in the Inclusive Classroom'. The issue of following instructions is possibly even greater for the dyspraxic student and so a greater range of options is included there, but some may well be what you want for your dyslexic student.

Reading and understanding

- When reading is slow and/or comprehension hazy, consider using highlighters for key words and sentences; get the students used to doing this for themselves. If books cannot be marked in this way, which will be the case if it is not the student's own book, judiciously placed Post-Its work well (and can have the student's own explanatory note jotted on them, too).

- If accessing information through textbooks is a problem (which it probably will be), perhaps point out that textbooks often contain useful previews, summaries, and overviews, often at the beginnings and ends of chapters; consider this point when ordering new textbooks. No one is pretending that it is as good to read only such sections, but it may be a reasonable piece of pragmatism to say, on occasions, that it is all right to do so.

- Similarly, is it possible to point out to a student the key or most important parts of a chapter? Is it always essential that every student wades through a whole chapter if this is going to take an undue amount of time, and possibly induce stress that could be avoided?

- Or are there other ways entirely in which the information could be accessed by the student, and which could be actively encouraged, for example, the Internet (although quite a lot of reading is still probably going to be involved), DVD, audio media, observation, discussion?

Time and the slow worker

- If you can possibly manage to give extra time for the completion of some tasks (even at the expense of omitting other, less important, ones), a lot of pressure may be taken off students. Somewhere there is a happy medium, but it is more than possible that for some students bad past experiences induce a sense of anxiety (which gets in the way of functioning and learning) as soon as time limits are set, so within reason, flexibility is desirable. Fear of failing simply by not being able to complete work is not constructive.

- If a piece of work or a test has to be timed, even if 'timed' only in the sense that it has to fit into or be completed by the end of the lesson, and the work consists of a series of questions or is in different sections, consider identifying the most important, the key questions or parts of sections, and allowing the dyslexic students to do those first. This does make for difficulties with the awarding of marks, but it also means that the students are sampling all the activities within the exercise and are able to demonstrate competence at all the levels within the exercise, rather than just never getting to and doing anything within, say, the last quarter of it. If they do finish their allotted items, they can, of course, then go back and start the bits they were initially allowed to miss out.

- Ensuring that students who are entitled to extra time in public exams actually get it is, clearly, very important (the organisation of the assessment, communicating with the Examination Board(s), etc. is normally the responsibility of the SENCo) – but students may well need specific advice about how to use the extra time to best advantage (and, consequently, quite often advice about how to manage the time constraints of the whole exam). This is much better started long before, say, GCSE or SATs, so that they develop a feel for managing the exam room situation.

Your general approach (teaching style) in the classroom

- Give a preview and summary before and after going through a passage with the class. (Thus, we see that items on the menu apply to many subjects; dyslexia is not dealt with only in English lessons.)

- Be multi-media and multi-sensory (chatting while writing on a board is unlikely to be being effective for students with dyslexia). Try:
  o audio recordings, DVD
  o highlighters
  o Post-Its
  o charts
  o illustrations and diagrams
  o verbalisation whilst demonstrating or showing and showing and demonstrating while explaining.

- Be practical:
  o use a hands-on approach
  o make things (3-D)
  o do practical demonstrations.

- Allow movement at times.

- Consider some of the simple aids to be found in most educational catalogues, for example:
  o reading rulers, which help them focus on the specific section of a page
  o small personal whiteboards, which can be used at the desk, which allow for swift and easy correction to be made and a fully correct final version to be shown unsullied by previous crossings-out
  o dictaphones for taking down homework tasks, essay titles etc., as well as possibly being an interim aid (alleviating the need for written notes) in planning and producing a piece of work.

- Try always to remember the students with dyslexia.

In the primary school, try to do something specific with regard to their literacy skills everyday; in the secondary school, where subject teachers may see students quite infrequently, try to do something supportive for your dyslexic students in every lesson you do have with them, or within every piece of work you set for them.

Absolutely frequent drips of support may be the way forward for these students in the long-term. Developing their reading, writing, spelling, and language skills in a meaningful, purposeful way within the overall, daily curriculum may be as important as, say, the one-to-one lesson they get with the specialist dyslexia teacher once a week. (Ideally, of course, the two are liaising.)

In the classroom, the teacher might well include revision and review rather frequently (while avoiding boredom and repetition) or skills may evaporate.

Enjoying your choices

Remember to choose sparingly; a plethora of strategies is not what you want. Remember to temper every choice of an item with the particular student, and only that student, in mind. Consider the general menus on classroom management earlier in the book; there may well be strategies there that fit your particular bill. Scan the other menus with regard to the other disabilities dealt with in this book; remember the notion of overlapping disabilities, and that at least trace elements of a range of disabilities can often be found within a single student. You may find items in another chapter which suit; this applies to all the disabilities featured in this book. The choice is always yours. Remember to put the strategies into operation over a reasonable period of time; what this constitutes is one of the things you have to decide for yourself. But you do have to decide. It will depend largely on how often you teach this particular student, which could vary from literally almost every hour of every school day to one lesson of 30 minutes a week. Then use your strategies consistently and regularly, and do not muddy the waters by suddenly introducing new ones (you would be unlikely suddenly to switch to a spicy curry while already enjoying roast beef).

A La Carte for a choice of ways of thinking about students with dyslexia

Now we have another menu of a different sort. It doesn't give you precise, hands-on strategies, but it does give definite, alternative ways of thinking about what may make the students tick, and a different perspective.

Think of your student(s), and choose from the list below those negative descriptors which fit. Then look at the alternative descriptors immediately underneath the ones you have chosen, and ask yourself if you could begin to think of the student(s) according to these instead, and if these would help you choose some strategies to counter the problems being experienced.

- He doesn't listen to what I say.

  o *He can't remember the instructions or he doesn't fully understand what you're saying (possibly because he has poor auditory processing skills).*

- He's lazy.

  o *He has an organisational difficulty.*

  o *He's all right if you can get him started.*

  o *He can't manage to write down and show all that he knows.*

  o *The less he writes, the fewer mistakes he makes, so he doesn't allow himself to write much.*

  o *The less he writes, the fewer mistakes he makes, so the less he gets into trouble.*

  o *The less he writes, the fewer corrections he has to do.*

- He doesn't concentrate when he's reading.

  o *He loses his place, and so loses the thread, can't pick it up again, and so loses engagement with the work.*

- He's careless with his written work.

  o *He's got innately poor control when he's writing, and so his work turns out looking a mess.*

- He won't check his work.

  o *He does check but he can't see the mistakes.*

  o *He's given up checking because he knows from experience he won't see the mistakes.*

- He won't look carefully at the work.

  o *He does look, but he's got a very poor short-term visual memory, so he quickly 'loses' information just acquired from what he's just read.*

- He's got a behaviour problem.

  o *Schoolwork is such an effort for him, he gets tired and then fractious.*

- He's so disorganised.

  o *Thinking in a sequence is a skill he doesn't yet have.*

- He's really not very bright.

  o *This could be true, but it is at the very least equally likely that all these superficial 'symptoms' are giving a false and depressed impression of his true abilities and potential (for instance, he cannot write to the same level that he understands and speaks).*

If you can carefully select some descriptors from the above menu which put a different slant on the life and times of some of your students, and consequently perhaps how you view them, you are more than halfway towards supporting them.

Conclusion

A sense of humour is one vital ingredient in the make-up of most happy and successful teachers. Another is the ability to look on the bright side, and to trouble to look for strengths, skills, and attributes within students with difficulties. This is true for individual students of all disabilities, but as a group, there is some truth in the view that students with dyslexia tend to be: creative, imaginative and innovative; good lateral thinkers; to have good visual-spatial skills (depending on the nature of their dyslexia) and to be practical and good at mending things. Sensitive teachers will not allow difficulties the students have in performing within the formal curriculum in the ways we (and they) wish they could to submerge these qualities, if they are discerned.

Along with all students with disabilities, some dyslexic students may be exceptionally industrious, and show great determination to overcome difficulties that are not of their making.

A large number of famous, talented, and highly successful people have succeeded in life despite their dyslexia. From time to time, a 'celebrity' reveals this; it may well be worth bringing this to the attention of your students with dyslexia, or making them aware of some of the famous people, past and present, who have had dyslexia.

Chapter 3

≈

A Menu for Supporting the Student with Dyspraxia in the Inclusive Classroom

First concerns

It is a nice point of philosophical debate as to whether we have always had as many SEN students in our schools as we feel we do now, or whether they were always there but went definitely unlabelled and possibly unrecognised. 'Dyslexia' and 'ADHD' provide fertile ground for continuing such a debate.

However, everyone acknowledges that we have always had 'clumsy' children. Then, we became a little more sophisticated and started talking about 'clumsy children syndrome'. Other, more sophisticated terms, such as motor learning difficulty and minimal brain dysfunction, were stirred around in this pot until dyspraxia emerged, followed by Developmental Coordination Disorder (DCD), while in the Health Service, in the UK at any rate, we might find Specific Developmental Disorder of Motor Function (SDDMF). Such is progress!

So, who in our classrooms are these students? It is very important indeed to appreciate that there may be no distinguishing, obvious physical disability or malfunction. Dyspraxia is more to do with a minor neurological lack of organisation than with visible physical defects. This cannot be stressed too strongly. Equally, do not assume that somewhat poor neurological organisation in this regard, with a consequent clumsiness in large and small movements (and possibly speech difficulties) necessarily means poor intelligence or limited capacity to attain.

I will not say at this stage, 'How shall we know this is a dyspraxic student?' But I will say, 'How will I know that I should consider that this student *may* be dyspraxic?' And as soon as a teacher asks a question like that, the next one has to follow as day follows night, 'And can I at least try to do something to support him?'

I well and vividly remember the first dyspraxic student I ever met; at least, I think it was the first, but I can't be sure because I can't know about any I never recognised previously. (That's one of the difficult issues one has to live with in teaching.)

Jack, aged 12, sat at the back of my class for slower learners. I took them for virtually everything, and we did it all in the same room. Paintings to dry and 3-D work to finish were laid out on a wide shelf which ran the width of the room along the back wall. Several times a day, as Jack pushed back his chair to leave his place for a perfectly valid reason in our active room, he would, in standing or turning, send someone's half-dry picture spiralling downwards to be hopelessly smudged on the dusty floor, or someone's model of the Eiffel Tower crashing to that same floor with a spectacular array of flying balsa wood and a shower of half-set glue droplets.

Then Jack would half-turn and look me in the eye, with anguish written all over his face. And what would I do? I would treat Jack to a repertoire at full volume of the (now outmoded) standard teacher clichés about carelessness and, 'Why can't you think what you are doing?'

And what would Jack then do? Two things: one, become distressed; two, carry on knocking down other people's prized treasures. Why? Because he was dyspraxic, I now realise, and I was doing nothing to support him.

Actually, two more things did happen. Jack became (a) increasingly embarrassed and self-conscious, and (b) increasingly unpopular with classmates, whose hours of labour and patience he had rendered null and void in one 'careless' moment. ('Careless' is the worst label we can put on a dyspraxic student.)

The next step

So, what are the sort of things that teachers might see that might make them wonder about the presence of dyspraxia? Here are some:

- The student is generally clumsy (has poor gross motor skills). He or she drops things and bumps into things.

- The student has very scruffy, ill-controlled handwriting (poor fine motor skills). There is difficulty in labelling diagrams, shading maps, representational art and drawing, clumsy use of scissors. The word processor may not necessarily help because of clumsy use of keyboard. Presentation of work may be a big issue, especially in the eyes of some teachers.

- The student may have poor balance (quite possibly including riding a bike), and poor catching, along with throwing difficulties in Physical Education (PE). He or she probably runs awkwardly, typically with legs splayed out at the knees. They may have a degree of difficulty going up and down stairs.

- The student is not good at practical tasks, such as holding a camera steady. Similarly, adjusting a microscope; unscrewing things; using locks and keys, even use of cutlery can be a source of difficulty.

- In the younger child, there may well be difficulties in dressing, at least with regard to continuing difficulties with zips, shoes and shoe laces, etc. (Such difficulties can make life very difficult, trying, and frustrating, and are not to be underestimated.)

- Instructions may seem not to be understood or responded to. (This is because there is too big a time lag required for the student to absorb and organise incoming information.) So dyspraxia is not always just a 'physical' matter; it may have verbal connotations, and this is another very important consideration.

- There is often what at first seems to be a paradox, in that the dyspraxic student may be a fidget, and unable to sit still for any length of time.

- They may appear not to foresee danger, as in not judging distances well; this could lead to fraught situations ranging from road safety to reaching out for a Bunsen burner.

- Certainly, they are likely to be accident-prone, as evidenced by frequent cuts and bruises.

- Learning may not be generalised: for instance, with the dyspraxic student, having learnt to catch a beanbag may not automatically lead on to catching a ball easily.

- There may be exceptional avoidance of some tasks (where difficulties particularly present themselves, as in the large gym or sports hall, or with Design and Technology, needlework, woodwork, etc.) or even with construction toys, jigsaws, drawing, colouring, tracing, etc.

- They may have difficulty in addressing a task systematically (this is because they cannot wholly conceptualise it, and thus cannot sequentially plan what is involved in completing it, or how to complete it in stages).

- There may be a verbal dyspraxia, which is a degree of difficulty in producing words or syllables due to difficulty in organising and coordinating the muscles of speech and the lips, tongue, and jaw.

- There may be social connotations for the dyspraxic student, as with the older student who remains a messy eater.

- There may be psychological repercussions too (one of the worst of which would be if teachers made, for instance, erroneous assumptions about a student's level of intelligence based on the superficial evidence of the neatness of his handwriting).

- These problems arise and occur over and above normal and typical laziness, boisterousness, and cantankerousness, which teachers are familiar with, but which must not be used to write off the dyspraxic student.

- These characteristics have no physical explanation (such as poor muscle tone), and no medical condition is present (such as muscular dystrophy).

So, problems can arise in every subject and area of school life, especially if staff are not in the picture.

And, more generally, the following may be observed:

- Poor sense of direction, possibly including getting from lesson to lesson in a big school.

- Poor self-organisation, losing things, including schoolwork.

- Poor sense of time, including realising at what rate to work in order to complete on time.

- Untidy appearance (can lead to uniform issues).

- Poor sense of rhythm: the student stands out at school discos.

So, such students may have difficulties with – and personal disappointment with – the everyday activities of childhood (some of which may remain significant in practical and personal terms in adult life) as well as with educational problems. If students have difficulty with drawing and writing, have difficulties in PE and games, have difficulty negotiating a space (between desks or through a crowded doorway), are awkward with a knife and fork, are clumsy in handling coins, etc., life is hard.

The result may be embarrassment, self-consciousness, social gaucheness, or withdrawal. Young people may become socially self-conscious to the point of low self-esteem and lack self-worth because of so many everyday things they find difficult – and the reaction this provokes in others who notice.

However, teachers can make small but sensitive and significant adaptations which help dyspraxic students thrive.

Having decided that perhaps you really should consider the possibility of dyspraxia being at work here, you will want to place this into a context. As with dyslexia (with which there is, in general, a correlation, although assumptions cannot automatically be made about an individual) there are no immediate links with intelligence, and it is important not to let one's perception of what students may be capable of achieving be over-dampened because of what one witnesses when they are in particularly dyspraxic mode. Incidentally, the dyspraxic student is four times more likely to be a boy than a girl (but, there again, do not rule girls out).

There is a tendency for dyspraxia to run in families to some extent, but, in saying this, one then has to add the big, cautionary footnote about not jumping to conclusions about young Ben because of what you knew about big brother Matthew, and how dyspraxic *he* was.

It has already been acknowledged that surely every teacher must have met such students, and if one accepts a national incidence of perhaps some five to six per cent, then this must be the case.

As always, the question comes back to, 'Have I at least recognised the possibility of this condition being present and responsible for these things which are happening, and which we do not want to happen? And what have I done, in my classroom and in my way, to try to improve the situation?' This always automatically leads to the next practical stage, where you ask yourself specifically *how* the dyspraxic (coordination) difficulties manifest themselves in ways that immediately concern you in so far as this particular student is concerned, for example, in handwriting, PE (hopping, balancing), scruffy appearance, poor organisational skills (lost books, turning up without books). Now you are in a position to study a menu in the right frame of mind, knowing what type of dish you are seeking which will satisfy you.

A La Carte of teaching strategies

Here are some things to consider; a menu from which you can select some strategies, or pointers to ways of working with these students. They will be approaches which you choose just for this student, and which you will try over a period of time. Remember that these difficulties have been present since birth, so progress may not be dramatically quick (although sometimes it is quite easy to improve a situation, such as when just providing a more appropriate ruler; when this happens, it's surprising how much better student and teacher feel!).

- Use large diagrams to facilitate labelling.

- Consider word processing to replace handwriting (but check keyboard aptitude).

- Consider allowing the use of the notes of another student.

- Teach the use of Post-Its, highlighters, etc. to navigate the way through text. In fact, always be particularly conscious of potential pitfalls such as dropping notes, or getting notes in a muddle if they are giving a class presentation.

- If at all possible, devise safety measures to enable use of some equipment (in gyms, labs, etc.).

- Choose tasks wisely, for example, do not ask them to hand out the exercise books if the odds are on them spilling over the floor.

- Give very clear instructions; quite possibly in writing, so that they can refer to them as they proceed.

- Make sure they are clear about what they have to do, and know what the outcome has to be, for example, brief notes or long essay. Explain the sequence in which tasks have to be done.

- Give early and frequent reminders about deadlines. Perhaps have spare copies of the timetable, as the original may well get lost. Perhaps colour-code it so that they can navigate it more successfully.

- Ensure the workspace is uncluttered from the outset.

- Perhaps encourage written work being done on alternate lines for improved legibility.

- Consider the use of a sloping surface for written work.

- Ensure your own handouts are clear, plain, and uncluttered.

- Consider teaching the use of Mind Maps to replace certain aspects of written work.

- Monitor and support the student's filing system.

- Have spare equipment (pens, etc.) for the student to borrow when they forget or lose their own.

- Be sparing with criticism.

As always, choose lightly and choose with your own students, and your own circumstances, utterly at the forefront of your mind. As with every *A La Carte* menu, choose what is right for you – and for these particular students at this particular time.

Having made your general choices from the above and having got the taste of how to to respond to dyspraxic students, you can now move onto the more specific courses, choosing from particular menus that will satisfy the needs of your students and yourself.

A La Carte of teaching styles

Introduction

This is one of those menus where you will probably feel you want to choose everything that's on it! The beauty of this menu is that this is exactly what you can do! That said, remember you are a gourmet. Even when choosing many courses, gourmets savour each one; some are thought about even more than others; none are taken for granted; each is appreciated, and has its own rightful place and time during the meal.

- Be sparing with criticism.

- Don't be surprised that some things they can do whereas other things, which on the surface seem to be related, they cannot.

- Don't show *your* frustration when students with dyspraxia take a long time over a 'simple' task – think how *they* must be feeling!

- Keep an orderly classroom so that resources and equipment they need can easily be found, for example, reference books, globes, Science equipment, measuring and weighing equipment. Have clear labels on cupboards; perhaps have illustrations on the cupboard doors.

- Be ahead of the game and be aware of potential pitfalls in order to avoid them. For instance, do not expect dyspraxic students to give a class presentation working from notes if they are likely to drop them or get them into a muddle – use a flip chart or PowerPoint instead.

- Choose tasks wisely, for example, do not ask them to give out the exercise books if the chances are that the books will be dropped all over the floor.

- Be on the look out for ways to amend tasks so that students with dyspraxia can participate in a fulfilling – and not just a frustrating – way. This is an extremely apt example of where it is so good if you have managed to enlist the cooperation and understanding of the rest of the class – a delicate and sensitive process but, ultimately, so beneficial to *all* concerned.

- Try to give them time to:

  o come out to your desk unhurriedly so there is less chance of them knocking everybody else's pencil case skew-whiff or onto the floor as they pass by

  o get out the right books and equipment. This can be really difficult when the rest of the class are ready to start or move on, and you all have to wait for one or two students. In such cases, consider the deployment of a 'buddy'. Obviously, there may come a time when this is inappropriate, and total independence is the goal, but in a controlled way and at times when the students with dyspraxia are definitely likely to struggle, consider if this could not be a very useful, pragmatic way of offering support when needed. Remember that buddies do not do everything for dyspraxic students; they lend a hand.

- Allow them to complete tasks in ways they can cope with and are comfortable with. Ask yourself if it really matters, for instance, if students complete a piece of work in a thick pencil when you would have preferred it to be done in ink. At some point it may well matter, but does that mean it has to be an issue now?

- Only ask them to show their work to the rest of the class if it really is good.

- Avoid competition with others – but encourage them to compete against themselves and set goals, for example, 'I will not be late into my next lesson after PE.'

- Devise safety measures (where necessary – and it isn't always) to make possible the use of equipment in, for instance, the gym or the lab. There may still be occasions when only closely supervised use of, or even just observation by the students of the use of, certain equipment is the best that can be achieved. This is fair enough if you have thought about – in detail and positively – how to support the students' participation, but haven't been able to come up with a safe and satisfactory solution.

- On outings, field trips, etc. keep a special eye on the dyspraxic students, and have particularly frequent roll calls. Delegate an adult to keep this special eye, but ask that this be done in an unobtrusive way. The reason for these precautions is that the possible lack of directionality can lead to them losing their bearings and getting lost; there is also the possibility of a lack of appreciation of situations leading them into danger.

- Remember the possibility of dyspraxia evidencing itself in verbal clumsiness and awkwardness. Give them time to express themselves.

Try not to draw attention to speech or language difficulties; this only induces pressure and makes things worse. Do not put them 'on the spot' by how you ask a question, or want a verbal response.

- Consider forms of backward chaining. Students are given as much support as necessary in the early stages of a task, and then independently complete the final stage. In a setting which is probably just outside the 'educational', an example of this would be that for children who have great difficulty putting on their trousers, they are given all the help they need to do so up to the point where the trousers are safely above the knees, and then the children carry on unaided from there. In the Maths classroom, an example might be that students who have great difficulty in setting out their work and aligning their hundreds, tens and units (HTUs) are always given their 'sums' pre-printed, but do have to write the answers in. Later, they could be given the hundreds and tens (HTs) but have to complete the units (Us) in the body of the sum as they set it out. Ideally, as common sense would indicate, backward chaining always leads to the students gradually being responsible for more and more stages, working away from the end of the task towards the beginning, until they can manage the whole task without support.

A La Carte for giving instructions

Introduction

To follow and carry out an instruction, students have to be organised. (It is very helpful if the person giving the instruction is also organised!) To implement a sequence of instructions, students' organisation has to be satisfactory in quite a complex way. To follow instructions from a range of teachers in a variety of situations, with the instructions being given in a medley of different styles (the brusque and terse, the minimalist, the expansive, the verbal, the written, the implied, the explicit, the measured, the hurried), some of which are for immediate compliance, some for long-term, some for mid-term, all day long, can be taxing indeed for some students with dyspraxia, perhaps especially so for those with aspects of verbal dyspraxia.

'Instructions' can vary from a one-sentence instruction about the next Maths exercise to be started to instructions about how they are going to prepare for, undertake, and write up a fieldwork project. It certainly covers instructions about what homework will consist of, which is often a bone of contention for some dyspraxic students.

Difficulties can arise on at least two planes: understanding the instructions and what they really mean in the first place, and then remembering them and following them through.

Scan the following menu with the general (although not stereotypical) awareness of the potential responses of dyspraxic students, who have not assimilated fully, prioritised, or appreciated the chronological order of all they have been asked to do. Consider your own style of making your requests of students, and how you indicate your expectations of them. Put the two together, and see from the items below those you feel you most need to bear in mind.

- Give very clear instructions. It is possible that, in order to be entirely certain that these instructions are accessible to the dyspraxic students, they need to be made in ways which could seem painfully obvious. (Then comes the danger of 'talking down' to the students!)

- Clearly pause between instructions; allow time for one to be assimilated before giving the next.

- Give your instructions in the same sequence as you wish the students to carry them out. Avoid 'Before you do X, you will need to have done Y.'

- Be verbally uncluttered, that is, keep sentences simple and straightforward. Do not have lots of clauses within a sentence. Generally avoid the passive tense, and use direct instruction. Avoid 'By this stage the liquid will have been placed in the beaker, and the beaker will be being heated in the bunsen flame.' Use 'Place the liquid in the beaker – pause – Heat the beaker in the bunsen flame.'

- Particularly if there is a series of instructions, they may need to be backed up in writing, so that the students can refer again to them. Generally, this is simply a matter of writing them on the board – and leaving them there. However, it could entail a mini-booklet (bearing in mind any rules about how much help is permissible) if the instructions were in connection with, say, a longish-term project which was ideally to be completed with the students largely using their own initiative, and perhaps occupying several homeworks.

- Try to make sure the students are clear in their understanding of the instructions, and are clear about what they are being asked to do, and what the outcome will 'look like', for example, brief notes or a long essay. You may have given the instructions clearly, but that still doesn't necessarily mean they were clearly understood.

- Support the dyspraxic students in sorting out the sequence in which a number of tasks are best done or, probably more importantly, sorting out how to break down a large task into a number of smaller sub-tasks, and in doing those in the best order to complete the whole task. Project work and extended studies of all types are likely to benefit from this attention.

- Do not overlook the simple and obvious practice, which can be inculcated into standard working practice, of the students making 'to do' lists, keeping work diaries, etc. Not only may students need advice about starting to keep these, they may very well benefit from help about how to do so in ways which are orderly and efficient.

A La Carte for written work

Introduction

It is more than likely that written work, on a daily basis, causes more feelings of angst for students with dyspraxia than any other aspect of their school lives. By 'written work' we mean here anything the students have to present on paper to teachers: it includes pieces of extended writing in English, the setting out of exercises in Maths, the drawing of maps in Geography and diagrams in Science; representational drawing or painting in Art, etc.

Individual letter formation is likely to be quirky, while words are either crammed too closely together or spread out far too far apart, and the whole lot may go shooting all over the page or be minutely cramped. Pictorial interpretation of information is likely to be at a level where revising that information at a later date is going to be difficult, if not downright misleading.

The many students whose dyspraxia manifests in this way are bringing their dyspraxia daily to the attention of virtually all their teachers; it cannot be disguised, and it cannot go unnoticed. So, the reaction of the teachers is vital: how they receive the work, how they respond to it, how they mark it, what they say about it, will all send profound messages to the students with dyspraxia about how they are regarded.

Handwriting

Different teachers in different situations will either feel they know a good deal or very little about the teaching of handwriting, and may also feel they have different degrees of responsibility for it. To state the obvious, Key Stage 1 teachers are likely to have a different degree of expertise in the acquisition of handwriting, and a different perception of their professional responsibility in this regard, than a teacher of A-level Chemistry. However, both may very possibly encounter students with dyspraxia for whom handwriting is difficult.

This cannot be a book about handwriting (see Resources), but the following menu gives choices. As ever, you choose what is appropriate for you, bearing in mind the students you teach and how you have observed them.

- Be very aware of the school's handwriting policy. If you feel it necessary, discuss its appropriateness to the students you have in mind (this discussion would probably be, in the first instance, with the SENCo).

- You may think it appropriate to encourage cursive (joined up) writing, rather than print. Here you will want to be in tune with the school's handwriting policy but, notwithstanding, cursive writing is something you may feel the more helpful. This does assume that cursive writing is being or has been taught. Students with dyspraxia are most unlikely just to pick it up, or virtually teach themselves in any way that that is likely to be very successful; just the opposite, in fact. However, correct cursive handwriting, which gives the 'feel' of and the sight of the whole word (or syllable) is likely to be better than individual, isolated letters, which may seem unrelated.

- If the students are taught by a variety of teachers, you may feel that consistency from class to class is very important, and you may want to discuss with the SENCo how teachers' expectations can be coordinated.

- You may feel that the posture and sitting position of the students when they are writing is important, and that being slumped across their work has to be discouraged. You may feel you need to be clearer about matters such as posture and to consult other sources (see the Resources section). In the meantime, you may wish to note the height of the desk and chair, and how they match; how they fit each student (students vary tremendously in physique); whether the students are sitting with reasonably straight backs; and whether they can maintain this position throughout a piece of work.

- You may feel that the students are, probably each in a unique way, holding the pen or pencil wrongly. You may then feel it appropriate to recommend specially-shaped devices which can be affixed to the pen or pencil, and which can help by more or less compelling that the correct grip is assumed. You may think it advisable to go even a little further, and recommend that one of the specially shaped pens be tried (in both cases, see Resources). Always be prepared at first for the students to complain, 'It doesn't feel right', 'It's awkward' etc. In fact, these are the common cries when trying to modify any aspect of handwriting. It is quite important that the pen/pencil is gripped properly, so if you feel the grip is a real hindrance, and this may well be the case, persistence will have to be insisted upon. Use your natural teacher wiles! On the other hand, if the grip appears to you to be wrong but the writing is adequate in terms of legibility and also speed and, importantly, this particular student is reasonably comfortable when writing and not incurring too much stiffness or experiencing too much fatigue in the hand or wrist, to leave it alone may be your conclusion. Such a situation is unusual, but is possible. One of the arts of making life better in the classroom for students with disabilities is focusing upon a small number of core difficulties and working on them, not trying to improve simultaneously every single facet of a student's situation.

- You may observe that the students are positioning their writing paper at odd angles, which is generally hardly helping matters. For right handers, the paper should probably be angled at about 30 degrees to the left, and positioned somewhat to the right of the body. For left handers, between 30 and 45 degrees is probably suitable, with the paper positioned rather to the left of the body. You may think it important really to encourage good habits in this regard, and even to put markers on the desk or have little right angle 'frames' firmly positioned indicating, say, the correct positioning of the topmost corner of the paper.

- You may notice wayward left hands (in the case of right handers), particularly with the left hand carrying out that time-honoured function of being a resting place for the head (which is, itself, flopping to one side). The role of the left hand in holding the paper steady is something you may wish to explore. (For left handers, the same is true of the right hand.)

- You may wish to consider allowing, encouraging, or suggesting (there is often at least these three subtly different ways of providing support in all sorts of spheres) that students write on alternate lines, which can provide a degree of freedom which improves legibility. In fact, choosing the most appropriate writing paper is something you may wish to give some thought to. Taking it as established that lined paper is to be used, you may think that the amount of space between the lines is important. Also, lined paper can be obtained which indicates the length that the ascenders and descenders ('sticks and tails') should be – but don't expect pinpoint accuracy.

- You might well feel that writing slopes (see the Resources section for details) are well worth experimenting with.

- Mini-whiteboards (wipe-clean), on which the students write with a 'marker', are other aids you may wish to contemplate, feeling not only that they may aid the appearance and the quality of the handwriting itself (which the students can so easily remove and try again, with no tell-tale evidence remaining of earlier efforts) but also make the whole chore less burdensome and daunting, thus having a degree of a liberating effect. The drawback, of course, is that whiteboards cannot provide a long-term record (sadly, they are also easily besmirched by other students). Are digital cameras and photos of the work on the whiteboard too fanciful a solution?

Word-processing

This has, to some extent, been a contentious subject in the past when discussed as an alternative to handwriting, but it is a sign of the times that it now engenders much less in the way of heated debate.

However, even now, few go so far as to suggest that it is a complete alternative to handwriting, and you may wish to consider it in this context, namely, it is something to be considered as a very possible adjunct to handwriting, which may become increasingly used as the students move up through the school, but is very seldom seen as a complete replacement for absolutely all the students' written work. And so, the type of menu you will wish to find in this context is:

- Allow or encourage certain pieces of work to be word-processed.

- Check on the students' word-processing or keyboard skills to see if they are functionally useful. If they are not, consider the possibility of having those skills improved (bearing in mind that this may itself not be so easy for students with dyspraxia – a catch-22 situation).

- If a word-processor is really useful, consider whether the students may be entitled to use them in 'public' exams. Talk to the SENCo about this, and about assessment with this in mind. Do this in good time and, in fact, do it for school exams, too, not only for practice and improved in-school results, but so that this is known, if appropriate, as the students' normal way of working.

- If the legibility of handwriting is very poor, and word-processing skills are not yet of a high enough level, consider having someone else word-process ('type up') the work. Who that 'someone else' is and whether they would have the time and opportunity to do this word-processing is among the other practical points that would have to be considered. Another is whether they can read the students' handwriting, or whether it will be necessary or advantageous for the students to read out the work to the 'typist'. This may be typical of the sort of strategy that cannot be always employed, even if you wanted to, but is an option on certain occasions.

Notetaking and notemaking

- Should it be that notes are just to be copied into exercise books (surely not a common occurrence), consider whether this is easier for students with dyspraxia when they copy from a book or piece of paper on the desk than from the board.

- The skill of organising notes, and the whole concept of summarising, ordering and classifying information so that it is transposed into a brief and systematic format for future reference are things which, given their general difficulties with 'organisation', may well not come easily or naturally to dyspraxic students. If that is the case, consider if these things can be taught. See the relevant section in Chapter 2.

- Consider teaching the use of Mind Maps, flow diagrams, spider diagrams, or pictorial representations as alternatives to the more usual production of linear notes; these may be helpful to dyspraxic students. In fact, consider Mind Maps (see Resources) that are available as computer software, thus removing the need for the written planning of essays and projects, as well as written notes of work covered.

- Consider allowing them to photocopy the notes of another student who is able in this respect. Consider providing them with a set of notes. If you go along these routes, you could further consider doing so only after the dyspraxic students have had a go, thus generating their own familiarity with the original material, even if they are not able to make good notes about it.

Getting the work done

- Within reason, consider if you will be prepared to accept less written output. Similarly, you may decide not to impose sanctions (which for other students you might), so long as you are reasonably certain that best efforts have been made.

- Will you acknowledge that there is generally little point in asking or insisting that 'untidy' work is re-written because it probably won't be much better second time around, and a lot of time will have been wasted in the effort?

- Would worksheets that don't require too much writing by way of completion (without lessening their intellectual rigour) be helpful, and possible to provide? Such worksheets could utilise close procedure, or have mainly multi-choice questions, where the students just have to circle their chosen answers.

- Similarly, would it be helpful and feasible to provide large diagrams, maps, etc., which would facilitate students' labelling?

- Would you consider the possibility of the students with dyspraxia sometimes dictating their work? This could be to you, to a classroom assistant, or to other students who are good writers if they have the time.

- Or, would you consider allowing them to speak their work and their answers into a dictaphone?

- Would you feel that word-recognition software would be beneficial, at least on some occasions, so that students can dictate their work to the computer?

- Could computer software which provides writing grids (see Resources) be supportive and apt?

- In extreme cases, would you consider the provision of an amanuensis ('scribe') for external exams? (If so, remember the proviso about early assessment for this entitlement, and establishing this as a way of working, etc.)

Staple choices

In selecting from the above, there are certain staples that you will always want to bear in mind:

- An active awareness that handwriting difficulties can be very frustrating for students who may have lots to say and want to get it down on paper, but know they cannot do so in the same way that their peers seem able to do. In many cases, all your choices will be underpinned by this consideration.

- An active awareness of the dyspraxic students' own realisation of their limitations with regard to producing attractive and smart written work, coupled with a realisation of the way this can colour the perceptions of them that other people and students hold. This will lead you to make 'positive avoidance' choices, such as being very wary of asking them to write on the board in front of the class.

- An awareness that as dyspraxics' legibility and neatness of handwriting improve, their speed of handwriting may actually slow at first. This is probably because they are now concentrating so hard on the appearance of the writing. (Thus, if there was a problem with their not finishing work, this problem may increase.) So, while your choices will always reflect your ambitions for your dyspraxic students, they will always be tempered by an appreciation of the difficulties they face.

A *La Carte* for personal organisation

Introduction

There is a strong likelihood that students with dyspraxia will have difficulties with personal organisation. They tend to lose their possessions, their books, their pens, their sports gear (or at least they can never quite put their hand on them quickly); they forget their homework; they lose their way; they lose track of time; they may lose their friends, who get fed-up with all this; they may lose patience with themselves; they may lose their self-esteem.

Practical, pragmatic measures can help tremendously, but dyspraxic students may really need to be shown certain basic things which many other students just do without thinking about it.

In this area of personal organisation, it is particularly important that you first think about what it is that is really frustrating them, and quantify the areas where they will most benefit from changes being effected.

The following menu covers the main areas you are likely to encounter in school, and provides a choice of measures that may work to alleviate problems. The menu indicates the flavour of what is likely to be effective; feel free to garnish these strategies in any way that suits your students, your situation, and yourself.

Timetables

These are the students' personal timetables, which they often have to carry with them, and need to refer to often.

- Consider having spare copies of their timetables, as the original may well get lost.

- Consider having them colour-coded (e.g. English in red, Maths in blue, etc.) to make it a little easier for them to navigate their way through their timetable.

- Even consider having them more visual than this, with cartoon-type pictures representing lessons (e.g. a football and a cricket bat for PE, an easel and some brushes for Art).

- Think about whether timetables need to show more than just the lessons and their times. Do they need to show the locations of each lesson? Do they need to show the names of the teachers for each subject? What about the equipment needed? A homework timetable will probably be needed; is this a separate piece of paper; is it incorporated into the main timetable (two pieces of paper instead of one means one more piece of paper to go astray; homework and lessons, etc. on one sheet means more information to tease out).

- Can ICT help in getting all the information down clearly on one piece of paper?

- Consider discussing with the students the design of their timetables, what they feel it would be helpful for them to show, and how they would like it laid out. This may make it much more meaningful and, in fact, personal (or personalised) rather than just something that is presented to them.

- Once completed, consider how to avoid the timetables rapidly becoming unduly tatty, for they will probably get roughish handling. Can the timetable be mounted, can it be laminated, etc.?

- If problems over getting to lessons on time – with all the right equipment – persist, consider looking at the timetable layout again, but consider also other possible causes, for example, slowness in clearing up and, therefore, in getting away from the previous lesson.

Their workstation

- You may want to ensure their desks and workspaces are uncluttered. This needs to be the case from the outset of the work (otherwise things will probably just get more and more muddled), but also – and more difficult – this needs to be maintained throughout the task. One of the secrets is to make sure that equipment required is thought about before the task is started and is put in place ready while, at the same time, everything else is put away.

- You may deem the end of the lesson to be important, and feel that a routine, sequenced checklist with regard to putting things away and in their proper places would be supportive. If they 'tidy up' in a completely random fashion, they may leave part of the room untidy, take an undue amount of time, quite possibly put their own things in the wrong bags, compartments or pockets and, if they are older students moving to another lesson in another room, leave their own possessions behind.

Looking after school essentials

This means all the everyday items that all students need: pens and pencils, text books, exercise books, loose leaf files, etc. Any one of these items is in danger of getting lost, or at least being difficult to find, or having to be gone back for because not taken to the lesson, or retrieved having been left behind in the lesson. Other aspects of this sort of organisation – or the lack of it – is the time it wastes, the frustration it causes the students, and the inconvenience and annoyance it causes the staff.

- Consider having clear plastic wallets, one for each subject, ideally to contain all that is relevant to and needed for that subject – and that subject alone. The transparent wallet means that it is possible for them, and you, to tell at a glance that their atlases are in their

Geography wallets, and have not mysteriously got transferred to the History wallets.

- You may feel the wallets should be labelled. This would include the students' names but, in this context, the name of the subject is the more important because this labelling is for the benefit of the owners of the wallets. More significantly, you may think the wallets should be colour-coded, along with the books etc. that they contain. For instance, the Geography wallet could have a big red sticker on it, and all the Geography books and items each have a small one. It is immediately apparent that something is out of synch if a blue sticker is spotted, which it easily should be, in the Geography wallet. All the students have to think about when packing their bags is that all the things with red stickers go in the wallet with the red sticker – and anything with any other colour sticker does not!

- Perhaps you would recommend having several sets of pens, pencils, rulers, etc. – a set in each wallet or subject folder. This removes the need for transferring equipment from lesson to lesson, subject to subject, and means they are never without in any lesson – theoretically!

- Cases and bags which have sections or pockets are things you may want to recommend. They are likely to be more successful than holdalls into which everything is put, if not thrown. That is a recipe for clutter, and for equipment to become muddled. However, utilising the sections and pockets (possibly with zips) within bags and cases in a systematic and regular way is itself a skill which dyspraxic students may need help in acquiring.

Getting the work done

- You may choose to have spare equipment (pens, rulers, etc.) ready for dyspraxic students to borrow when they forget or lose theirs. A word or two about why they should need to borrow may be appropriate (and they do have to realise that they cannot forever be reliant upon someone else to bail them out) but just before starting a piece of work is probably not the occasion for causing a scene; the loan is a pretty matter-of-fact transaction.

- You may think it helpful to give early – and frequent – reminders about deadlines for the completion of work. You may feel these reminders need to be non-threatening but specific, for example, not, 'That's got to be in by the twenty-first" but, 'That's got to be in by the twenty-first. That's eight days from now, including the week-end.'

Storing and retrieving work

This refers to what we may term 'filing', which at the secondary level can be quite a complex task and involve a large volume of work and material while, at the primary stage, students will have to put work away appropriately and be able to bring it out again for continuation.

- So, you may feel it is necessary to monitor and support their filing systems. Therefore, you may want to check their understanding of what a filing system entails – and you may find that to dyspraxic students a filing system simply means putting every sheet of paper they write on and every piece of work they do into a file, possibly at any point in the file.

- You may feel that your dyspraxic students should work in exercise books rather than on loose paper for later filing. If exercise books may seem a little juvenile for older students, especially when others are carrying around impressive looking files, quite smart and sophisticated notebooks can be obtained.

- You may want to check that they have given thought to filing things:

  o chronologically

  o subject by subject in separate files or in clearly defined sections within one file

  o systematically on a daily basis.

- You may want to check they have thought about:

  o buying a new file when one is bulging to overflowing

  o buying files or exercise books of different colours

  o putting their names and other details clearly on the front

- o keeping a running *Contents* page

- o numbering pages as they are inserted (to match the *Contents*).

To be fair, it is completely true that few adults (including teachers?) manage to organise the storage – and, therefore, the retrieval – of their material completely thoroughly, but you may find some dyspraxic students particularly lacking in the concept of systematic filing. They may also lack the mental schema to compensate. They will need showing and training. If they can be helped to be successful, or at least less chaotic, in this regard, a lot of hassle will have been removed from their lives.

A La Carte for PE

Introduction

It is in the PE, games, and dance situations that the dyspraxics' difficulties are most likely to be obvious and noticed (by other students as well as teachers), which is why PE deserves a special short general introduction.

Dyspraxic students are, in the normal course of events, almost never in the School or House team. If they are, their lack of skills or competence may 'let the team down', or they may fear that that is what might happen. Of course, many dyspraxic students might love to be in the team, if only things were different.

In fact, though, they may fear the assembly hall, the gym, the sports hall, the playing field, or the tennis court which can be threatening places, where there is equipment they cannot manage, and activities they cannot do.

So, before choosing some courses from the following menu, here are one or two *hors d'oeuvre* for you to sample to whet the appetite before your main decisions.

- Think very hard before allowing students to pick teams, or even partners. The dyspraxic students will usually be among the last to be chosen.

- In some activities, students can have a choice of how they complete them, thus partially removing 'failure' from the dyspraxics' agenda. For instance, rather than tell a class, 'Tightrope-walk your way along the balance bar,' you could allow all the class to travel along the bar any way they like, but specifically encourage the more able to tightrope-walk it, while allowing the dyspraxic students quietly to carry on crawling along it, or to be pulling along it on their stomachs. There is an important point here about emphasis. This way you are not saying, in effect or by implication, 'Everyone should really be able to tightrope-walk this, but there may be just one or two who can't, so they can crawl if they need to'. This is OK up to a point (better than insisting everyone tightrope-walk), but it is still something of a put-down for the dyspraxics. Putting it round the other way (just saying, 'Travel along the bench') makes it seem as if this is fine and then it's a bonus (which they are certainly entitled to) for the children who can tightrope-walk it, but the dyspraxic students still feel they have achieved something, too. When they compare themselves with the others who are more able, which they will certainly still do, they may, at least, not do so in quite such a negative way.

- Always consider the possibility of adapting or amending an activity. One example would be where the net could be lowered or the court made smaller (or bigger!) Another, more problematic, example could be in skittles, where some students are allowed to take aim from a shorter range. This is fine if that is appropriate to all the students in the group in that particular game, but what about if some students are very competent and have no need of this concession? This is a philosophical point that always provokes discussion about 'fairness' and 'equity', etc. But if you can get it across to the class that they can have a meaningful game and competition even when different students roll from different ranges (determined in all probability and practicality by the teacher), then you are teaching something much more profound than how to knock down a few skittles. This principle and practice can be replicated over and over again throughout a range of activities, such as throwing a bean bag into a bin or through a hoop, throwing a ball at a target, kicking a ball into a goal, etc.

- Remember that, certainly in some peer groups, proficiency in games and PE gives students kudos within that group. The opposite may well be true. Who'd be a student with dyspraxia in such a social setting?

Now here is a sample menu. Particularly where PE is concerned, there are many variations on any one theme. Choose your fare, but once you have got a taste for it you can be your own chef and simply adjust the mix slightly to fit a number of situations.

- Space (1): Give dyspraxic students their own space – a relatively large one – for changing. If you do this, you might want to do the same for every student in the class. This alleviates feelings of being different for the dyspraxic students, but is difficult to police.

- Space (2): Whether in individual or group activities, students with dyspraxia are likely to appreciate working within a defined space (chalked on the floor, marked with gym tape, indicated by cones, or on specified mats) rather than in the whole of the vast space of a sports hall or gym full of activities.

- Stamina: Consider, on the whole, having shorter rather than longer periods of activity. In a group or class situation, it may be necessary to engineer discreet intervals of rest so that dyspraxic students can continue to participate usefully.

- Strength: Certainly at secondary level, consider if (wisely) building up strength might help. (Consult with the occupational therapist or physiotherapist, if such other professionals are involved, before embarking on any particular programme.)

- Balance (1): Remember that balance activities may present a real difficulty for dyspraxic students, and a partial blind eye may be turned to some students who just cannot maintain balance. As ever, sensible, professional awareness is crucial in judging how far to go with this for a particular student.

- Balance (2): Consider literally providing support, even to the extent, in the case of students who cannot balance on one leg, their being allowed to rest the foot which is supposed to be off the floor on something (perhaps first a cube, later a ball).

- Hopping: If they can't hop at all, let them rock from one leg to the other.

- Freezing: In games where students are required suddenly to freeze, that professional blind eye used in Balance (1) may need to come into play again, but if it's a competitive game that professional sensitivity about how far to go will also have to be ready to spring into action.

- Catching: This is another activity that may be particularly fraught for dyspraxic students. Consider not expecting them to catch balls thrown by other students. Instead, they may be happier working at the level of simply dropping a ball onto the floor and catching it as it bounces up, or throwing the ball against the wall and catching the rebound. In these ways, they are more in control of the activity; as the teacher, you can move them on (e.g. use a smaller ball, stand further away from the wall) as you judge.

- Throwing: As indicated above, you may consider it best to treat this as an activity in its own right, and not to link it with catching. You may want to think about a range of targets (large hoops, small skittles), a range of 'projectiles' (bean bags, beach balls, tennis balls), and a range of distances. And you may want to think about having a number of ability groups working with different combinations of these, thus allowing the dyspraxic students to be progressing at their level without in any way impeding the progress of the more able. This is another example, also, of where the motor activity is best carried out on an individual basis, but that does not mean working in total isolation; perhaps one student can hold the hoop steady while the other tries to lob ten beanbags through, before reversing their roles.

- Climbing: You may want to think about climbing, in that climbing does not always have to mean climbing *upwards*; it could be, for instance, climbing *around* an array of boxes, if that is what the dyspraxic students are able to do.

- Crab football: This is mentioned as just one example of how a game can be adapted in order to allow the dyspraxic students to participate without making any really material difference to the game. In crab football, the rule generally applied is that all players maintain the crab position all the time (i.e. bottoms off the floor) but some players could be given the referee's permission to rest and remain stationary with bottoms on the floor, but have to assume the crab position when moving or kicking.

- Obstacle courses: You may think it would be helpful to have two, or even three, obstacle courses being used simultaneously. The courses would be of different levels of difficulty, and the aptitude of the students would be matched to a particular course. It is facile to deny that the able children will not appreciate that they are negotiating the difficult course, and even more so, that the students with dyspraxia will not realise they are doing the easiest. You will feel that if only your class can have really healthy attitudes and outlooks, this will not matter. And you may feel you have to confront the alternatives. Have dyspraxic students attempt hard courses on which they will fail? Have no obstacle courses at all so that no one fails (and no one succeeds)? Thinking through issues in this sort of way, you will expect to come to a suitable compromise, in which there is something for all students.

- Swimming: You may wish to decide not to be over-fussy about technique. A certain level of technique is desirable, but perfection is not required in order to enjoy social swimming (look in on any general public swimming session at any public pool). To an extent, swimming is a physical activity that can be accomplished by students who are not over well-coordinated, and still give a lot of satisfaction and self-confidence. That said, you may want to acknowledge swimming may well have to be taught if it is to be efficient, even if the dyspraxic students do 'take to the water'. If you do opt for specific teaching of swimming technique and stroke-making, you may want to think about teaching arm and leg movements separately if you think that coordinating the two may initially be too difficult. If you do feel this, you might feel that it is better (easier and more fun) first to get them moving forward with leg power (moving on the stomach while holding a float, probably) before introducing arm movements. You might even think it is better to progress to moving on their backs, using the same method as above, before introducing arm movements. Anyway, you are making choices as you think best, things are not sliding, and you will be prepared to adapt quickly depending upon what you see.

A La Carte for Maths

Introduction

Perhaps the immediate significance of dyspraxia upon students' performance in Maths is not always immediately apparent when one thinks about it in the abstract (the same may be said with regard to students with dyslexia, too). However, even relatively casual observation in the classroom will soon show otherwise.

As with handwriting and letter formation, dyspraxic students may well have difficulty with acquiring the ability to write numerals. If they can do this, they may then have difficulty keeping them in columns as they do their 'sums', with some catastrophic answers.

The fine motor skills needed to hold a ruler steady, either to draw a line or in order to measure, say, a side of a parallelogram in the calculation of its area, may be lacking, and very imprecise results may accrue.

Drawing diagrams, as in Geometry, also requires a fairly high degree of fine motor skills, and possibly spatial awareness comes into play here, too. The same remarks could be applied to the use of a pair of compasses and the drawing of circles and arcs.

In fact, the whole notion of organising a page of Maths, and the logic of the way such a page is set out step by step, are concepts that students with dsypraxia may find difficulty either in appreciating or implementing.

And, is it not true that Maths teachers in particular do recommend, and really like to see, well-ordered and neatly presented work? If students do not supply this, there is the potential for a certain amount of misunderstanding, not to say conflict.

However, there is much that can be done to ameliorate these problems. As ever, the answer lies in observing the students in question and thinking about what skills would be really helpful for each of them to acquire to ease their lot in the classroom. Apply some insightful common sense, allow some time and do not expect instant miracles, and you will be supporting your students.

Here is a menu of the sort of things that will be helpful. Depending upon what you see in your own classroom, you may wish to adapt these dishes, or invent new ones along the same lines which will suit your particular palate more aptly.

- Consider having students paint digits with big brushes using thick paint. This can help with number recognition but, more particularly, can be useful in learning to write numbers (simple calculations can also be set out in this way). Not only is this a useful ploy, it is likely to be good fun, too.

- Similarly, consider encouraging students to write numbers in sand using either their fingers or a stick. A development of this could be to ask them to write numerals with a thick pen on coarse sandpaper.

- The personal, relatively small whiteboard could be useful at this stage, too. Here the students can use, in contrast to the previous two activities, lovely, smooth, easy-flowing wipe-clean felt-tip pens to write, erase, and practise again many numerals in all sorts of delicious colours to encourage them in the mastery of this task of forming numerals well.

- In each of the three above activities, ideally the movement of the fingers, the brush, the stick, the felt-tip pen (and, later, the pencil and the pen) should be the 'correct' ones from the outset. (If you are unsure which are the correct ones, please see 'Handwriting' in Resources.) This is vital in handwriting but, also, highly desirable in the writing of numerals. The final outcome is the most important thing, of course, namely, that numerals are clearly and neatly written, but this is much more likely to be the case if the correct movements are being made in order to produce these numerals, and this may well have to be specifically taught. It is a case of the process being important as well as the product.

- Think about the use of stampers to avoid the need to write numerals on some occasions. Or, in much the same vein, you could consider the use of magnetic numbers and boards. If the teacher needs to see the answers, as is likely if actual calculations are being done, the students can set out the 'sums' on the board but just copy the answers into their exercise books or folders for the teacher to check.

- You may think that stencils have a part to play to help students with the writing of numerals. (The same may be true when it comes to the drawing of squares, triangles, etc.)

- Squared paper is likely to be used in the early stages of Maths for all students; you may consider it advisable to persist with it for much longer for some students.

- Worksheets on which the students have to do their calculations, you may feel, need to be adapted, literally to give them room to do these if their numeral writing is erratic and not well controlled.

- You might think it worthwhile having worksheets where, for instance, the *hundreds* are presented in one colour, the *tens* in another, and so on. If appropriate, in fact, in order to help students with their place value and keeping to columns, students can do their own written numerals similarly (whether or not the original 'sum' is thus 'colour-coded').

- Consider highlighting the 'procedural' words and signs (*plus, add,* +, *minus, subtract, take away,* etc.) really to draw the students' attention to them. Again, a different colour for a different sign may be worth thinking about.

- In considering all Maths worksheets and, even more particularly, some Maths textbooks and workbooks, you may wish to think about clarity and simplicity (in the sense of it being easy for the students to discern what is required of them). Font needs to be large enough, and the pages not too cluttered. It may be that you feel that some textbooks which are generally considered to be attractive, and have been designed to have student-appeal, may be difficult for the students with dyspraxia to cope with because there is actually too much 'going on' on each page, with too many illustrations, too many colours, too many little tips, etc. (The same could be true, of course, for students with dyslexia.)

- Depending on your students (or rather each student as an individual), have a think about any small practical ways in which they could each be supported, such as by having suitable blobs of Blue-Tac under their rulers to help keep them in place and stable.

- Consider particularly the possible place and likely effectiveness of structural Maths (e.g. Cuisenaire Rods, Stern Kits, Unifix, etc. – suppliers can be found in the Resources section at the end of this book) and whether these might not be very appropriate for students with dyspraxia, in that they they are not merely abstract. Dyspraxic students will quite possibly have some manual difficulties in handling and manipulating the materials, and allowances may have to be made for dropped cubes and spilt equipment, but the way in which they address mathematical concepts may be thought so appropriate that this is a price worth paying.

- For students who have real difficulty in organising their Maths on the page, especially when it comes to rather more complex Maths, such as when an example has to be solved in several stages, you might consider trying giving the students an acetate sheet the same size as the paper they are working on. In the acetate, a rectangle has been cut out. The students position the acetate exactly on their page and then confine the workings out they are immediately engaged upon to within that rectangle. As each stage is completed, the acetate is, of course, moved down the page so that the cut-out is appropriately positioned on the page, ready for the next stage to be written within it. This may help the students organise their pages and still enable them to see and refer back to the earlier stages of the problem.

- Calculators are likely to be useful in avoiding the need for a certain amount of written Maths. It is possible, though, that students with dyspraxia will have difficulty with small keys. That is not, of itself, a problem in that calculators with fairly large keys are readily available. Depending on the fashion of the day, however, a large calculator might be seen as distinctly not the thing to have. A possible answer to this is to have outrageously, humorously large calculators, quite possibly in garish colours. They may make an alternative, or anti-, fashion statement, and be acceptable, especially if presented to the students with a light touch.

A La Carte for Art, Craft, Design and Technology
Introduction
These umbrella terms cover the multitude of activities that go on in schools involving painting and drawing, plasticine and clay, cutting and sawing, sticking and glueing, designing and decorating, in primary school classrooms and in secondary workshops and hi-tec CDT (Craft, Design and Technology) studios.

Largely because of a cocktail of visuo-spatial difficulties, fine motor control problems, and imprecise hand-eye coordination these are all likely to be difficult areas for students with dyspraxia and so, as ever, the first desirable feature is for teachers, without despairing of their dyspraxic students, nevertheless to be sensitive to this.

Following close on the heels of this awareness, it is really helpful if teachers can remember that dyspraxic students may wish to be creative, and may have lively imaginations, but that it's doing these justice that is the problem. It's a problem in that the students cannot perhaps create anything that looks or feels like the thing they have in their mind's eye (and may even know, theoretically, how to produce), and it's a problem in the frustration this can engender (sometimes exacerbated by the reactions of classmates).

Given the range of subjects, activities, and locations we are talking about here, the following can only be a taster menu. It is illustrative, and you will be able to draw upon it to create your own strategies as befits your particular circumstances.

- Consider helping to keep the paper in place in Art (a type of matting is one way to do this – see Resources).

- Consider:
  o chubby wax crayons rather than fine pencils
  o chubby chalks rather than fine pastels
  o hard-leaded pencils rather than soft.

- Consider use of a wide-toothed comb, or fork, or even fingers instead of a brush (in, for instance, pattern work).

- Consider thick paint rather than poster paint (soda crystals thicken paint).

- Consider plasticine and clay (the deep pressure of pressing down into these may be appropriate).

- Consider adapted equipment, for example:
  o different types of scissors are available, such as those with a spring-loaded action, or ones that are designed so that all four fingers can be used in the lower grip (see Resources)

- o larger bodkins

- o material of bigger mesh

- o embroidery hoops (can be useful for organising and holding steady work other than embroidery)

- o embroidery hoop with attachment or foot which is sat upon to give even greater rigidity and stability.

- Consider alternative media, for example:

  - o photography could be a good option (rather than Art). Digital cameras can make this more feasible (although the degree of finesse required in operating could be something of a problem – if so, perhaps the use of a tripod could help)

  - o displaying these images on the computer screen, and enhancing, altering, printing, and displaying the images can all be part of this, and be a creative outlet which leads to a good result.

- Consider that students with dyspraxia may be happier to concentrate on abstract rather than representational work (although the abstract may still not turn out as the students wanted, but this will be less obvious to the casual observer or classmate).

- Consider computer design programs.

- Consider (even if you have a syllabus to follow, and you would want your students to experience a range of media and methods) allowing dyspraxic students to some extent to utilise their own preferences.

A mixed salad of subject considerations for the student with dyspraxia

Introduction

This chapter opened by suggesting that it has long been acknowledged that we have always had students with dyspraxia in our schools (even though they may just have been referred to as 'clumsy'). This final section of the chapter will indicate how this condition does permeate the whole of the curriculum and, indeed, the whole of the students' school experience. It will certainly, though, comply with the fundamental messages throughout this book, which include the belief that students with SENs can be given a worthwhile degree of support by all teachers who are prepared to see the world through the students' eyes, and then have a positive and constructive think about what measures it is within their powers to implement to make the classroom a better and easier place for such students.

In Science, as a generalisation, dyspraxic students tend to drop things, spill things, shake things too much, and knock over experiments and apparatus. Certainly, these are not insignificant matters, with 'Health and Safety' being a very reasonable concern. Knowing the students is, of course, half the battle (some might say that remembering them is the other half); once the Science teachers get to know the students, they can work out which are the situations where greater vigilance must be exercised, and where steps must be taken such as making sure the dyspraxic students are not stood too close when observing any 'volatile' experiments, or are working with a very reliable partner when conducting such an experiment. On the smaller practical level, Science teachers will want to think about working practices such as test tubes being worked with in racks rather than in the dyspraxic students' hands.

Dealing with dyspraxic students at their desks, they may be helped by being provided with blank diagrams which they have to label, but which they have not been expected to draw. Or, perhaps diagrams could be provided which are partially drawn but which are for the students to complete.

Addressing the possible educational consequences of dyspraxia, in Biology the students are likely to understand 3-D anatomical models better than diagrams. In fact, in all aspects of Science, models are likely to be more meaningful than diagrams.

In Geography, the idea of not expecting too much by way of map drawing is probably wise on the teacher's part; again, maps already drawn but ready for labelling are generally a good idea, or perhaps partly drawn ready for the students to complete; this latter does have the merit of probably making the students pay a closer attention to the details of the map. Completion, of course, does not just mean outlines or coasts, but can include contours, mountain ranges, lakes, etc. More sophisticated skills of map reading, for instance, are likely to be difficult, and a patient step-by-step approach will be called for.

In Music, a lack of a strong sense of rhythm can pose problems, and basic rhythm work is probably the only way to address this. Again, one must emphasise (a) teacher frustration must not, if humanly possible, be allowed to show, and (b) exposing the dyspraxic students to any ridicule from other students has to be guarded against by not drawing too much attention to the students' lack of rhythmicity. Use of a variety of instruments makes Music more fun for the dyspraxic student, as it does for any other, and so far as rhythm work is concerned, different types of drums (and drum sticks), tambourines, maracas, even castanets, clapping hands, stamping feet, palms of hands tapping on thighs (seated), different surfaces (desk tops, trays, possibly glasses, triangles, large balls) all add not only interest but also different, but linked, types of feedback. And perhaps the voice should not be forgotten, not here for singing, but for *dah-dah-dah*, *dee-dee-dee* type rhythms.

Beats of regular intervals, differently spaced intervals, heavy and light stresses all need to be woven into a planned pattern of slowly increasing complexity, but never presented as a chore or a test; indeed, the art is to try to present such exercises as a form of music making.

Music can actually also play a part in developing dyspraxic students' hand-eye coordination and aspects of motor control. Think, for instance, of what is required in asking students to 'play' a short sequence of given notes on a piano or, more likely, an electronic keyboard, perhaps first with the preferred hand, then with the other. It may well be necessary to number the notes with 'stick-ons' in the order in which you are asking the student to 'play' them. Probably it goes without saying, do not be too ambitious in the early stages of the length of the sequence of notes you are asking them to 'play'; it may be very short indeed to start with. Once teachers begin this sort of work, developments of it often become apparent; not only could the number of notes to be struck be increased, but their distance from each other on the keyboard could also be extended. Use only white notes in the sequence, use only black, use a mixture. Varying intervals between the strikes could possibly be introduced (this is rhythm). Students could 'play' along with a recorded sequence.

This type of work can certainly be extended, and again made more fun, on the chime bars, and even the xylophone, if the school is lucky enough to have one.

In several subjects, there may be difficulties for students with dyspraxia over 'reading and understanding', by which is meant more than just word recognition, but the understanding of the sense of a piece of writing, the ability to extract salient facts, the appreciation of context, etc. Subjects such as English and History are very much in mind here. Dyspraxic students may benefit (as may dyslexic) from being taught little techniques to help them in this regard. The use of Post-Its, judiciously placed in margins, possibly with the students' further reminders noted on them, or highlighters (possibly colour-coded) to make important sections jump off the page and into the students' consciousness are also beneficial (so long as marking the text is acceptable). Summarising reviewing, and making notes as valuable study skills (not just as set tasks) may have to be encouraged.

In a more general sense, when providing information which is mainly to be accessed by reading, such as handouts, all teachers need to ensure that these are clear, plain, and uncluttered. They can often benefit by being further delineated by the judicious use of different fonts, different colours either to link or separate points, and by underlinings, italics, capitals, asterisks, etc. to make points stand out. Guard against going overboard in these respects, but if they can be made just slightly visually distinctive, dyspraxic students are likely to benefit. For more discussion of all these points, please see the 'Notemaking and notetaking' section in Chapter 2.

School consists of a great deal more than classrooms. In fact, the rest of the school environment and the time outside the classroom can be fraught for the dyspraxic students. This leads to the conclusion that not only the students' main teacher need to be aware of them, but all teachers, and all staff. For instance, can the dyspraxic students carry their trays successfully from the serving hatch to the table at lunchtimes, or is this just an accident waiting to happen? Even if they do manage not to drop the tray, and not to have to endure those awful ironic cheers that this can provoke, is this daily experience stressful? Only in extreme cases would you want the students to have no responsibility for their trays, but a suitable dining room assistant could be prompted to keep a weather eye out for these students, and lend a tactful hand. A really good friend could serve the same role, and this is much to be encouraged, but proceeded with only cautiously, out of respect for the feelings of both students. Depending on the seating and dining arrangements, ideally it should be possible for dyspraxic students to sit nearer to, rather than farther from, the servery, with a shorter distance to walk.

Of such measures, are disability-friendly schools made.

Chapter 4

&

A Menu for Supporting Students with Attention Deficit Disorder and Attention Deficit Hyperactivity Disorder in the Inclusive Classroom

First concerns

Attention Deficit Disorder (ADD) and Attention Deficit Hyperactivity Disorder (ADHD) can be difficult to diagnose and in the minds of some, the jury is – at best – still out on whether these are real disorders. Consider the following which a teacher friend of mine recently told me:

> That Mrs X! She's at it again. That elder boy of hers, we all know he's a pain. Can't sit still for two minutes, and always upsetting the class. Well, it's a bit better now she's got him Statemented, and we've been able to get an LSA. So now she's trying to say the little one is ADHD, too. She's just playing the system.

So, who are these children who provoke such a reaction? As with all children, there is not a single set of descriptors which totally fit a particular child (all human beings having that annoying characteristic of each being unique) but it is possible to give some fairly good indicators, so that we know who we are talking about. In fact, at one level (and without committing the cardinal sin of jumping to conclusions), this is not difficult because every teacher is likely to recognise these provoking students.

ADHD

Let's consider ADHD first: does the following sound familiar when you think of students you know or have known?

- They are always fidgeting with something or squirming in their seats; in fact, with younger children, they have difficulty remaining in their seats. If this is not the case for older students, they nevertheless strongly evince an air of general restlessness.

- They are easily distracted by almost anything: workmen in the playground or the groundsman cutting the grass on the playing field means the end of any learning in your lesson as far as these students are concerned. If they are paying a degree of attention, they blurt out answers to questions, and never really take fair turns in any situations such as group work, class discussions or activities, or games. If they are paying attention, they can't sustain it; again, this goes for work and play.

- They make what seem to be just careless mistakes.

- They seldom complete work, but will flit from one task to another. In any case, they probably have not listened to the instructions in the first place, and if they have, they still will not fully follow them. In fact, they seldom listen to anything, but they talk excessively, and at inappropriate times, often interrupting others, and intruding into situations that do not concern them.

- They lose things, or do not arrive with the equipment they know they will need.

- They are disorganised, poor planners, poor starters, and poor at working in an organised, logically sequenced way, especially over a period of time, and quickly become bored.

- They do not learn from mistakes, or reflect upon them in order to avoid them in the future; they just do the same thing over again, and this is likely to apply to behaviour and conduct, as well as to learning. One result of this is that they experience lots of failure, which leads to frustration, and poor self-esteem, although because they are often so boisterous this is not necessarily immediately apparent.

- The way that they are always 'on the go' may even lead teachers to suspect or feel that these students, especially when they are senior students, are 'on something', that is, taking some illegal substance.

- They are excitable, and they may get themselves into dangerous situations, such as when climbing on apparatus or trees; they are regarded as risk-takers.

- They are prone to accidents, they don't stop to think of possible consequences, and thus dangerous situations can arise.

- In class, they are difficult to manage, they distract other students, and greatly disrupt the smooth running of the lesson, and the learning of other students.

Although the above rather long list of ADHD-type behaviours does make negative reading, it could equally be said that all students, and indeed all people, display some of these behaviours from time to time, or that all students are naughty from time to time, so how do we decide if the behaviours are real problems, and possibly ADHD? It is also necessary to keep such behaviours in proportion; we are not entitled to bandy the term 'ADHD' around the staff room without good reason, or to jump to conclusions.

So, we need to consider if the student is showing a range of such behaviours, and has done so for a period of time, such as for at least six months. It is generally accepted that such behaviours will have been present from an early age (before seven) for ADHD to be a real possibility; 'newer' behaviours probably have some other cause. Also, for ADHD to be at least on the cards, the behaviours must occur in different situations and environments (that is, they are not situation-specific), the school and the home being the obvious ones. Most importantly, the behaviours must interfere 'significantly' with the students' emotional, social, and educational functioning – and not be explicable by any other disorder.

If we think along these lines, it is entirely possible for the teacher who was quoted at the beginning to accept that ADHD is definitely not a term which can be applied to, or even 'excuse', the behaviour of any or every occasionally naughty child, but also to agree that there is a significant number of children whose unsettledness, distractibility, and capacity to disrupt is of a different order and magnitude; who are not merely restless; are not in a class where the teacher is poorly organised (so that students have time when they have nothing, or nothing 'stretching', to do) and so are just bored; are not in a class with a teacher who is unable to maintain normal classroom rules (a situation which if it does occasionally unfortunately occur is likely to be taken advantage of by the majority of students); and for whom traditional discipline might not be enough. These may be our ADHD students.

Albeit fairly briefly – but adequately enough for teachers to get the flavour, and quite possibly to be reminded of some difficult students and situations – we have described the presenting behaviours of ADHD students, but we can look now just a little beneath the surface to see what are the consequences for these students.

Learning

As has already been indicated, many ADHD students are very inefficient learners (they quite possibly cannot concentrate long enough to read a book, let alone produce some worthwhile work). Their actual learning is almost certainly impaired, but this does not mean they have neither intelligence or ability. They may have both but it is understandable that these never surface, are masked by all the ADHD behaviours, and are recognised by neither the student or the teacher. This is very frustrating to both, but particularly to the students who, understandably, get low marks, lots of criticism, and no satisfaction from their school tasks.

In fact, they may be able to concentrate on some things on some days in some subjects or activities. This means they present a confusing profile to their teacher(s). Perhaps they can concentrate on what they are interested in, which we can all do. What they can't do is concentrate on what they are not interested in; most of us find this hard, but manage to do it, or to learn to do it. For ADHD students it is impossible without support (see menu later!). But, again, this frustrates teachers who feel that if students can concentrate in one situation it is reasonable to expect them to concentrate in all situations. This can lead to teacher–student conflict.

Social implications

After a while, ADHD students tend to have few friends, or few friends who are themselves of stable dispositions. Why is this?

Other students may laugh at their inappropriate behaviour, and possibly set them up to do inappropriate, or silly, or naughty things. Eventually it is entirely possible that the ADHD students annoy their original friends and, basically, come to be rejected by them. ADHD students are not good in teams or corporate activities, which causes peers simply to get fed up with them. ADHD students can make life very difficult for their peers both in the classroom and at breaktimes, and peers may well find them very hard to understand, let alone tolerate. A possible result is that they become so unpopular that they are not just rejected, but actually bullied.

Outside of school, they may find social groups very difficult in anything except the short-term. Yet, they desperately need to learn to socialise in conventional ways. For some, the activities of Cubs and Scouts, for instance, might be very appropriate, yet difficulties are always likely to be just around the corner. The children and young people, and the clubs themselves are likely to need support – from some quarter. *Individual* or semi-individual activities *within* a club setting may be one of the best solutions, so we might be thinking of weightlifting, art, perhaps photography, a craft activity, possibly learning an instrument, ten-pin bowling, etc.

School implications

Given that ADHD students can be verbally and emotionally impulsive, they will tend not to obey the rules (or rather, not think to heed them), and also be rude to staff. These incidents can lead to explosive situations, with the ADHD students oblivious of rational argument, and in lots of disciplinary trouble. ADHD students can be aggressive towards other students and very oppositional to staff, and come to be seen as 'a behaviour problem'. Theoretically, one should interject at this point that 'behaviour problem' is merely a description (and a fairly vague one at that) and not an assessment that carries one forward, but one does have every sympathy with the school and the teachers at the chalk-face; these can be very annoying students for teachers honestly trying to run a smooth classroom for the benefit of the whole class. Anyway, this can all certainly reach the proportions of school suspension and exclusion.

ADD

The ADD students present so differently from ADHD students that initially some people cannot understand why they are, to some extent, bracketed together. ADHD students are totally in your face for much of the time; the ADD students are totally the opposite. It is impossible to overlook the ADHD students, who strike such a high profile. With ADD students, it is all too easy to overlook them as they maintain the quietest of images. When we look later in a little more detail at the constituents of ADHD and ADD, it will become apparent why they can be thought of in the same category, but let us first paint a picture of ADD students.

The ADD students certainly can sit still and quietly, and exhibit none of the 'on the go' behaviours of the ADHD students. However, although sitting in just the way many teachers would like their students to sit, the ADD students are not focused, and they are actually completely missing important points of the lesson. This inability to keep their minds on the subject and settle down to their work is their chronic and serious disability They are like their ADHD counterparts in that they will, therefore, miss instructions, be unclear about what is to be done, how it is to be done, and by when, and they will also make 'careless' mistakes (because their concentration on the task in hand is so tenuous).

In fact, the ADD students simply do not engage with the curriculum or the life of the classroom in any really meaningful way. They may well be regarded as day-dreamers, and they may also be regarded as lazy.

Clearly, they are not disruptive but this can mean that they do not attract the teachers' attention, and the depth of their problem may be entirely unrecognised.

They are, in fact, distinctly dysfunctional. They forget to do things, or forget what they are supposed to do, largely because it never fully registers in the first place, forget their kit and equipment, and are unable to get organised.

So, like their ADHD peers, they are inefficient learners, and very likely to underfunction. Teachers may despair of getting a worthwhile amount of work out of them, and their inability to concentrate long enough to complete tasks may easily result in low marks, and their being regarded as uninterested.

Although they will avoid the disciplinary incidents which befall the ADHD students who upset their friends or confront teachers, ADD students will not gain much satisfaction from their school life, and will not be held in very high regard by their teachers, who see them as not being industrious or motivated.

ADD and ADHD characteristics

So far we have described our ADHD and ADD students in ways descriptive and almost anecdotal. It is time we were a little more precise in thinking about these behaviours. How can they be categorised?

This is usually done under three headings:

1. *Inattention/inattentiveness/short attention span.* This leads particularly to those careless mistakes, the lack of maintained focus, the not listening and the day-dreaming, not finishing work, being disorganised and, very importantly, being distractible.

2. *Hyperactivity.* This is revealed by the excessive fidgeting, leaving their seat in the classroom, excitability, coping neither with quiet work or quiet play, being always on the move, and talking excessively and in the wrong situation at the wrong time.

3. *Impulsiveness.* This is seen in the students who speak out of turn, call out answers and, quite possibly questions, in class, and who cannot take a fair turn in games or group activities.

There is always the possibility of overlap between these three categories, none of them is absolutely watertight, but the ADD students, as is pointed out in the National Institute for Health and Clinical Excellence guidelines (NICE 2008), clearly come mainly in the *Inattention* category, and it is this which distinguishes them from the ADHD students. But the essential condition of seriously lacking self-regulation is common to both.

The next points we must consider are (a) why is it that an ability to regulate their own behaviour is so lacking in some students, and (b) are the reasons for, and causes of, this particular lack of ability the defining characteristics of ADHD and ADD?

Causes and 'cures': possible and probable

As has already been indicated by the comments of the teacher quoted at the opening of this chapter, the cause of ADD/ADHD (or the types of behaviour, and learning, associated with these terms) has certainly been contentious and, to a degree, this remains the case.

Deficiencies that can be rectified by a particular diet, for instance, have been claimed to exist. Advocates of this theory tend to suggest that certain items should be avoided because they either cause or aggravate the condition, while certain others should be taken or added to the diet because they either cure it or greatly ameliorate it. Typically, among the items which proponents of this approach recommend children have in their diet are vitamin (B6) supplements and megavitamins, zinc supplements, and fish oils. They would, probably even more strongly, suggest that many or all artificial colourings and preservatives are avoided, along with sugar-rich foods. The topic of diet with regard to ADD/ADHD has been much debated, but most would agree that the case for has not been proven for the majority of students. That said, there are certainly people (including parents) who swear by its beneficial effects. Perhaps common sense strongly suggests that, say, large amounts of extra sugar (some sweets, some drinks) are not likely to help a child who already has a predisposition to ADHD.

In fact, there is a range of treatments and cures, each with their own supporters. Another of these, for example, is the giving of an anti-fungal medicine to stop the growth of candida, which is a yeast that naturally grows in the body and which may produce harmful toxins. Another is cranial osteopathy, which includes realigning certain bones in the skull through manipulation.

It is fair to say that none of these has very wide support, but perhaps their very existence indicates the concern that ADD/ADHD provokes, especially among parents, how seriously these conditions are viewed, and the lengths that some people are, therefore, willing to go to search for solutions.

Teachers will tend to be more pragmatic or prosaic, and to espouse the virtues of 'discipline', and it is fair for them to question the quality of the parenting, which is where most discipline starts. What is not fair is for them automatically to blame the parents. It may be difficult to accept that ADD/ADHD children are not simply naughty children who have been allowed to behave badly from an early age, and who now need even more discipline from parents who seem unable to administer it. It can be hard to accept that they are in a different league, and although behavioural management certainly has to be part of a long-term strategy for supporting these students, that it may well not be the fault of the parents that normal disciplinary and child-rearing approaches have not worked (quite possibly to the despair of well-meaning parents).

So, what is the explanation of the origins of ADD/ADHD that is most widely accepted today? It is that there is a neurological cause, and that it is a neurobiochemical condition which is genetic and biological in origin. There is no diagnostic blood test or scan or anything of that ilk which will identify ADD/ADHD, but it is believed that there is a malfunction in the neurochemical messengers that regulate concentration and the control of impulses.

Thus, ADD/ADHD is not a mental illness, is not psychological or social in origin, and is not a result of a poor environment, poor parenting or, for that matter, poor teaching. It is an inability to inhibit inappropriate behaviour and to control impulses, and there is a biological basis for this inability.

Medication

In some circles, the rights and wrongs and the desirability or otherwise of medication are much debated, and strong feelings can be aired. It is not unknown, also, for couples to disagree as to whether or not their ADHD child should take medication, and for this to generate great tension and discord between them.

'I don't think children should be sedated.'

'I don't believe children should be drugged.'

'I don't believe we should turn children into zombies just because we can't control them.'

'It's not right to drug children up to the eyeballs and turn them into cabbages.'

These are some of the sorts of comment one might also hear, perhaps particularly from those who don't really believe in the existence of ADD and ADHD, and who feel the problem can be explained away by lack of early parental controls.

And so it comes as quite a surprise to a number of people when they learn that most medications are actually stimulants. Admittedly, this does sound odd at first: children are massively overactive, so you give them a stimulant to calm them down! In fact, what seems to be happening is that all medications work on some of the natural chemicals (such as noradrenaline and dopamine) in areas of the brain which seem to be underactive in doing their job of balancing impulsivity. In other words, the areas of the brain which are stimulated therefore include those which help with concentration, and regulation of behaviour. As a result, those who advocate at least some medication claim that all the typical aspects of ADHD and ADD, which may perhaps be summed up in the word *distractibility*, will generally improve. Putting it another way, the core symptoms will come under much better control.

Virtually no one advocates that giving medication is all that one does for ADD and ADHD children. It is important to place the giving of medication in a broader context, and to appreciate how most people view its purpose. This is more constructive than just decrying medication, yet does not imagine that medication is the total answer.

In a nutshell, the results of the medication mean that teachers (and parents and the rest of the family) have a young person with whom they can work, and for whom educational intervention might actually achieve something. Once the educational intervention (a synonym for good teaching) is felt (although probably not articulated) by the students to be working, a virtuous circle is set up. The students do better in school, gain success and confidence and grow in self-esteem, so are more receptive to more educational intervention – so they do even better. And so it goes on. The need for medication is thus diminished, and the actual medication is reduced.

This view of medication as an aid to education, and not a replacement for it, is worth emphasising. The idea is, then, that medication, and its calming influence (which has been achieved not by dumbing down but by helping the student's own brain to work in the balanced way it should) provides a window of opportunity for educational measures to gain a toe-hold. Once that level of engagement has been made, perhaps student and teacher can begin to move forward in a way that was not previously possible. If, in the past, the ADHD was so severe that the student never really made contact with education, all strategies may have been pointless. Now, perhaps, they can have a chance to support the student, and to show the student what education can offer.

An appropriate metaphor which is sometimes used to sum up what it is that medication makes possible is that it provides a calm sea in which the student (and teacher) can control the navigation rather than just be permanently tossed around in a tempest.

Allowing for the above, concern is often expressed about the possibility of side effects resulting from taking the medication. These concerns include: reduced appetite, weight loss, slowing of growth rate; stomach ache or abdomen pains; difficulty in getting to sleep; tics and jittery movements; irritability; and headaches. One has also heard of fears about addiction, blood disorders, and liver and kidney problems.

Possibly the most common side effect is weight loss due to appetite repression. To observe this worries parents, and teenage boys who want to develop their bodies and their masculine image may be put off taking the medication for this reason. There may be some evidence that medication contributes to a later entry to puberty in the case of younger children. That said, it is possible that weight will increase in the case of some students because their appetite improves because they are now able to settle to eat properly. With regard to failure to sleep, it should be remembered that poor sleep patterns are relatively common in ADHD students, anyway. If there seems to be a change in personality, perhaps with the child becoming either fractious or rather the opposite and somewhat passive, these side effects can probably be rectified by adjusting the dosage (rather than simply stopping the medication).

Although it is, of course, absolutely right to be concerned about side effects and – very importantly – to be vigilant and to look out for them, the consensus is that any side effects are most unlikely to be long-term but to be present for only the duration of the medication, and to be minimal if the dosage is right.

In fact, from every point of view, the level of the dosage is crucial. It has to be acknowledged that it can take a long time to get this right, and that it varies a good deal from student to student; sometimes the beneficial effects can be immediate, or it can take weeks for them to become apparent (during which time the right dosage is probably being sought). So, dosage levels may be adjusted, and should always be kept under review. It has to be recognised, also, that medication may need to be taken long-term, although an annual pause, quite possibly in the school summer holidays, is often prescribed, partly in order to observe the children and their demeanour when without medication.

From the above, it becomes apparent that not only is the medication not an antibiotic, it does not work like one. It does not provide a cure, but it may provide daily relief, and in order to obtain the relief the medication has to be taken regularly for as long as it is necessary.

The medication may be slow-release, and the morning dose, taken at home, will last the student through the school day. Other medication may require a midday top up. This will be less convenient for the school, which will have to have regard to its policy over the administration, and probably storage, of medication. Quite possibly, there will be issues here for the students, too. Being ADD or ADHD, they may well not be able to remember to go to have the medication, or there may be personal feelings of self-consciousness about being singled out and having to do so.

If the school is not involved in the administration of the medication, it should still know whether or not the student is receiving it. If that information is not apparent, the school should ask. If the student is taking medication, this is probably straightforward enough, but if he is not (and, of course, initially the school does not know either way) it is rather more delicate. By the school asking, parents can infer that the school is saying that the student should have medication. This, in turn, can make the parents anxious, or they can take offence at what they perceive as a suggestion that they are not providing properly for their child. Great tact is, therefore, needed on the part of the school, with the approach probably being one of the school simply seeking information so that it has as full an understanding of the student's situation as possible.

In fact, although the school does not have a role in the prescription of medication, it should have a role in feedback with regard to the apparent efficacy of the medication. After medication is first prescribed, the school should report either to parents and/or clinician any differences (or not) which they notice in the student's demeanour, while long-term it should also feed back any changes which might suggest that the beneficial effects of medication are wearing off and an adjustment might be called for. Perhaps most importantly, the school should consult with parents/clinician if the student has a particularly unsettled or unproductive spell; the reason for doing this is principally to check (as far as possible) that the medication is actually being taken.

Another topic of much discussion can centre around the question of whether medication should only be prescribed, even though ADD or ADHD has been formally recognised, after teaching and behavioural strategies have been consistently tried over an extended period and been seen not to work, or whether it should be tried early so that the teaching and behavioural strategies can have the best chance of working, and so that negative cycles of failure and low expectations are not set up. The actualities of such a decision will depend upon several factors, such as the student and the severity of the ADHD, and the attitudes of the parents towards medication, but the consensus leans towards relatively early medication (with a view towards lighter dosages and earlier removal from it being, therefore, more likely).

Finally, what of the students in this debate about whether or not they should have medication? Ultimately, it will always be the decision of the parents and the child as to whether they accept the option of medication if it is recommended. Equally importantly, if medication is used, someone should be making it clear to the children that they are not being 'drugged'; teenagers, in particular, may well resist the medication, which they do not trust, feeling that they are being controlled and made docile. It should be explained to them that the opposite is the case, and that the whole idea of the medication is that it gives *them* control. It follows from this that, certainly, older students should be given an idea of how the medication actually works, and if their medication is changed, it should be explained to them why this is being done. Schools must be very wary in 'meddling' in medical matters, but they may have a role here, not necessarily in providing this sort of information but in ascertaining what the student's perception is, and discussing this with the parents and the medics.

Co-occurring conditions

ADHD students may well be difficult to manage in the classroom, where their over-active, non-conformist behaviour prevents the teacher teaching and, indeed, other students learning. Thus, they may come to be labelled generically and informally as *behaviour problems* or possibly more formally as having either Oppositional Defiant Disorder (ODD) or Conduct Disorder. The excessively quiet ADD student may be referred to as withdrawn or even depressed. Also, they may be thought to be students with Asperger Syndrome, and they certainly may share some of their characteristics, such as being particularly upset by a change of routine and functioning better in an environment which is always the same.

It is certainly possible that within any single student, elements of different conditions can exist and, indeed, mingle and mix so that there is an omelette of behaviours that cannot be totally separated any more than one could part the yolks from the whites of an omelette once it is made.

Specialists and clinicians may at least to some extent theoretically argue otherwise with regard to the previous paragraph, but the teachers in the classrooms are best advised to be aware that this complicated mixture may be cooked up or bubbling away in the students before them, especially the ADD and ADHD students, and then constructively adopt the working philosophy advocated in this book, view the menus offered reflectively, and adopt and offer the strategies they choose in the light of their experiences to date with the students and their pragmatic appreciation of what it is they would like to achieve for and with them.

It is also true that ADD and ADHD students very often have either dyslexia-type and/or dyspraxia-type difficulties, so it would be useful to look into the sections in this book which cover those disabilities. Again, it may be difficult to tease out the relative weights with which each strand of disability contributes to the student's whole being.

However, if teachers consider what it is they would most like to change at the current time with regard to a particular student (bearing in mind very much that they cannot change everything immediately, and being quite conservative in how many fronts they feel it sensible to work on) they will find menu choices here worth trying, regardless of disability labelling.

Assessment

ADD and ADHD fall, like the other conditions principally covered in this book, within the remit of the Disability Discrimination Act (1995). That said, the possibility of students in schools not having been formally assessed, let alone Statemented, has always to be borne in mind – and there are students who may never go for a formal assessment for whom some of the menu choices presented as options in this section of this book would be appropriate, whether or not the formal label of ADD/ADHD is applied (as I am sure numerous experienced teachers would testify).

In fact, assessment or formal diagnosis can only be carried out by a child psychiatrist, community paediatrician, or specialist clinician. It follows that for this to happen, referrals need to be made, and it is likely that a referral will be made by the GP. It may sometimes be the case that parents do not want to take their child to the GP for this sort of matter, which they do not really recognise as GP territory, or because they are fearful of their child being regarded as ill, particularly mentally ill. In a sense, they are right about a GP's scope in that a GP will not 'treat' ADD/ADHD, but it is the GP who is most likely to make a referral to a 'specialist'. We should add in here that it is by no means unknown for adolescents not to cooperate either formally or even informally with assessments, which possibly they are very unsure about, and may regard with suspicion. This would mean, of course, that some ADD/ADHD students are never diagnosed as such. To state the obvious, this does not mean they are not ADD/ADHD, or that they are not in our schools. The onus is back on the teacher to make provision, regardless.

The actual assessment, then, is carried out by specialists with a medical/psychiatric background, but they should not (and generally do not) act entirely alone. Indeed, the clinician who makes a diagnosis may well not personally see the child in ADD/ADHD mode because in the consulting room the child may conform, cooperate, and focus. This is because of the novelty of the situation, perhaps its formality, perhaps because of a sense of the importance of the occasion, perhaps because of what they have been told beforehand by the parents, and so on.

For this reason alone, and in order to gain a rounded picture in any case, the clinician will probably collect case histories from the parents and from the school; in fact, the possibility of other agencies having been involved (such as speech therapists) should be checked, and they, too, should generally be asked to contribute information to the clinician. So, history interview forms will probably be distributed by the clinician, preferably well before the actual appointment with the child, so that returns can be thoroughly and carefully considered, and can be up-to-date yet reflect a period of time.

Formal assessment procedures are also implemented by the clinician; one that is frequently used, and which does have specific home and school sections, being the Conners Rating Scales (Conners 2008). However, such scales are not used in isolation.

The outcome should be that, following a thorough assessment, a management plan is devised for the individual child, using the most appropriate combinations from a wide range of strategies. This, in fact, virtually sums up what this book is about, except that the assessment may have to be provisional and informal through the teachers' observations and wisdom, so that attempts may be made to meet children's needs (rather than wringing hands and actually trying nothing specific) while time is slipping by waiting for appointment dates to arrive (assuming parents and students are willing even to step out on such a route).

The management plan might include medication, and this would be prescribed (which particular medication, the dosage) by the diagnosing clinician, but routine subsequent prescriptions would probably then be overseen on a regular basis by the local GP. Some parents and children resist the notion of medication; others welcome it.

A *La Carte* for ADD and ADHD teaching strategies

Whether or not medication has been prescribed (and whether or not it is being taken regularly), and even whether or not formal assessment has been or will be carried out, we now definitely proceed on the basis that specific teaching strategies must be adopted in support of ADD and ADHD students. Of course, if an assessment has taken place there will be accompanying management recommendations from the clinician, and the teachers will have to familiarise themselves with these, and work to them. It is likely that the SENCo has a strong role here in helping the staff in general, or the class teacher in particular, become aware of how they can translate these recommendations into practice in their own classrooms in their own subjects. However, even when there is such management advice, it is likely that teachers will need to see this advice as a guideline, and still need to flesh it out in a detailed, everyday working way.

Of course, there may be no formal assessment in the pipeline (or a long way off), and thoughtful teachers are then entitled to say that some of the strategies we know to be useful with ADD or ADHD students should be tried with students who exhibit similar behaviours. This is *not* to say that teachers are trying to make a diagnosis, or are even interested in trying to do so. It *is* saying that we know of these methods, and we think they might well work with these students. In short, labels on students do not much interest us; practical strategies that are worth trying because we believe they will support the students do interest us. Also, doing nothing to support students until they receive a formal diagnosis does not interest us.

As is often the case, the support needs to be aimed at improved learning, but with a particularly strong acknowledgement that for ADD and ADHD students it may be improved behaviour that has to come first, before students are in a position to learn. In using the term *behaviour* we may be meaning better conduct (less calling out, less talking in class, etc.), but we may equally be meaning less daydreaming, better concentration, improved personal organisation. The teachers (if there are any) who simply say *I teach my subject,* and give no regard to wider aspects of student support, are likely to be unhelpful to ADD and ADHD students, and to find in due course that they have a very hard job managing the ADHD students.

Teachers' everyday behaviour management should, as ever, be rooted in *precise* observations. In dealing with undesirable or unproductive behaviour, teachers will need to look at the location in which this behaviour occurs, and the activity going on in that location; an overview of the types of place and types of activity which seem to provoke the unwanted behaviour may emerge (and a converse pattern of places and activities where such behaviour is less frequent). Along with this should go an *exact* description of what the behaviour is, what the student is doing, and what effect this has. This all takes a little time but is an investment, and more productive than just wading in not knowing quite what is being dealt with, or what the desired outcomes really are. So, teachers need now to decide what a good solution would amount to; this can be summed up by saying there will be either an elimination of the current behaviour, or a substitution for it by an alternative behaviour (decide which). Now we are in a position to work towards our solution. For example, if the problem is very frequent calling out in class, do we want the student simply to stop calling out, or is what he calls out of some importance to him but done in an inappropriate way in a whole-class situation? If we decide that his calling out has some intrinsic merit (but disrupts the class) perhaps we would encourage him to write it down every time he goes to call out, and then the teacher can manage to look at what he has written and deal with his various questions altogether at some rather more convenient point in the lesson.

So, let us now turn to a menu of strategies that are each worth considering for ADD and/or ADHD students, with the teacher, as ever, being the expert in the sense of knowing the students, what they need at this particular juncture, and being able to judge which of the following would be useful given the current state of play.

Some of the following will more generally apply to ADD students, probably rather more will apply to the superficially more problematic ADHD students; some will apply to both. Teachers will, as ever, use their judgement and discrimination to choose those which fit their particular bill.

General strategies

- This first option may work particularly well if ADHD students can be collected into a small group, and the principle which underlies it is connected with the notion of developing students' own understanding of the condition of ADHD. Build up two flow charts with the student(s). At the centre of one could be *ADHD*, but possibly better would be *Lack of self-control*, and in sequential fashion explore the consequences, and how one thing might lead to another, for example, *poor behaviour in class – exclusion from lesson – falling behind with work – poor exam results – poor employment prospects – lack of money, reduced standard of living.* This example may be a little too long-term (long-term thinking is definitely not normally a strength of ADHD students) so another avenue might develop as *poor behaviour in school – school exclusion – time on hands – hanging around – getting in to 'bad' company – drugs – crime – imprisonment (Youth Offender Institution).* This one may be a shade extreme; the teacher must judge, although it is best if it is the student(s) who forecast these routes, in which case they will be meaningful. Of course, the opposite exercise should probably also be done, so that at the centre of the chart is *Lack of ADHD,* or *Controlled ADHD,* or *Good self-control.* Routes that might flow from this would probably be along the lines of *good behaviour in class – good learning – good marks – good exam results – good job.* Another might be, *being responsible around the school – popular with staff and well-regarded by students – school responsibilities (prefect?) – participation in clubs and teams – satisfying, rewarding lifestyle – good school references.* The principles are those of the vicious circle and the virtuous circle, of how consequences, whether good or bad, flow from one's own actions and attitudes. They will not solve ADHD problems, but they do provide a format within which ADHD students can usefully think about being ADHD.

- It can be discussed and analysed with students what and when it is that make things more likely to go wrong, that is, if the students are mature enough, it is always worthwhile trying to develop their own individual recognition of these places and times. Also, of course, if the teacher can get this far with the students, alternative strategies need to be available. For instance, waiting for the teacher to arrive to take a lesson can lead to problems, either because the ADHD students get bored (which they generally do very quickly – it's virtually part of the condition) or because they get carried away with typical pre-lesson playing around, which the rest of the class can switch off on the arrival of the teacher, but which the ADHD students may not be able to. Our friend the doodle may be very appropriate here.

- Another strategy which may be better done by a group of ADHD students (although it can be carried out by a single student) is to arrange for them to meet with a group of the staff, or possibly the whole staff, and discuss in a 'neutral' sort of way what it feels like to have ADHD, what it is that provokes the ADHD into a dominant position in which the students cannot control it, and to explain to staff what helps. It is also very enlightening to have the staff come with questions for the students about their ADHD.

- Many ADHD students present an unfortunate image. They come across in too volatile a way, are too loud and too talkative, while they possibly gesticulate rather wildly, with waving arms and nodding heads. In other words, their body language is wrong, and can provoke adverse reactions from those on the receiving end. How to look and talk, how to be more still and to keep the shoulders down, how to appear less confrontational (especially when making a request) are all skills that it is worth trying to teach some ADHD students. Clearly, there is a place for role play and, possibly, drama here.

- Weekly reviews with the students, particularly if this can possibly be arranged on an individual basis (or is this over-optimistic?), whereby teacher and student(s) review how the week has gone, the high spots and low spots, and reasons for, may be thought to be useful. Not only strategies for coping next week with the things that went wrong this week can perhaps be worked out, but it is part of a process of the students developing a consciousness of their own behaviour. Giving positive feedback about relatively stable weeks can mean that this pattern becomes the norm.

- Preparing these students for any change of routine can be helpful in avoiding or minimising 'wobblies'; by and large, ADHD students do not react well to alterations to their structured day, but such alterations are, of course, unavoidable from time to time and, indeed, desirable for some other students. For example, special assemblies, talks by visitors, carol services, visiting drama groups are all positive variations which enrich school life and expand the curriculum, but are likely to 'throw' the ADHD students. Making the students aware of the changes in advance, preferably in a matter-of-fact sort of way, may be seen to be the best teachers can do here to support the students. However, these events do need to be managed (or perhaps it would be more accurate to say that the ADHD students do) rather than just allowed to occur. So, let the students know in advance, talk them through what to expect, and remind them of previous similar experiences.

- In fact, the whole notion and concept of 'structure' might be regarded as the watchword in successfully accommodating ADHD students and, to a lesser extent, ADD students in school. 'Structure' here is applied to the timetable, to lessons, to the classroom in general, to school routine, in fact to all aspects of school life. There are here great similarities with the guidelines for the successful management of students with Asperger Syndrome. The ADHD students may not, initially, like the structure, but if they cannot, as it were, structure themselves, they must be given a structure. But it can be given in a positive, matter-of-fact way ('That's the way we all do things here, Luke') and not in a punitive or threatening tone ('Everybody else does, why can't you? What's so special about you, everybody else manages?').

- It may be unavoidable, but schools should at least acknowledge that ADHD students are unlikely to be helped by travelling around the school to different rooms for different lessons and subjects. Whether the students spend lots of their time walking around the school in this way or whether the teachers do so is an old organisational issue, whether or not students with special needs are involved. Sets and setting, with students constantly forming and re-forming into different teaching groups for different subjects can make for further complications for ADD and ADHD students. It is not suggested that the school reorganises itself around the minority of students (i.e. the ADD and ADHD), but it is suggested that schools recognise that they are, in effect, creating difficulties for these students, that they cannot simply expect such students to fit in with the school and that they, therefore, provide such support as they can. This latter is difficult, but could involve measures such as instructing the ADD or ADHD student to walk with a designated 'reliable' student when trekking from lesson to lesson, or to have a card on which the time of leaving one lesson is written by one teacher and the time of arrival at the next lesson is written in by the new teacher.

- ADHD students do seem to vary from day to day. They have 'good' days and 'bad' days, and it may be impossible to say why. Accepting this may be one of the first strategies that teachers need to be prepared to adopt. There is not much good (probably the reverse, actually) in merely reminding them about the good days when they are having a bad day. 'Yesterday was such a good day; why can't you be like that today?' They don't know the answer to this. But there may be some mileage in mentoring them or counselling them on a good day, and then discussing their bad days, how they feel on the bad days, and if there is a trigger (although, in fact, they probably won't be able to identify it even if there is); such discussions can be couched in terms of helping them *begin* to move to a *degree* of greater self-control on their bad days.

- Another general problem that teachers have to be prepared for is the likely poor time management of ADD and ADHD students. They do not, on the whole, think long-term and, particularly in the case of ADHD students, they are usually reacting to immediate stimuli (probably multiple!). They cannot plan, but, also, they do not reflect; they do not learn from the past or profit from previous experiences. This presents a behaviour management issue for teachers. 'Remember what happened last time you did X and got into trouble' is not a particularly effective ploy. Punishment is, therefore, not much of a deterrent.

Managing behaviour

- It may be very helpful, although often difficult in a busy day, to remember that ADHD awkward behaviour is almost always impulsive, and not premeditated. Understanding where behaviour 'comes from' does help in dealing with it. And if teachers do not deal with it very well on occasion, as is almost inevitable, they should not worry. They should be confident enough to try to learn from the experience and, in a relaxed way, look at some of the other strategies here, and see if one or two of them might be worth trying in similar circumstances next time.

- The oldest trick in the book may be useful for the ADHD student when he is getting over-excited: 'Count to ten!' The skill for the teacher is in either being able to say this to the student at the opportune, crucial moment or, of course, working with the student so that, after a period of time, he can say it (and do it effectively) without the teacher's prompt.

- Equally much-used, but none the worse for that, is the deep and slow breathing technique when a student is getting 'hyper'. It can work if the student wants it to work. Initially, the teacher may have to supervise and more or less insist that they do it. Do not debase it and use it when it is not really needed. Obviously, the aim is for the student to take the idea on himself, and come to his own appreciation of when it would be useful.

- Some teachers may be interested in the *Sollocks* technique. This comes from Noel Coward's *Private Lives*; when Amanda and Elyot, a couple who enjoyed a tempestuous relationship, were rapidly building up to yet another flaming row, one or the other would call *Sollocks*, and that would remind them both of how they now had a situation which was rapidly getting out of hand, and they would cool things. A word other than *Sollocks* might advisedly be chosen, and in school it will really only be used by the teacher (although conceivably the student could say it to himself) when a ADHD student is close to going over the top. Perhaps this sounds trite on paper here, but if the relationship between student and teacher is really strong, and if the student really does want to help himself, it can work. It is the use of a code word which reminds the student that he needs to calm down. This will not happen instantly, but on hearing the word perhaps he can manage to turn his back on the contentious situation, and take alternative action, such as taking himself off to his *time-out* area (see p.128), and there begin to lower his temperature.

- Unobtrusive management of behaviour is almost always desirable. An exception to this might be when the teacher wants to make sure that a student is rewarded for good work or, possibly, good behaviour in front of the class; that it is done in front of the class is actually part of the reward (even if the reward is 'only' praise). A particularly unobtrusive strategy for managing behaviour is the traffic lights system. The teacher has a supply of counters or tokens, red, amber and green. For students who are operating this system (it could be the whole class, it could be one student) the teacher just places a counter on the student's desk as he moves around the room. A green counter means that the student is doing really well (e.g. working quietly and conscientiously); an amber one means that things are so-so, but could be better; and a red one means, of course, that things are not going well, and the student needs to think about how he is not behaving or working appropriately. Not a word need be spoken, although a meaningful look is likely to pass between teacher and student. The system can be extended by the student collecting greens, and avoiding collecting a certain number of reds. It is probably too much to ask that a note is kept of why each green or red was given, but it would be informative.

- Managing behaviour always involves devising ways of reinforcing desirable behaviours (as opposed only to reacting to undesirable behaviour). Delayed gratification, rather than the giving of instant rewards, is something else to work towards. Thus, the time might come when in order to receive a reward for sitting still with hand up and not just calling out, the student has to do this a certain number of times before the reward is forthcoming. Either the teacher, or the student, or both has/have a simple checklist so that each successful instance can be ticked off, and the student knows how close he is to achieving the goal.

- Teachers will probably decide that the wisest and most effective course is not to involve themselves with the student in lengthy discussions when a difficult, and possibly confrontational, situation arises. Teaching is not a power struggle. Quickly taken, quietly firm action will be the order of the day. Probably, teachers will want to talk things through with the student later, although even here, if the waters have calmed, teachers might decide it is just as well to make no further waves; if this course is followed, though, it should ideally be as the result of a definite decision, not because a situation is really only being allowed to drift.

- However, ADHD students do need to understand that there are consequences to actions. If, while in aggressive mode, an ADHD student breaks something, teachers will probably rightly feel he should – putting it simply – pay for it or repair it. The general approach to ADHD students in particular can be misinterpreted as just making allowances for them. This is not the case, although committed teachers will try to understand them, both as people with a disability, and as individuals.

- Discerning teachers will wish to judge when it is all right to turn a blind eye, and when to intervene. The latter is likely to be much the more prevalent, but that is not to say there is no place for the former. Deciding between the two is a matter of empathy and sensitivity; things text books can raise awareness of but cannot teach. However, there are dangers here, for inconsistent attention is very reinforcing of undesired behaviour, so the teacher does need to try to be very wise and considered in this area.

- Making ADD and ADHD students aware of their own behaviour, and whether it is appropriate and called for at any one time, is something teachers may choose to foster. One possible way of doing this is for the student to have a timer or bleeper (or the teacher could have it if that is more practical), or for the alarm on a watch to be set, and re-set. Anyway, there is something audible going off (not to the extent or volume that it disturbs the rest of the class), say, every 15 minutes. The noise provides a reality check; on hearing it, the student has to ask himself what he is doing, and if he is doing the right thing. Obviously, gradually the interval between bleeps is extended; also, it can be varied for different lessons and locations, depending on the students' performance and reactions. This idea can be taken a stage further, if it is thought useful, by the student and/or the teacher having a simple scale (1–3) with which either of them, or both, rate how well the student was meeting the criterion at that particular moment. If teacher and student both give a rating, the similarity or otherwise of their scoring can be very interesting, and perhaps reveal something of the student's perception of what is expected and acceptable. If a record can be kept of what was actually happening (e.g. working through a Maths exercise, watching a History DVD) on each occasion, this is also very informative, but requires quite a lot of efficiency to keep up; again, either the student or the teacher could be the recorder.

- Students could prepare their own checklists of what they find difficulty in tolerating in the classroom and of what calms them or keeps them calm. Teachers also have copies. This is not a students' charter for students having everything exactly their own way; items on the list should be agreed between staff and students. But it is a way of students and staff working together (both parties, of course, need to be willing to do this, and this does not always prove possible, especially initially). If the student is aware of a deteriorating situation in the classroom and he can see he is going to blow a fuse soon, he may be able to see why this is from the checklist, and be able to bring it the attention of the teacher. An example of an item on the 'what winds me up' list might be, 'too long a period of silent reading' and a very typical example of an item on the 'what helps' checklist would be 'five minutes "time-out"'.

- When beginning to feel stressed in class, it is helpful if the student has simple personal strategies that may help. It is unlikely, however, that they will develop these independently; they need to have been talked about and discussed as possible helpful devices beforehand. Such strategies can be performed by the students at their desks without the rest of the class knowing, which is usually a great advantage. The perceptive teacher, who should certainly be aware of the strategies, may well notice, though, and that, of course, is a good thing as he or she is, thereby, alerted. Such strategies are very simple and might include: steadying the breathing rate; rhythmic flexing of the ankles and feet; and gentle stretching of the arms behind the chair, with hands clasped lightly. With this type of activity, no one is claiming the problems will be cured but, for some students, such strategies do lower the temperature just a little, and make it that much more likely that a crisis point will pass.

- Students who find it very difficult not to call out to the teacher (a very common occurrence) can be given cards which they hold up. On each card is written why they are holding it up, for example, 'I want to ask you a question.' The fact that they are conveying their needs to the teacher by holding up not just their hand but the card may well persuade them that they do not need to call out.

- For the student who simply will not/cannot stay in his place, as a last resort a rectangle of tape (brightly coloured) can be stuck to the floor around his desk and chair area. Only with specific permission does the student move outside this rectangle.

- If a student disputes that he is being noisily disruptive, teachers might consider telling him that they will record him (audio). This may be difficult to accomplish from an operational point of view, in which case do not use this strategy, but if it can be done it can be salutary.

- If a buddy system is operated, teachers will feel that it is important that *both* students know what particular things the buddy is helping with, for example helping check that the ADD/ADHD student has all the right books and equipment for the next lessons and homework. A buddy must not feel he is totally responsible for everything the partner does, or does not, do.

- As has previously been pointed out, ADHD students can make themselves so unpopular by their 'over-the-top' way of conducting themselves that they can become victims of bullying. The bullies have, of course, to be dealt with but the ADHD student also needs advice about how not to be provocative, about not interfering, about following the rules in a game, about how to see things from other students' points of view.

- With more mature students, teachers might consider exploring the nature of ADD and, more particularly perhaps, the nature of ADHD. Has anyone ever explained anything about it to them? They may know the terminology, they may use the label(s), but do they have any concept of what the condition is. Do they have misconceptions? Teachers might be surprised at the answers to such questions (e.g. 'I'm a bit mad'). Do they have any idea of how common it is? Does each individual think he is virtually unique? Do they realise that many people feel the way they do, go through what they do? These are sensitive areas, and teachers must not rush in here, but they are areas that teachers might feel it valuable to explore with certain students.

- If behaviour problems seem to be escalating, especially if a group of students rather than just an individual is involved, teachers might think it wise to have a staff meeting. This may well be called and led by the SENCo. This meeting must be structured and professional (not just a moaning session, although there may be room for just a bit of that).The meeting will look for positive, although probably simple, management strategies. Also, the meetings should continue if the problem is not resolved. Thus, definite monitoring of the student(s), and how this is done, are inherent outcomes of such meetings.

In the classroom

Introduction

So far as the classroom is concerned, it is straightforward enough to state the principal aims for ADD/ADHD students:

> To get their attention, to keep it, to keep them on task, to stop them being distracted, and to keep them focused on the topic in hand.

Achieving this is not so easy. Selecting wisely some of the items from the following menu will help. Remember to follow those excellent axioms of: consider your student; consider your situation; choose sparingly; implement consistently.

School organisation

- The first point is very obvious, but is stated just to be on the safe side: a small class is almost always preferable where ADHD/ADD students are concerned. In as small a class as possible, teachers will feel they have the best chance of managing the ADHD students productively, and of monitoring the ADD students effectively.

- The second point is virtually equally obvious: if it is possible to spread the ADHD students thinly through a number of classes, life may be smoother, and learning easier, for *all* students, and no individual teacher will be under disproportionate pressure. ADHD students tend to spark each other off when clustered together.

Classroom organisation

- Teachers will probably feel, particularly for ADHD students, that the best classrooms are well structured, with well-rehearsed routines. Also, an orderly classroom means that ADHD students, who tend to be quickly frustrated, can easily find classroom equipment, if that is applicable.

- It is hoped that nobody wants a classroom which has a moribund atmosphere, but teachers may want to operate a classroom where the noise level is fairly low, finding that this is more conducive to the settled atmosphere that ADHD students need.

- Individual desks and serried rows are probably better for easily distracted students. This, of course, can present a practical problem if the teacher generally prefers groups around tables, and if the majority of the class really can cope with this. However, it is possible discretely to have individual students alongside groups and yet separate from them with some careful manoeuvring of the furniture. Fully open-plan rooms are probably best avoided.

- Whatever the classroom arrangements, teachers may wish to consider how they can have the ADHD students not sitting too close to any other student, without in any way segregating them. This could be to the benefit of all students, with the ADHD students being somewhat less likely to be distracted, and the other students less annoyed by the ADHD students' fidgeting.

- It is generally better for ADHD students to sit near to or at the front of the class. If not near the front, it needs to be a place where the student can be monitored, although generally not in an unnecessarily overt way. Crucially, a regular place is the thing. No fuss need be made about this; it is just a matter of fact that this is where such and such a student sits: 'This is where you sit, Dan. This is your place, Sharmini.'

- Naturally, teachers will almost always want to sit their ADD/ADHD students away from distractions, such as windows, wherever possible.

- Without putting unfair pressure on any students, teachers may like to sit an ADD/ADHD student near to a 'well-behaved' student. If that student can actively be encouraged to try to exert some benign influence on the ADD/ADHD student, so much the better, but just to have nearby students who are good role models may well be thought to be sensible.

Managing the students

- Another basic point teachers will wish to cover is whether (or not) to have available spare pens, pencils, rulers, etc. which are freely accessible to ADD/ADHD students who turn up without such items. The issue here for teachers is that it is virtually inevitable that quite frequently these students will be lacking in such equipment, which will probably prevent them carrying out the teachers' tasks fully. Teachers will have to decide whether making a fuss about it every time, bringing the student back to finish the work, etc. is profitable, or whether a more pragmatic, less stressful approach might be more useful, while they work on general organisational issues in other ways.

- Teachers might wish to insist that desk tops are kept rigidly uncluttered, having on them only the essential or agreed items. Every other object is something to fiddle with, manipulate, and quite possibly drop on the floor so far as the ADHD student is concerned.

- Use of the student's name very regularly, even frequently, is another elementary technique to keep pulling the student's attention back on course. The tone in which the name is used is also important; as far as possible, it should be used with an encouraging intonation (difficult to achieve sometimes – everyone's only human!) and not hectoring.

- Keeping good eye contact is generally reckoned to be an excellent way of keeping a student with you and concentrating. Teachers may feel they wish, therefore, to achieve this particularly with their ADD/ADHD students, but may also wish to bear in mind that a few students find eye contact off-putting and they are, in some way, made uneasy by it. As ever, it comes back to knowing the student.

- Teachers may feel that it is best generally to speak to their ADD/ADHD students in plain, concise English, especially when giving instructions, or explaining something (these two things being what teachers spend most of their lives doing). The reason for the desirability of this plain language is that, putting it plainly, ADD/ADHD students may not 'bother' to spend the time unpicking unnecessarily complex sentences.

- Having certain students repeat to the teacher instructions just given may be useful. Of course, even if instructions are repeated accurately, it does not absolutely prove that they have been fully understood. It is a help, however.

- Non-verbal signals can be extremely useful – a writing motion mime which passes from the teacher to the student indicating, 'You seem to have stopped writing,' attracts less attention, which is usually negative, from the rest of the class. Further examples could include: thumbs up if the student has been working well for, say, ten minutes; a finger to the lips if the student is beginning to talk; or a signal rather like that of a policeman on point duty stopping the traffic means, 'Stop what you are doing. It's out of order'; or a downward motion of the hand, palm down, perhaps followed by a pointing motion, if the student is out of his seat. So the advantage of all of these, and many more teachers can invent and convey to the students in question is that they do not in any way disrupt the class. The difficulty may lie in the fact that the teacher has first to attract the students' attention so that they actually see the signal! It is hoped that if eye contact cannot quickly be made in order to do this (which it may not – these are ADHD students and they may have forgotten about the teacher) just a quiet calling of the student's name will suffice, followed by the signal.

- Getting ADHD students to wait their turn (to speak, to ask a question, to have their work looked at, to use the computer or a piece of apparatus, to listen to instructions before starting work, to queue in the dining hall or on the way into assembly, etc.) may be one of the most pressing everyday problems teachers find they have to confront. Teachers will, perhaps, feel that they must have an expectation that ADHD students will wait, yet appreciate that they cannot wait for periods of time that will seem never ending to them. The secret to extending the students' capacity to wait may lie in giving them prompt attention but, tiny bit by tiny bit, extending the time they have to wait (if others are also pressing for attention) minutely day by day over a considerable period of time. As a feature of low-level disruption which is probably unintentional, this inability to wait may score very highly, and it is important that teachers do devise a strategy for improving the situation, not least for their own sanity. Having something else to do while waiting, and cooperation from peers who will allow a little 'favouritism' from the teacher towards the ADHD student so that he does not over-react, is also very helpful.

- It's very easy – and very understandable when it does happen – for teachers always to be criticising, or for it to sound this way. So teachers may want to consider going out of their way to give approval when the ADD/ADHD students have listened, and have remembered something they might just as easily have forgotten.

- It is greatly to be hoped that teachers have some support in the classroom from non-teaching assistants, and teachers may find that if they can deploy these extra people to work alongside their ADD/ADHD students, the performance of the students may well rise very significantly. Someone who does not nag, but who keeps turning the switch back to the 'on' position when the ADD student has allowed it to slip to 'off', or to turn the re-focus wheel when the ADHD student has spun it into the wrong position, can be worth their weight in gold.

Lesson planning and task setting

- It sounds trite and is, indeed, a truism but, for these students, teachers may wish to acknowledge that they really do have to go out of their way to capture their interest, which means being innovative. This is most likely to come through the visual medium or channel.

- Different media and, indeed, different teaching styles may be found useful in encouraging these students to pay attention (although this should not be overdone as it can become over-stimulating in its own right and, hence, counter-productive!).

- In lesson planning, teachers will probably want to reflect that generally ADD/ADHD students have more difficulty concentrating on the verbal than the visual.

- All teachers know that it is good practice to make sure they have the students' attention before they start. They may think this is particularly important with ADD/ADHD students as if they start without their attention, these students are most unlikely to tune into them subsequently.

- It may be thought useful to preview a lesson at the start of it so that students are comfortable with what is to come (although there may be a contrary argument that it is unwise to display your wares at the outset in case students decide in advance that they are not going to like them; once again, teachers will decide in the light of their particular students). However, it is almost certain that teachers will forewarn students if anything drastically different from the usual is going to happen in the lesson.

- Following on from the previous point, without going into ridiculously fine detail teachers may choose to explain at the beginning of the lesson how long the various stages of the lesson will last. Thus, if a student decides that a certain part of a lesson is 'boring', he will know for how long he has to 'endure' it before getting on to something he feels to be more appealing. These sort of strategies need to be carefully thought about, but it may be they are helpful to certain students. Teachers will decide.

- ADD/ADHD students will almost certainly, in effect, miss parts of a lesson when they are not concentrating or are distracted. Summaries of lessons may, therefore, be particularly useful to them.

- In the all-important matter of setting tasks, teachers might like to consider setting closed, and not open-ended, ones for ADD/ADHD students. These students have a better chance of completing tasks where what the outcome is to be, and what will be encompassed and involved in reaching that outcome, is clearly discernible (probably having been spelt out by the teacher), along with when it is to be finished by, than any tasks which are, to them, vaguer, ambiguous, and capable of being done in a variety of ways. Initially, at least, teachers may feel justified in being prescriptive.

- While always wanting to provide a lively environment, in the case of ADHD students it may be thought wise not to offer too many options or choices.

- Teachers will feel they should have different expectations of different students, but that they should have *some* expectations of each student, which the student is aware of. Teachers will not normally accept the production of *no* work, or of *no* concentration from any students just because they carry the 'ADD/ADHD' label. As with all students, the adage, 'What you expect is what you get' has some mileage.

- Nonetheless, teachers will want to be prepared for ADD/ADHD students going off-task. They will want to decide if it is then justifiable to allow the student to move onto another activity, or to force the issue, insist he stay with the task in hand, and risk the student still not concentrating, becoming more and more restless and, possibly, disruptive. Teachers will want to consider allowing the student to move onto some other work, probably in another subject (this, of course, being much more likely a viable possibility in the primary school) or perhaps, especially in the secondary school, sticking with the same topic, but working on a different aspect of it, for example, 'All right, Sam, you can stop your writing for a while about why Henry VIII went to France for the *Field of the Cloth of Gold*, and do an illustration or diagram of the scene.' It would, of course, be generally highly desirable that the work which has been left would be returned to at some point.

- Long, sit-still lessons can be very difficult for ADHD students, who may get very restless. Teachers may wish to consider allowing them to have a break (in an agreed way) or, better still, not to deliver lessons which are over-long (whatever that means), and to have a variety of activities. In their teaching styles, teachers may wish to acknowledge that ADD/ADHD students are hands-on learners, and not passive listeners.

- Allowing ADHD students to have some individual time-out, even though the rest of the class continues working, in order to break up long working sessions may be found to be practical. It does have potential difficulties in that some classmates would undoubtedly also like a break, although they don't really need it, and so their cooperation is a requirement here, and the relationship between the class as a whole and the teacher is crucial.

- An alternative to the above, which some teachers may prefer for some students, feeling that it develops more self-discipline, is for them to have a break at a designated time, which has been stipulated in advance.

- Yet another variation is to tell the students they can have a break when – and only when – they have completed a certain amount of the work.

- Particularly, though, when students do have to sit still and listen, teachers may allow or encourage an agreed physical activity to be simultaneously undertaken by the student. A typical example would be permission (even encouragement) being given to the student to manipulate a squeeze ball or bean bag, or to doodle.

- Wholly, never ending didactic teaching will generally not work well for either ADD or ADHD students. The former will soon drift away, possibly even lulled by the teacher's voice, and the latter will be unable to sit still and listen.

- As is often the case, teachers may feel that most tasks are likely ultimately to be successfully accomplished if they are broken into stages and segments.

Written work

- When setting written work, teachers might wish to consider not allowing some of their students to start writing immediately, but for a known period of time to have to elapse before they do so. This is in an effort to make them think about and plan their work before they rush into it.

- When students are supposed to be producing relatively lengthy pieces of work, teachers may well wish to check frequently that ADD students are actually keeping their mind on the job in hand and producing a sufficient amount of work, and that ADHD students are producing work that is relevant to the task in hand, and not shooting off at some unrelated tangent. Thus, their work may be called in for checking more frequently than is usual, and teachers may not want to wait until the whole task is (supposed to be) completed before looking at it. If teachers can also check the quality of the students' understanding of the work as well as the volume, it will probably be considered even more useful, although difficult to achieve in a busy working life.

- With regard to the production of longish pieces of written work, teachers may feel that writing frames are useful, and they may perhaps be continued with for longer than is usual (although care and tact would, yet again, have to be used here).

- Generally speaking, if possible, teachers might wish to opt for the setting of shorter pieces of work, which have to be finished within a stipulated period of time, that period of time being one that is well within the students' ability to grasp and focus on. Teachers may feel there is no harm in encouraging a relatively short timescale, in which there is, therefore, a built-in need to concentrate and work over a manageable period, if the target is to be hit and the work finished.

- If longer pieces of work are inevitable, or if the teacher is wishing incrementally to build up the students' capability in this respect, teachers may try to give extra support over the time management aspect of getting it completed (if the over-worked teachers can themselves manage to do this!).

- A device which teachers might care to consider when students are (supposed to be) engaged on lengthy or other individual pieces of work is the students wearing ear plugs or sound bafflers in order that they are less likely to be distracted by conversations and other noises inside (or outside) the classroom. Obviously, great care would have to be taken here; the student would have to be comfortable with the idea, parents would have to give permission, use would have to be relatively limited. A possible disadvantage is that the teacher cannot attract the student's attention by calling his name, so the teacher would have to move to the student, if necessary.

- It is possible that teachers might decide to give ADD/ADHD students slightly easier work so that they become used to working for longer periods; they are more likely to stick at it if, initially, they do not have to keep stopping to work out too many difficulties. Obviously, there are inherent difficulties: if the work is too easy students will become bored with it even quicker (more fine judgement needed by teachers!); and the quality of the curriculum must not be diluted just to help these students, or to keep them occupied. However, there may be a time and place for such a strategy.

- If students are expected to take notes as the teacher is talking, this will be very difficult for ADD/ADHD students. Their attention can flicker away so frequently they are almost bound to miss some points or, indeed, their attention may wander off completely, in which case they will miss all the points. There are ways of easing such a situation, if the lesson really has to be delivered via the notetaking method. The student could be given a list of pointers or hints as to what the teacher really wants them to listen out for, for example, the name and 'number' of the king they will be talking about (Henry VIII), when he came to the throne, the name of his first wife, the reason(s) why he wanted to divorce her. Advantages of this method are, also, that the teacher can see at a glance from the students' notes how much has been assimilated, and the students could fill in any blanks from their own research afterwards because they know exactly what they are looking for. This method can also be used when students are watching educational DVDs. Another method is for the teacher to stop, say, every five or six minutes approximately to give students the opportunity to review and note what they have heard in those previous minutes. It is possible to produce pro forma recording sheets that students can use with either of these methods.

- Teachers will probably find it much more effective to get marks and marked work back to these students quickly (this is a general truth for all students). What an ADHD student wrote ten days ago is unlikely to have much significance now, even though it did when he wrote it, if he has had no feedback since.

Further choices

- Teachers may feel it is not productive to expect ADD/ADHD students to gain too much information by reading it up, largely on their own. This is because it is too easy to let attention wander from the book (have we not all done that?) or to read without absorbing, while the ADHD student simply has not the patience to persist with lengthy reading. This is not to say reading is not important to these students, but teachers may perhaps particularly consider in these cases encouraging them to supplement their information from books with complementary material gathered from, particularly, the Internet, DVDs, and computer programs.

- Teachers may find that ADD and, particularly, ADHD students respond well to teaching programs on the computer, which often do seem to succeed in engaging and holding their attention. Teachers may find this an avenue they can pursue very positively with these students, and design or buy quite a lot of work that can be presented via the computer and computer programs. On the other hand, they will not want students to sit for hours gazing at computer screens. And they will not use computers as a way of just keeping ADHD students out of their hair, and the hair of other students, too, however tempting this may be. That said, computer time could very legitimately figure as a reward within a systematic reward scheme.

- Teachers may feel that failure to get their thoughts organised, and to make a constructive, logical start to pieces of work is one of the main things that prevents ADD/ADHD students getting into a piece of work; if they never come to terms with it, they are never going to complete it satisfactorily. If this is the case, teachers may like to consider helping the students construct tables or frames in which they can sort thing out, for example, in Biology a tabular display may be more productive for such students than a descriptive piece of writing identifying differences between mammals, reptiles, and insects.

	Mammals	Reptiles	Insects
Hair			
Scales			
Vertebrate			
Invertebrate			
Warm-blooded			
Cold-blooded			
Live young			
Egg laying			
Produce milk			
Do not produce milk			

(With apologies to real biologists!)

There is, of course, nothing unusual about the above approach, but who has shown it to the ADD/ADHD students, and suggested it might be particularly suitable to them? What it does is focus thinking, which is something they tend not to do for themselves. Ideally, the students come to construct the tables themselves, but the teachers could provide it if that level of direction was needed. However, just thinking about the way the table needs to be so that it will do the job, and then physically drawing it up, may make them stop and think, and think relevantly. Here's another example from a totally different subject.

	Socialism	Capitalism
Private ownership of production and distribution of goods		
Nationalised industries		
Government in charge of economic planning		
Free markets		
Government in charge of production and distribution of goods		
Operated by laws of supply and demand		
Competition		
Individual enterprise		

(With apologies to economists and historians!)

- Rather similarly, teachers may feel that Mind Maps could be very useful in helping ADD/ADHD students organise their thoughts, and get some logic into them. They may wish, however, to take time (if they have any) to ensure that these students do not, in fact, shoot off further and further away from the locus.

- If students have an ability in one (or more) subjects, or a particular interest or even hobby (and this is possible) it may be wise to try to allow them to pursue these to some extent in school. It will make them a lot happier, whereas ADHD students in particular tend to be pretty disenchanted with school. The teacher may be able to incorporate such abilities or interests into the curriculum, for example an interest in cars might come into Maths (numbers of cars produced, mpg, cost of cars, running costs, etc.) or into Geography or Economics (where they are made, materials used, where the materials originate), or in 'free' or 'club' time.

- It is probably stating the obvious that for impetuous ADHD students in some activities special consideration has to be given to safety aspects – without, if at all possible, debarring them (when, apart from the educational considerations, there may be legal implications also – see Chapter 7). Subjects such as Science, PE, and Design and Technology (DT) come to mind – but these are lessons where the students can be physically active so, in that sense, they are likely to be popular lessons.

- PE and Games may be seen as valuable to many ADD and ADHD students. The former may actually get involved in a physical activity, and cooperate with and relate to their peers in a team situation. This may be different for the ADHD students, who generally do not thrive in a team situation, and more individual activities may be more productive, for example weight training, martial arts. I know of one very successful boxing club for ADHD teenagers (using only punch bags, punch balls, etc.). Contrast this with, say, fielding at cricket (unless the student has a particular interest, which is possible) and one can see the difference. As always, inactivity is the thing which ADHD students cannot tolerate.

- The thought of taking ADHD students on field trips, camps, and out of school visits can fill teachers with foreboding, and special arrangements may well have to be put in place to accommodate them, such as extra non-teaching assistants being deployed, or possibly the parent(s). Another section of this book (Chapter 7) deals with the legal expectations with regard to including all students in all activities. However, it is possible that teachers can be pleasantly surprised by the success of the ADHD students on such trips. Some of the secrets of a successful venture are likely to include thorough preparation of the students beforehand so that they broadly know what to expect (and what is expected of them), lots of activities on the trip and little free time, and well-organised, well-supervised activities. Specialist instructors can be surprisingly well-received, too. Although ADHD students actually depend on structure, such trips do provide new and interesting things to attract their transient attention.

Rules, instructions and sanctions
Rules

- Teachers will almost certainly feel that school rules should be particularly clear – and concise and unambiguous.

- Following on from the above, rules should be written down, aptly phrased, visible but not dominant, with each student having a tidy copy.

- Teachers may also feel that it is both kind and expedient to give reminders about what the rules are, particularly with regard to rules of the type which tell students about what they are expected to bring to lessons, which days they are expected to have their PE kit in school, etc.

- As with their lessons, teachers may wish to ensure that the rules accurately reflect the structure of the school and/or classroom organisation. They indicate clear expectations; this makes it more likely that rules will be complied with. In lessons, clear expectations make it more likely the students will achieve.

Instructions

- Perhaps teachers will want to give consideration to the way they phrase their instructions, on the basis that there is a line that can be drawn to distinguish a positive instruction from a negative one, although both have the same objective in view, for example 'Keep the chair still' is subtly more positive, and effective, than 'Don't swing on the chair.'

- Teachers may wish to be quite extreme in the directness of their instructions. Thus, they may even avoid, 'Will you now, please, open your books at page 72?' by cutting out the 'Will you now?' that is, cutting out the question leaves no room for a negative answer or action.

- In giving instructions, especially ones in connection with what is expected by way of behaviour and good discipline, teachers may wish to be particularly aware of their tone of voice, and the manner in which the instructions are conveyed. It will probably be thought best that instructions are not spoken in a patronising way, and yet are issued politely. Shouting will be seen as pointless (although one appreciates teachers' frustrations); these students will not listen to what the teacher is saying (shouting) but, one way or another, they will react to being shouted at, either by becoming oppositional, or distressed. It will be thought best that instructions are issued in a calm way, with no sign of a hint that they might not be complied with! Similarly, they should be specific, and brief (but adequate). Instructions given one at a time (no long chains) may be found to be laborious but more effective in the long-run.

- If failure to 'hear' instructions is a particular problem with a student, the teacher may well decide upon a particular rule to get round the problem. For example, the teachers may allow that they will repeat an instruction just once. If the student has still not attended, a certain consequence will ensue. That consequence will be known to the student and teacher, and will be implemented. Of course, it needs to be made absolutely clear to the student from the outset that this mini-system is in place.

Sanctions

- Knowledge of sanctions on the students' part may well be seen as integral to a system, and particularly important to ADHD students.

- Teachers, though, may recognise, or soon come to realise that, although sanctions certainly are part of rules, punishment alone is unlikely to be very effective.

- If it is thought necessary that consequences of more general non-compliance should be spelt out, teachers will probably feel that this should best be done at the outset. What those consequences will be should be made entirely clear – but this can be put to the students in language which is factual, explanatory, and in an almost helpful tone, rather than a threatening one (which is quite likely to provoke ADHD students).

- Particularly when rules have been broken, and teachers have to take some action, they may try to adopt and practise the adage, 'The teacher keeps calm when the student does not.' Calmness on the part of the teacher, no matter how agitated and excited the student gets, may be a virtue much to be sought (if difficult to obtain). Courtesy, but no pussyfooting, may be the style to adopt in administering sanctions.

- While always being firm, seldom, if ever, be confrontational.

- Sanctions – which the students are aware of – do need to be administered. However, it has to be acknowledged that the threat of punishment is generally not very effective; a threat of what might happen in the future is seldom strong enough to inhibit behaviour of ADHD students. The reality or actuality of punishment is, in practice, often not all that much more effective (even though punishment must be administered) because these students, at the precise moment when they need to do so, do not inhibit their behaviour, even if it is behaviour which has previously attracted punishment and will, therefore, certainly do so again, and probably even more so. Thus, teachers will wish to administer and enforce their sanctions systems, but they will not set too much store by them, particularly where ADHD students are concerned. They will look for other strategies.

Conclusion

- Above all, teachers may want to try to master that great alchemy whereby even when bad behaviour has occurred and sanctions have had to be imposed, the behaviour is separated from the student, namely, it is the behaviour which is bad, not the student.

- In doing so, teachers may wish to carry this mystical art still further and, even when having to impose sanctions, demonstrate to the student – and to the rest of the class – that they are not writing off the student. Teachers may choose to show, even after a bad lesson and/or when sanctions have been set and complied with, that they are always prepared to start again, working from a clean sheet.

Motivation and rewards

- Praise may not be enough on its own where ADHD/ADD students are concerned – but teachers may, nevertheless, not wish to underrate it, either in its own right, or in conjunction with any other reward system(s) they set up.

- When the student has done well, teachers may wish not just to tell him (i.e. give praise) but also point out (if appropriate, which it probably will be) that he (the student) is now feeling quite good about himself. This is a feeling that ADD and ADHD students are not particularly familiar with, as so much of their work turns out to be much less than wholly satisfactory.

- What do teachers want to reward? In the case of ADD/ADHD students, one of the very best things to reward is the actual completion of a piece of work on time!

- Teachers may feel that they have to devise individual reward schemes for individual ADD/ADHD students over and above the ones they already have running in the class. Alternatively, and perhaps rather better if the current system is sturdy enough and adequately wide-ranging, teachers may wish to use any existing system very extensively with the ADD/ADHD students, and to a degree that would not be appropriate for many others in the class, who are more able to motivate themselves, concentrate, and complete their work with less external encouragements.

- Teachers can select from, or use in combination: individual daily charts and records; points and tokens, which can be earned according to a tariff, and perhaps traded in for rewards; House points; and points awarded at the end of each lesson for hitting the targets, for example staying in seat, not talking to neighbours.

- In due course, tokens, for instance, have to be earned and accumulated for the known reward to be forthcoming. Perhaps there will be different rewards for different numbers of tokens, and different actions may earn different numbers of tokens; hence, a full tariff scheme can be operated.

- The above needs, obviously, carefully recording, and the students need to know how many tokens they have acquired. Teachers may decide not to do this on a large chart on the wall if it is a largely individualised and personal system. Once such a system is set up, whatever the exact details of how tokens (or points, or whatever) are earned, teachers will probably feel advised (a) to operate it thoroughly, and (b) not to discuss the actual system or negotiate it further with the students.

- Rewards (and sanctions, too) can be individualised; different students like and respond to different rewards. And rewards are for achieving students' personal targets, these also being different from student to student. Each student should have a copy of his current targets; this does not guarantee they will work towards them or consult them, but they just might, and they are there for teachers' and students' reference.

- Within the activities of a busy classroom, teachers may want to try to give immediate feedback to the ADD/ADHD students. This is possibly more frequently done when behaviour has to be restrained, but is at least just as important when praise or reward can be given. And it applies as much to 'work' as to 'behaviour'.

- In fact, knowing that they are being constantly monitored can be seen by the students themselves to be supportive, so long as it is done in a helpful spirit. Knowing they will get a grade or mark for 'quality of work' and also for 'effort' at the end of *every* lesson can focus the mind considerably.

- 'Contracts' are agreements drawn up after discussion with the students about how they will behave or work in certain situations, stating what rewards they will obtain if they achieve the stated goal(s), possibly stating what they will lose if they do not. Naturally, contracts can only work if there is at least a degree of a real determination on the part of the students that they should do so, and if they are realistically framed in the first place, and then implemented and adhered to.

- Teachers may feel that a Home–School Diary is particularly useful when working with ADD/ADHD students and that, since it is supposed to be a positive device, it can appear in this section of types of strategy. Although, no doubt, it may often have to contain brief reports from both home and school about things that have not gone well, these can be couched in non-judgemental terms, with indicators of how improvements might be made next time. Additionally, the Home–School Diary is an excellent place to point out when things go well; this makes home and school feel positive, and gives opportunity for positive feedback to the student to be doubled. Underlying the Home–School Diary, whatever it contains, when working effectively it shows to the student that there is a strong bridge between home and school across which he walks on a daily basis; there is not a chasm between the two.

- Similarly, teachers will want to set goals to these students; this applies to conduct, and to the satisfactory completion of tasks. However, teachers may feel that it is practical to set goals in the students' minds which are achievable in the short-term (and that to ask or expect these students to think long-term is, at least initially, pointless). The teachers' art comes in timing and calculating how and when to begin to turn the short-term goals into mid-term and, then, long-term ones. For some ADHD students, this may always be optimistic, but then teachers also need goals, too, and to judge whether such transitions are viable for their ADHD students, and to move them on accordingly if appropriate, is a worthy goal for the teachers.

Time-out

This is yet another contentious matter in the minds of some, who feel that it is unfair for certain students (i.e. the ADHD students) to be able to take a break, apparently just whenever they feel like it. Others feel that it is unprofessional for teachers just to throw students out of the room for a spell when they are getting difficult. Both points of view are understandable, but both fail to appreciate what 'time-out' really is, and how it should be used by both students and teachers.

Time-out should be a constructive strategy whereby student or teacher can, in an agreed way, nip in the bud a developing and potentially damaging situation, with no confrontation, with no loss of face on either side, and with no consequences.

- Thus, it is axiomatic that the best time-out is set up with the teacher and the student agreeing that each can choose when the time is right for the student to take advantage of this facility.

- Time-out can actually even be with the student remaining at his desk, but not having to work for a few minutes. This would be because the student knows that he is beginning to feel volatile, and needs a few minutes to compose himself. Engaging with some other (non-disturbing) activity, such as a doodle – which tends to be very popular with ADHD students – may also be beneficial.

- The time-out area may be partially screened off. There are obvious dangers in this, and teachers will want to do a cost-benefit analysis to weigh the pros and cons.

- Whether screened or not, it will probably be considered effective if the area is clearly identifiable as distinct from the rest of the classroom. Along with this, ideally teachers might like to induce a suitable atmosphere of calm, and lack of external stimuli, by having soft flooring (i.e. carpeting, even if the rest of the classroom has a hard floor surface), blinds to any windows which can be used if appropriate, blank walls with no pictures or posters, and all in a 'quiet' colour, probably a pastel, and almost monochromatic.

- The time-out area can be located outside the classroom – if it can be satisfactorily arranged. It is almost certain that supervision will be required, so that's a problem. A colleague's classroom is a possibility, but that is imposing quite a lot on a colleague. The Headteacher's study or office could work quite well (given the right Headteacher) but is too often seen as a place, even a last resort, where students are sent for disciplinary action, and this is not quite what is wanted here; also, of course, the Headteacher is often either not in his room or is seeing visitors in it. Most importantly, the ambience of the time-out location has to be just right, remembering that it is not a punishment as such, and the idea is that it is a place where the student can pull himself together without too much input from anyone else.

- Although teachers may often have to separate the ADHD student from the rest of the class (although not necessarily by actually utilising a time-out location, but through in-class seating arrangements as already described) they will probably believe that somehow these students have still got to feel part of the class. Part of achieving this may lie in not singling out the ADHD student in front of the class even when sanctions have to be imposed. If control of the student can be achieved unobtrusively, it will help. Not forgetting to reward the student whenever it is possible to do so will also greatly assist.

- It may be thought that time-out, although accurate enough, is not a name that appeals to all students. Perhaps an alternative should be found. What about 'Personal Study Area?'

Group work

ADD/ADHD students may not function well in groups. ADHD students, with their lack of ability to share, to take turns, to listen to others, may prove disruptive (and unpopular). ADD students may simply fail to engage even more than in the normal class setting, with no one to pull their wandering attention back, and simply not profit or contribute. Yet teachers may justifiably say that they believe a proportion of the class time being spent on group work to be a good thing, and not wish to drop it because of a small minority of ADD/ADHD students. But good teachers are resourceful; they will adopt methods that, at least, greatly help.

- If the ADD/ADHD students are required to work in a group, the group should probably be as small as possible; this might well be even just two students, with the 'other' student being well chosen (by the teacher) and willing, but not imposed upon.

- The task of the group needs to be very specific and, preferably, the contribution of the ADHD/ADD student needs to be similarly explicit within the overall task. Note taker, scribe, secretary or recorder may be felt to be particularly apt because they are continuous roles, with the post holder always having something to do.

Homework

Homework can pose a great problems for ADD/ADHD students, who cannot settle to it, even if they have remembered to take it home, have remembered what they have to do, have all the right books and tasks to hand on the right night (which might be a different one from the day it was set). It is also a potential problem for parents who are keen that their children do their homework, and at their wits' end, perhaps, to know how to get them to sit still or concentrate long enough, and to be insulated from all the other distractions in a family home, to accomplish anything worthwhile, or to profit from the homework. Parental supervision can itself be a delicate matter: some supervision may be highly desirable; too much may lead to tensions and be counter-productive.

- Teachers may try to find the time to check the students' homework diaries to make sure they have the right homework in mind for the right night. They may, if they are able, even write it down for the students; this could be for the parents, as well.

- In fact, teachers may like to go further than this, and have a homework monitoring system set out on paper. This might well be a system for homework only, and separate from any other (very useful) system they might have for reminders about taking PE or swimming kit to school, or money for a trip, etc. The homework monitoring sheets would clearly record the tasks that were to be done, the completion dates, and be checked and signed by the teachers and parents (to show the parents are fully aware of what is in hand), signed by the parents upon completion of the work, and by the teacher upon the handing in of the work. Naturally, the monitoring sheets travel daily between school and home, morning and afternoon. The danger of their being lost, either genuinely (entirely possible) or accidentally-on-purpose is ever-present, but we have e-mails between teachers and parents and vice-versa that can be used to counter this, and the whole system could be wholly or partially electronic in the majority of cases. The student could well be involved in the design and layout of the monitoring sheets.

- At home, a particular routine (with regard to time and location) is probably desirable. The time for doing homework is likely to be earlier rather than later in the evening, and the location should not be too stimulating an area (is the child's room actually the best place?).

- 'Time off' within the homework slot may possibly be necessary, but preferably always at the same time. But this whole routine may be very difficult for parents to enforce or impose, especially if harmony is to be maintained. Teachers may feel they have a role here with regard to parents and students.

- Within reason, teachers may be prepared to accept (and, possibly, even to set) smaller amounts of homework if they believe that a small amount of work accomplished may represent quite a lot of effort on the student's (and perhaps the parents') part.

- Some latitude not only with regard to the homework itself but, also, to sanctions for failure to complete homework might be thought appropriate, at least for some students on some occasions. Quite possibly, this will lead to cries of unfairness from other staff or even other students and it is, indeed, a tricky situation. A partial answer may be not to impose the sanction(s) but to mark only the work that is handed in (thus, only a low mark can be awarded) while indicating what the predicted (presumably much higher) mark would have been awarded if only the work had been completed.

- Homework clubs, with ADD/ADHD students, and others, staying behind in school voluntarily to do their homework may well be worth considering in some cases.

Exams

Regardless of ability, exams can be a problem for ADD/ADHD students. No matter how important the exam, it is not unknown for students to lose concentration: for ADD students, in the quiet of the exam room to drift off into a reverie, while ADHD students simply cannot sustain their concentration, or even bear to sit for the length of the exam. Alternatively, they are on an examination 'high', rush through the exam paper, and finish in no time at all, probably not doing themselves justice.

- In public exams, ADD students may be helped by extra time, which will probably be granted to them if proper application is made. But it is still possible for them, in extreme cases, to daydream through the extra time as well.

- It is an even more difficult decision as to whether extra time is useful to ADHD students, regardless of whether they are officially entitled to it. The ADHD student who finishes very quickly is unlikely to spend extra time patiently reading through his exam paper, deciding where he could improve it; instead, he is rather more likely to get thoroughly fed up just sitting there, especially if the situation is that he sees all the regular time candidates leaving before him. On the other hand, some will not finish because they have lost concentration during the course of the exam and had unproductive batches of time when they were writing very little. Perhaps if it is possible for them to have extra time, they should take it. Once again, it is largely going to come down to the teacher's knowledge of the student.

- Pre-exam counselling may well be thought to be called for to discuss the sort of issues raised in the above paragraph.

- An awareness of exam 'tactics', centring on time management, is, perhaps, particularly important to these students. Like many students, they will probably be lacking in insight in this regard, and it may be thought desirable to try to teach tactics (answering the requisite number of questions, answering the questions as asked, allocating and managing the time, etc.) specifically.

- Similarly, particularly careful analysis of how they perform and achieve in exams, and scrutiny of their past exam papers and how they were functioning throughout the exam, may prove helpful. This really needs to be done on an individual basis and is, therefore, labour-intensive. Can a classroom assistant, following guidance, be utilised here (and with other strategies in this section)?

Breaktimes

With their reduced level of structure and instruction, teachers may feel that breaktimes offer many opportunities for things to go wrong for the ADHD students and for them to get into all manner of scrapes, especially with unstructured games becoming rather wild and a recipe for disaster, and that a degree of support and supervision has to be built in.

- Getting the dinner ladies and the midday supervisors on board will probably be seen as very advantageous; they can ease students' way through breaktimes greatly by involving ADD and ADHD students in activities, by deflecting ADHD students from troublesome scenarios, and by calmly absorbing their outbursts. However, there are practical questions raised about training (when, by whom, to what depth?). It may be necessary to break down any attitudes which say, 'The children should be able to occupy themselves without all this trouble.'

- It is possible that support can come via a 'buddy' – someone who is willing to relate to the ADD or ADHD student throughout the break, involve him or her in their activities, or go along with (sensible) activities that the ADHD student wants to instigate. Of course, this arrangement must be acceptable to both students, and there must be no undue responsibility placed on the 'buddy'. A way of avoiding the latter may be to have the 'buddy' duties carried out by a small group of students (two or three) in a 'corporate' fashion. This strategy may be found to be useful in the classroom, too.

- The simple idea of asking the ADD/ADHD students what it is they like, or would like, to do in breaktimes should not be forgotten. It may prove fruitless (in which case, nothing is lost) but it may give a handle on how breaktimes can be more positive experiences for these students.

Colleagues and the whole school

- Consistency with regard to how ADD and ADHD students are managed is likely to be very advantageous to them, and it may be thought that an awareness on the part of every member of staff, and some standardisation of how they each react to ADHD students, is a very desirable aim. Teachers of this view may like to be a little pragmatic at the outset, and have some expectation that some colleagues may not be entirely sympathetic, preferring to advocate discipline and sanctions as the entire answer.

- Extra-curricular activities provided by the school may be thought to be beneficial. They provide opportunities to students who are not good at occupying themselves, mop up free time in useful ways, and consume energy!

- Some colleagues may be reluctant to take ADHD students on school trips. Generally speaking, such a view is not sustainable (see Chapter 7). However, it is sensible to acknowledge that one or two special rules and arrangements may be necessary, not least for reasons of safety as well as the smooth running of the trip. Perhaps an additional non-teaching assistant may need to be drafted in, perhaps the teacher may need, if possible, a parent present (without singling out the student or the parent – more teacher magic needed).

Parents

- Teachers will always wish to communicate with parents, and to agree some regular way(s) of doing so; they may also decide that it is important that the student is fully aware of these communications, which should be almost always entirely open, and not concealed from the student.

- Teachers will probably decide that they will seek all opportunities to give the parents *positive* feedback (it being all too easy to give negative). Not only does this boost the frazzled parents but it makes it much easier when the teacher does have to give a bad report.

- Parents do need to be in the picture. They must not be able to say, 'Why didn't you tell me this before if it's been going on for X weeks?'

- So far as the students are concerned, this regular school–home link represents a bridge they cross daily; they know there is not a complete divide between the two (and, also, cannot play one off against the other).

Conclusions

The contention is that most teachers will, as a matter of fact and as a matter of course, meet ADD/ADHD students. In a school of 1000, approximately ten will have severe ADHD, and at least a further 20 will have less severe, quite possibly undiagnosed, ADHD. Indeed, perhaps up to 5 per cent of school students will have the condition, and this makes it one of the most common conditions that teachers will encounter.

The hyperactivity may go unnoticed in young children, possibly because nursery schools, etc. are generally very active, mobile places, but these children behave in virtually the same way in Infant and Junior School. Even if the condition does become toned down, they may, at best, be 'fidgets', and that, in itself, can be disruptive enough in a classroom.

Perhaps years will go by before busy teachers, understandably, come to realise that the very 'good' child sitting quietly day after day in class is daydreaming their time away, and that school and lessons are going on around them, rather than their participating in them, and that they are producing very little, that it is difficult to get a sense of their true potential, but it is pretty clear that they are not reaching anywhere near it.

Teachers, quite possibly, feel that children can make themselves concentrate, even in subjects they are not interested in and not good at or – heaven forbid – even if they are taught by boring teachers. 'Should concentrate more. Could do better,' may be comments that appear very frequently on these students' reports.

ADHD students certainly can make life very difficult for teachers trying to run a smooth classroom and deliver well-planned lessons. However, it will be very beneficial indeed if teachers can empathise with ADHD students especially (although we must never commit the cardinal sin of overlooking the ADD students) realising that, for ADHD students, school can be an alien environment, as they develop at least a degree of awareness that they're not fitting in.

We have to acknowledge that there may well be an increased risk of young ADHD adults moving to lives which are prone to problems (Irving and Bloxsom 2002). Looking on the black side, these could include their social integration, economic status, housing, relationships, crime, alcohol and drugs. Of course, there is not an inevitability about this progression, but we must be aware of its possiblity, and determine all the harder in the school years to do all we can to make our students with ADHD less susceptible – and one further way to do this is to recognise, and show them, that having ADHD does not have to be all bad and negative.

If their social skills are all right (admittedly, a big *if*), they may have lots of social contacts, and be involved in lots of things. In fact, there can be some virtues in having ADHD. These students have, clearly, lots of energy, and they may have many enthusiasms and interests. If these attributes can be harnessed and tweaked into multitasking skills and put to good use, they can achieve much in a modern, fast-moving world.

If they get the 'right' job and career, one that interests them, probably one with lots of variety to hold their attention, one in which they need to be really busy, they can do very well, but they need to be employable, and to secure the job in the first place. How they leave school may be a big factor here.

ADD students will lead less colourful lives, but if they can be engaged increasingly with activities, they can come to function more and more efficiently and productively. The hope is always that, as they engage more with one activity, it is that much more likely they will engage more easily with another or the next. And so it goes on, building up, bit by bit, over a long period of time, until engagement becomes the norm, and not the exception. So far as it is possible, finding and following their interests in school, and in career choice(s), is crucial. A final thought with regard to ADD students: they do not need to be treated as shy, or even introverted, psychologically withdrawn students.

The National Institute for Health and Clinical Excellence (2008) states that 'Teachers who have received training about ADHD and its management should provide behavioural interventions in the classroom to help children and young people with ADHD' (p.5). As a whole, the document from which this quote is taken is a useful one, but this particular statement will beg a few questions in the mind of the committed, positive teacher. What about the children who are in classrooms of teachers who have not received training? What about children in schools where no teachers have received training? What is this training, and where is it? How accessible is it to large numbers of teachers? Are untrained teachers to do nothing positive? Are teachers, knowing the troubled, or unfulfilled, futures that can unfold for these young people, to sit back and do nothing? Or are they to use their considered judgement, carefully apply some of the strategies of the types described in this book, and try to make a difference?

In the meantime, one final thought and idea. Without trespassing into the realms of slander, ask the older students to speculate which current, famous, probably wealthy, people might just be ADHD!

Chapter 5

&

A Menu for Supporting the Student with Asperger Syndrome in the Inclusive Classroom

First concerns

Not too far away from where I live there is a 'convenience store'. It's not actually on a corner, but it's what we used to call a corner shop. That is, it sells pretty much everything you might want for everyday living: papers, groceries, frozen foods, wine, birthday cards, stamps, paper towels and tissues, lottery tickets, and I'm afraid inevitably, cigarettes.

I go in there pretty regularly. More accurately, I go in there pretty frequently, but I go at all sorts of different times of day: at whatever time I happen to be passing by, or when it occurs to me that I need something, or when it's just handy to pop in.

The staff seems to be a shifting one now. Working long-term in a corner shop doesn't seem to be what people want nowadays, not in this case, at any rate, so staff and service are variable. Sadly, mostly staff are not too interested in serving you (it's more or less self-service, anyway). The job is only temporary or part-time or filling-in or while waiting for something better to turn up. Getting a smile or a greeting at the single check-out is is unlikely. The shop does provide a uniform but, regardless of the age or sex of the wearer, it's worn in the way a rebellious 15-year-old would.

As for the shop itself, it is generally quite a mess. With the range of things it sells in a small space, and no one much interested in keeping it neat and tidy, the shelves soon get in a muddle, stray brussel sprout leaves remain unswept on the floor, and the pile of the local newspaper tips ever more precariously as copies get yanked off the top and wire baskets brush past it.

That is except at one particular time of day, if you happen to go in then. The difference is immediately noticeable. Everything has a place, and, at this time of day, everything is in its place. The whole shop has a sparkle about it, and a nice fresh smell.

At this particular time of day, apart from the general manager, just one chap will be on duty; it's clearly his 'shift'. Unlike everyone else, he's been there years from when he was quite a young man (although he doesn't seem to have changed much even now). He's tallish, and carries himself very upright. He's always smoothly clean-shaven, and his hair is 'short back and sides' with a parting. His top button is done up, and he wears a tie. If he is not actually behind the till, he will be neatening the rows of cigarette packets, or making sure no tins of pears are muddled up with tins of peaches. If he is behind the till, he will invariably pass the time of day, comment on the weather, say please and thank you throughout, tell you the total, count out the change into your hand, and wish you good day. This conversation is entirely appropriate; it is, also, always virtually to exactly the same pattern and sequence, and always has been.

I've been going to the shop for years; it's a pleasure to do so (only) when this chap is on duty. Eventually the very 'sameness' of every time I saw this chap, and made purchases from him, his sense of orderliness, the slightly old-fashioned appearance, the marginally stilted conversation, struck me. He's absolutely brilliant. He's also Asperger's – in my opinion!

But, if everything is so great, why am I including this man under 'First concerns'? The concern is a 'What if...?' concern. What if, more or less as soon as he left school, this job had not come up? Or he had not got it? What if this small shop should close down, as so many have done? Would he be happy in a large supermarket, doing much the same tasks, but in a much different environment? Would he be OK working with a lot of other people; would he manage all the different personal relationships? Would everyone else allow him just to get on with his work, or would there be the occasional jibe from time to time? Would he be ruffled if there was?

And a final set of concerns. How many other people are in our communities like this? And how are they getting on? Are they employed? Are they happy? If there are a significant number of people around like this, they must have been at school once. How many students like this are there in our schools today? Are they recognised? Are they supported? What do we do for them?

Perhaps it seems that I am being over-sensitive here, and getting worked up about a man who is actually a 'one-off'. So, I refer briefly to the National Audit Office report (2009), *Supporting People with Autism through Adulthood*. This report has several interesting examples (brief case studies).

There is a description of one man who was, indeed, diagnosed with Asperger Syndrome – but not until he was aged 30. (I very much doubt if my local chap has ever been.) This man attended mainstream school, and went right through to 18. He excelled at Maths and Physics which, no doubt, was great, but he struggled to make friends and, in fact, was frequently told he was 'strange'. Nonetheless, he went away to university, which proved to be a fairly disastrous experience. He couldn't make friends, control his time or his money, and he did not like lectures in large and noisy halls. As a result, he became lonely, and then unhappy. Probably wisely, after one term he dropped out but, fortunately, was able to return to the family home. Obviously, there was at this point some enlightened support for this guy because he was able to transfer to a local university, and to live at home.

Although he, therefore, went on to get a good degree, his problems were not over. Now he couldn't get a job. One of the main problems here was the interview situation. Without a job, he had little alternative but to stay in the house a great deal. Thus isolated, he began to experience mental health problems and depression, to the extent that he was admitted to hospital. There something happened which it is feared is not all that unusual; he was diagnosed as schizophrenic. This diagnosis was not corrected to Asperger Syndrome for two years, and then almost only by chance. Given some appropriate support, he was at last able to find a job in a local government office. He continues to make use of that support, and now lives in his own flat. Perhaps he is another of the lucky ones for whom things happened to have worked out all right – eventually.

There is another instance of a young woman who, again, went right through mainstream schooling. This time there was a diagnosis, but not until the age of 15. Still, not only was there a diagnosis, but it was actually of autism, and a Statement of Special Educational Needs resulted which, in turn, produced some classroom support. Leaving school at 16, she continued to get support and some appropriate Further Education, but she cannot find a job, despite good administrative skills. Again, the problem is largely the interviews, and the anxiety they, the new people and the different environments produce.

So, these are two examples which are highly pertinent to mainstream schools, and here is one that is possibly even more so. It was reported in The Guardian of Monday 20 April 2009 and concerns the instance of a boy who was refused a place at a local secondary school because of his Asperger's (Siddique 2009). Hence, he studied at home, obtained excellent A-levels and is now more than likely off to Cambridge. The Special Educational Needs Disability Tribunal got involved and ordered the school to apologise (see Chapter 7).

In fact, Asperger Syndrome is beginning to assume a higher profile. It seems as if one is beginning to hear it referred to in ordinary conversation in everyday life and – so far as adults are concerned – now we actually have the Autism Act (2009) (England and Wales), following high profile debates in the House of Commons and the House of Lords. The need not to forget people with Asperger Syndrome, who were described as being at the more able end of the autistic spectrum, especially as they were less likely to have been statemented as children and young people, was certainly referred to in the course of those debates. This Act led directly to the publication of the government's *Adult Autism Strategy* (Department of Health 2009) so, at last, necessary key actions and recommendations for central government, local authorities, the National Health Service (NHS), and – almost most important of all – Jobcentre Plus are itemised, and it is law that such a strategy must exist (in England only).

Certainly, an Asperger Syndrome person made the headlines (unwittingly) when a national campaign was started in July 2009, particularly by the *Daily Mail*, to try to prevent him being extradited to the USA and placed on trial there. The issue arose because this man, now aged 43, fascinated by the possibility of alien life and possessing good technology skills, succeeded in hacking into computer systems in the Pentagon and NASA, possibly thus compromising security and causing expensive damage to the systems. It is claimed, though, that he was virtually unaware of the criminal nature of his activities as he pursued his interest, and it is thought by many, including Jane Asher, President of the National Autistic Society, that the strange, unfamiliar surroundings on extradition would be more than he could accept, and that the change of routine and absence of familiar faces around him would lead to breakdown of such communication skills as he does possess, and possibly a more serious breakdown of his mental health (Asher 2009). Nonetheless, the High Court has ruled that the Home Secretary and Director of Public Prosecutions were right in not opposing his extradition and in not bringing the charges in the UK. This resulted in debate and questions on two of the country's national institutions, the radio programme *Today* and the television programme *Any Questions?* (both 27 November 2009). Then, it was decided that a High Court judge would review the Home Secretary's decision (to extradite), and this resulted in the further decision that there does exist a right, via Judicial Review, to challenge the Home Secretary. It seems more than likely that months of renewed legal argument will follow. This mishmash of a situation may never have arisen had the man at its centre been assessed and diagnosed with Asperger Syndrome before he was about 40 years of age.

It does begin to sound as if there is quite a lot of 'it' about – although crucially, often unrecognised – and, in fact, the National Audit Office quotes the estimate that 1 per cent of the adult population should be regarded as autistic, with 50 per cent of that 1 per cent being 'high functioning' (2009, p.14). I reckon that means that this last group have virtually all been through mainstream schools.

According to these figures, most teachers will meet students with Asperger Syndrome. Incidentally, it is generally reckoned that the prevalence of boys compared with girls is high (about ten times), but teachers should not ignore the possibility of meeting Asperger girls. Boy or girl, these students may not be diagnosed as Asperger and not, officially, be entitled to any extra support or provision. Teachers may not recognise them. No need to feel guilty about that; it took me years to work out the chap in the shop. This book will help, but, as always, an alertness to the possibility has to be the starting point on the open-minded teacher's part.

What is Asperger's?

So, what is it, this Asperger's? Where has the term come from? Although it's been around for some little time now, it's still relatively new; generally speaking, people have only become familiar with it recently, or what it means. Let us, importantly, clarify what Asperger's is not, and dispel some possible misconceptions that certainly have been heard in some quarters in the not too distant past.

Indeed, is it just a new(ish) term, or is it actually a new condition? It is probably not a new condition, but the reason why the term has come into being is that the first work on what was to become known as Asperger Syndrome was done towards the end of World War II in 1944 by Hans Asperger (see Frith 1991). It was done in Vienna, and written in German. It was translated into English much later (Asperger 1944), and only came onto our radar in the early 1980s.

There is still a degree of debate about what Asperger's is caused by. For instance, Hakonarson (2009) believes that his research strongly points to a genetic cause, with many genes being involved, whereby tiny genetic changes have an impact on the likelihood of autism, and related conditions, developing. Everyone accepts that this is most interesting work, but not everyone, including the National Autistic Society (Campbell 2009) accepts that this can yet be regarded as a total explanation.

Investigating possible causes, and looking not even at the child but at the foetus, Auyeung *et al.* (2009) suggest that autism, including Asperger Syndrome, could be linked to unusually high levels of testosterone in the womb. This raises tremendous questions around the early identification and prediction of autism through amniocentesis, and a profound debate about consequent abortion, as well as the possibility of pre-natal treatment through drugs that block testosterone. Less powerful now, but a controversial and contentious debate (argument) has run for years over the possibility of a link between autism and the MMR vaccination.

The work of Ecker *et al.* (2010) suggests that there are minute differences in the anatomy of the brain which account for autism and Asperger Syndrome. To date, this work has only been carried out with adults (and a small sample at that, of 20 people with autism and a control group of 20) but the authors express a degree of optimism that their techniques, which closely involve magnetic resonance imaging (MRI), will prove to be applicable with children. Should this be the case, and should the findings that there are observable biological markers achieve a wide degree of acceptance, the implications are considerable. The MRI scanning is done very quickly, within about fifteen minutes, and opens up the possibility of speedy and relatively easy diagnosis (as opposed to what very often happens at present). In fact, it opens up the possibility of routine screening. However, these are very early days; sight of Ecker's work most certainly should not be lost, but it is unlikely that we shall notice any practical ensuing benefits at the chalk face in the immediate future.

Where there is common accord nowadays is that Asperger's is not a mental illness (although mental health problems may develop later if appropriate support is not provided). It is also very widely accepted that there is not an underlying emotional cause. Similarly, Asperger's is not due to social conditions, and cannot be accounted for by the way someone has been brought up.

In short, then, what it is is a developmental disability. It is a developmental condition, and what this does is affect the way that information is processed, and causes people, adults or students, with Asperger Syndrome to react (or not react) slightly differently from most people to all or many of the signals received from the environment, from the world around them, and the people, places, and situations within that world.

Asperger Syndrome in mainstream schools

Let's turn to the school situation. Shortly we will come on to some menu choices you can make which will provide support to your Asperger's students. The contention is that Asperger's students are particularly likely not to have a diagnosis, and not to have been previously recognised as such. Even if they have had a diagnosis, they will almost certainly, and rightly, be in the ordinary schools of the country, and the individual school will be expected to make appropriate provision and adjustments to cater for their needs. So the responsibility remains with the school, the SENCo, and the class and subject teachers. Furthermore, Asperger's is recognised within the Disability Discrimination Act (1995).

We will return to the issue of diagnosis shortly but, before that, what the teachers want to know (whether or not there is an existing diagnosis) is how they will recognise Asperger's students, what do they look like, how do they behave, how do they learn – and, of course, how can they best help them?

So, moving on from the adults already briefly described – and it's so important for us teachers to remember that our students do become adults – here's an initial thumb-nail sketch just to give the flavour of what we might expect in school, before we begin to think about these students more deeply.

1. You may quite possibly find that your Asperger's students want to be sociable (perhaps especially with adults). Difficulties can arise, though, because they don't quite appreciate how we generally go about this. Thus, they may not realise that they have to take turns in a conversation, or they may want only to talk about a topic (often a repeated one) of their choosing, or they may not be able to move a conversation along and progress it. They may not understand the non-verbal signals which accompany many conversations, such as frowning, pursing the lips, etc. and ignore them, which can lead to the conversation taking an unfortunate turn. Similarly, gestures used by the other parties are not responded to or taken on board. They may open conversations inappropriately, perhaps abruptly, and terminate them at illogical points, or, more likely, not terminate them at all. They give the impression often of talking at you rather than to or with you; and they do not maintain appropriate eye contact. They may have a poor appreciation of personal space, and almost barge in (unwittingly) too close, making others feel uncomfortable.

2. Nonetheless, and going on from this, you may initially have the firm impression that your Asperger's students speak fluently. If you are a teacher, perhaps in a large secondary school, who sees them only relatively infrequently within

the cycle of a weekly (or longer) timetable, this is particularly understandable; it took me years to pick up on the oddness within my shop assistant's conversational skills. What you may find in fact, though, is that their conversation is over-precise, rather formal, and over-literal. And you may become aware that they are not really understanding all you say to them. This remains true no matter how colourful or vivid and rich the language, full of examples, analogies and metaphors, you use in order to illustrate points; in fact, this makes things worse, as this sort of language possibly passes them by or, more likely, they take it at face value and try to understand it literally, and get further confused (which can lead to stress for them). It is also possible that they may scarcely listen to the other person, or hardly allow the other person to speak; the purpose of the conversation is to allow them (the Asperger's students) to have their say, and this can certainly come across as impoliteness; this, naturally, is another source of 'misunderstandings' and impaired relationships with peers and staff.

3. You may well find Asperger's students to be of average or good intelligence, but you may also find that this depends particularly on the task, or type of task, involved. This is true of everyone, of course; we all have our strengths and weaknesses, our preferences and dislikes, but not to the extent of Asperger's students. Their difficulty in some areas arises from their ability to think in the concrete, but not in the abstract. Facts and details may be assimilated, but open-ended or hypothetical tasks will probably throw them, as will those where they are asked to generate their own ideas.

Set alongside all of the above, their typical preference for routine, their need for structure, their fairly extreme dislike of even small but unexpected changes of lesson, teacher, location etc., and we are beginning to get a picture of students within the Asperger Syndrome. A little professional imagination applied at this point will indicate how school life can be fraught for them, perhaps particularly on the broadly social side, but also within at least some lessons.

The above should give a degree of awareness of and a 'feel' for Asperger's students, but it has to be said that the students do vary a lot, as is appreciated when one comes to consider an individual boy or girl, and to ask oneself if one is seeing an Asperger's student. They may as a group be stereotypical in their thinking – but there is not an exact stereotype. This exacerbates the difficulty that Asperger's is, arguably, initially the hardest type of disability to spot. One can only very seldom tell that a student has Asperger's Syndrome simply by looking at them – certainly not instantly, certainly not by looking only briefly (observation over a period of time is a different matter). Similarly, there is no medical test or blood sampling, etc. which will make a clear-cut diagnosis.

But needs must be met, and students must be supported, even if there is not a formal diagnosis. However, teachers cannot diagnose Asperger's. There are a number of rating scales which attempt to do this, but they are unlikely to be within teachers' remit. A teacher who is on the ball may wish to be instrumental, probably via the SENCo, in obtaining a formal diagnosis, and teachers are great at observations (i.e. qualitative assessment). These may inform part of a formal diagnosis, if one is arranged, but in any case are vital in helping them work out what support strategies to decide upon, whether or not a formal diagnosis materialises. Appropriate observations in the right areas and the significant aspects of Asperger's justify teachers in saying that an individual student *may* be Asperger's, or does have some Asperger Syndrome characteristics. This then carries the teachers forward in their attempts to support these students. They have not made any glib or trite assumptions about the certain presence of, or even the degree of, the Asperger Syndrome, but they have given themselves a provisional framework within which to think (constructively) about how they may now find ways at least to attempt to support these students (rather than do nothing positive).

So, whether or not the behavioural observations the teachers have made strongly suggest that the student comes within the Asperger Syndrome may not be the point (and questions the value of labelling). However, the teachers do need to assure themselves that the behavioural characteristics they have noted are *not* the characteristics of other disabilities:

• *Asperger's is not a specific language disorder.* Language may be limited in some form (as already indicated) but if gesture, facial expressions, body language, even signs and mime, are used to compensate and communicate, it is likely that the source of the disability *is* language-based and, therefore, *not* Asperger's.

- *Asperger's is not primarily a behavioural problem.* Although Asperger Syndrome students can certainly exhibit poor behaviour at times, students who are uncommunicative, withdrawn, possibly conduct disordered will not have the other Asperger Syndrome characteristics, and may have relatively obvious and relatively causative family, or social, or environmental circumstances, which the Asperger's probably will not.

- *Asperger's is not dyspraxia.* Asperger Syndrome students do tend to have problems with physical coordination and there is a higher incidence of motor coordination difficulties in the Asperger Syndrome population, and these may well need addressing. Dyspraxic students do *not* have most of the other Asperger characteristics, and so the two disabilities should not be confused, and the Asperger's students need supporting primarily as Asperger's, *not* as dyspraxic.

- *Asperger's is not ADHD.* The greatest potential for a seeming overlap may lie between ADHD and Asperger's. For instance, ADHD students may – like Asperger's – talk out of turn or to excess, may not apply instructions to themselves, may be able to do only their own thing and not conform, and generally behave in ways which are somewhat out of kilter with that which is the norm. It is the persistent way in which the Asperger Syndrome student is so often out of step over the years across a broad canvas that is the key to distinguishing between the two disabilities, but it is an area where confusion can certainly occur.

Fortunately, to practising teachers, although not exactly helpful, these areas of possible confusion will not matter too much, so long as the teachers bear them in mind, and then concentrate on the actual behaviours which can be observed, and intervene in ways which seem appropriate to the individual *student* as much as to the individual *disability*. This is not to say that knowledge of or awareness of the gamut of disabilities is not wholly useful, but it is to say that teachers need not agonise over the niceties of an exact diagnosis when they are in their classrooms, and under their noses are the behaviours and learning they would like to change and improve. An awareness of the disabilities, and the differences between them, is certainly necessary if this support is to be provided in a positive and sensitive way, and is highly desirable. But teachers should not hold back, paralysed by their own perceived lack of skills and knowledge, or in anticipation of an expert in the field (a) being parachuted in the near future, and (b) providing ready-made, neat, cast-iron certainty solutions.

So far as Asperger Syndrome is concerned, the crucial thing in understanding it in school is the appreciation that the manifest social difficulties which the students experience are *the* difficulties at the root of their problems. Their difficulties in language and behaviour are *not* caused by the social difficulties; it is the other way round. This is a shade simplistic, but provides a useful handle on the disability, a clear indicator as to its presence, and an equally clear indicator as to how to prioritise intervention.

While formal definitions and descriptions of Asperger Syndrome do certainly exist, they do not of themselves make the Asperger's students immediately identifiable in school, especially within a large class. Students may well be undiagnosed; they may be very 'mild' Asperger's. Some teachers may see their classes infrequently; they may not have been told about the presence of Asperger's students. Teachers are only human: at the moment when a problem pops up (such as when the student has been impolite without realising that what he had said or the way he had said it was out of order) because the condition is not obvious and overt, the teacher might just forget that the student is Asperger's, and conflict arises (this is not to say that the student just 'gets away with it', but we deal with that later).

Recognising Asperger's

We have sketched in 'the Asperger Syndrome student', and begun to indicate how, by appropriate observations, teachers can recognise these students. Without in any way trying to place teachers in the position of diagnosticians with regard to Asperger's, it is now time to formalise something which approaches being a template by which Asperger Syndrome students can be acknowledged, and a more precise guide with which teachers can focus their observations. (When these steps have been taken, and this background has been provided, we can usefully get to the selection of menu items in order to attempt to support these students.)

On pp.146–147 there are three numbered paragraphs. This is done to cross-reference those paragraphs with the Triad of Impairments which characterise autism (and, therefore, in milder form, and perhaps in different ratios each to the other, Asperger Syndrome). This uninspiring-sounding but highly useful term stems from the work of Wing and Gould (1979). It is important to note from the outset that the three components of the triad do not exist independently of each other; they are linked and in a relationship with each other. They are impairments in or of:

1. social interaction

2. social communication

3. social imagination, flexible thinking, and imaginative play.

It may be worth just turning back to pp.146–147 to see how the behaviours described fall, in turn, paragraph by paragraph, into the above categories.

Because students fit in different ways into this triad but, nonetheless do have significant difficulties within it, terms such as 'autistic spectrum', autistic continuum', 'autistic spectrum conditions', 'autistic spectrum disorders' have come into being. The definition is, therefore, relatively broad, and the range of students relatively wide, but all such definitions remain, ultimately, based on the triad.

Generally, Asperger Syndrome students are included within the autistic spectrum, and can be regarded as a sub-group of it, but it is fair to acknowledge that there is some debate about whether this is the case or whether Asperger Syndrome is a different form of disability representing a separate group of individuals who have a few autistic characteristics. In this book, the view is taken that Asperger Syndrome students are on this autistic continuum, but the students are identifiable as a group, albeit a group that is a bit blurred at the edges, and that teachers can get on and make provision for them on this basis.

That said, therefore, it is time to be more exact about what, if students are to be regarded as being Asperger's, or possibly as having Asperger's characteristics, the behaviours we observe actually consist of. Indeed, Wing (1981) has a list of diagnostic criteria for the identification of

Asperger Syndrome, and other diagnostic instruments also exist and are used by clinicians, but here we are talking about what teachers are entirely capable of observing in the school and classroom. This they can do to confirm (or question) an existing diagnosis of Asperger's, to raise a concern about the possibility of Asperger's in a hitherto undiagnosed instance, and always and crucially to inform their teaching, anyway.

There are a couple of points which underpin all observations of behaviour; this is no less true of Asperger Syndrome than of any type of student or behaviour.

The first of these is to be very specific when 'reporting' what you observed; there is no room for vague statements. 'He was not very cooperative' may be OK so far as it goes, but exactly in what way was he not cooperative (not getting started on a task, repeatedly asking questions that did not seem to need asking about the task, fussing over his equipment, downright refusal)? In what lesson was this and what was the activity? What time of day was it? What lessons or activities had preceded this behaviour, and what was to follow?

These are very precise and necessary requirements. There are one or two more which are equally necessary if the observations are to lead to anything of value, but they are a shade more speculative. The level of speculation is reduced, however, if the observations upon which they are based are really precise in the first place.

So, think about your observations in at least two further, linked dimensions. What does the student (the Asperger's in this case) get out of the behaviour, that is, what is the consequence of this behaviour that the student finds rewarding? We, and perhaps most students, may not find the consequence rewarding, but is it rewarding, perhaps in a rather obtuse way, to this particular student? If students get into trouble but thus get out of work which they find embarrassingly difficult, this might well be reward enough (the lesser of two evils, although probably not appreciated at a conscious level in this way by the student).

Another legitimate piece of speculation that teachers should positively engage in is, 'What was the immediate trigger for the behaviour?' Caution is needed; triggers can be imagined or invented. If the original observations, though, are crystal clear this is much less likely to be the case. If triggers are correctly recognised, it may well be possible to ensure they are not provided in future.

The above comments are true of all high quality teacher observation, but they are particularly important, perhaps, in the slightly blurred world of Asperger Syndrome.

A La Carte

An appreciable time has been spent outlining a profile of Asperger Syndrome and, indeed, filling in some of the details. This has been done in the hope that this will help alert teachers and others to this group of people and students who do merit a degree of extra and additional support but who are often in danger of being overlooked, either because they are not recognised at all, or are recognised only as being rather different and individualistic but not as having a degree of disability which can make life difficult for them, not least in school.

Now we come to the crux of the matter. What menu of strategies can this book offer teachers so that they – having had the customary think about their student or students, and their mutual situation – can then offer support to students who display observed and identified behaviours characteristic of students within the Asperger Syndrome? It is true for all students that if we cannot settle them socially they are much less likely to thrive in school and to learn; because of the nature of their disability, arguably this is particularly true for students within the Asperger syndrome. And so we must deal with the social side of life with and for these students, and all the following menus really should be read before making selections for particular students. That said, schools are about learning and teaching, so let us start with choices teachers may want particularly to consider which will make both of these two more likely and less stressful.

A La Carte for Asperger Syndrome
Teaching styles to fit learning styles

- Asperger's students often really like to 'work'. This is because they like the structure of a set learning task (so long as they are completely clear about what they have to do and what the outcome should be). Therefore, teachers may well wish to consider if this is true of their Asperger's students, and to plan to keep them busy, and contented, with lots of structured (but worthwhile) tasks (possibly even when others in the class are having freer activities).

- Although there may well be merit in keeping Asperger's students busy with lots of learning tasks, teachers will always want to consider the quality of learning that is inherently possible within these tasks. This is because the tunnel vision thinking of many Asperger's students may lead them to learn well by rote, but to miss the connections that lead to worthwhile understanding. So, in choosing tasks for the Asperger's students, it may be necessary to check that they are not being fed, say, a diet of isolated worksheets, which they may happily do, but only in a mechanistic way, and which they do not join up to provide an all-round understanding, or a set of skills.

- Teachers may come to the conclusion that their Asperger's students are POP artists, that is they have difficulties with their work related not so much to their actual educational ability to do the work but with Planning it, Organising it, and Prioritising the component parts of the work in order to accomplish it. Teachers may choose to keep this dimension of the way Asperger's students may be functioning in mind as they choose their approaches.

- Since there is a distinct possibility that skills and understanding, although apparently acquired, are not necessarily generalised and utilised in linked areas, teachers may opt to check on and demonstrate these connections in as concrete a fashion as possible. Thus, if the effects of drought on the farming and then the wellbeing of the population in one part of the world have been studied, teachers may feel it appropriate to check that the Asperger's students are not starting from scratch when they later study a similar phenomenon on another part of the globe.

- Whether or not teachers find that their particular Asperger's students really are happier when they are working, they may find that the students have difficulty in actually getting started. Largely, this is because, as is mentioned above, they often have difficulties in planning or organising a task, or even how to approach the task. Teachers may want to consider two options, or an approach which blends these together in proportions appropriate to the individual student. If it seems right to do so, teachers can defeat the students' procrastination at the very beginning of the task, and brook no argument. On the other hand, lots of guidance may be needed as the students struggle to plot a way of tackling, and starting, a lengthy project requiring their own research and investigations.

- Thus, teachers will wish to consider whether their students need help to see 'the big picture', and if they need to be guided away from irrelevant lines of enquiry, or dissuaded from focusing on inconsequential detail.

- Structuring tasks for their Asperger's students will be something many teachers may wish to consider so that separate, clear, sequential steps are (it is hoped) delineated for the students. Having done this, teachers will probably want to consider celebrating with the students the completion of each step, so that the students get a sense of progressing through the whole task.

- Asperger's students may get stuck, and do nothing about it, or scarcely realise that they are stuck, or that anything can or should be done about it. If this is the case, teachers may wish to tell their students that if they haven't got anything to show for the last, say, five minutes, then they are stuck! And they should do something about it, which will probably be to tell the teacher, and that it is all right to do this. There is always the possibility of pitfalls opening up, though. In this example, it is possible that the students will devoutly watch the clock to count exactly the five minutes. Or they may not quite understand what 'anything to show' means. Teachers may need to say, 'If you haven't written down anything for five minutes, you must tell me'. Sensitive teachers will develop an awareness of how to deal with this, and the example is quite an extreme one (although entirely possible).

- Bearing in mind that the visual channel tends to be stronger than the auditory channel or at least more effective than the exclusively verbal (despite perhaps superficial indicators to the contrary), teachers may consider writing instructions, learning tips, pieces of advice for their Asperger's students, and may find that they perform better as a result. Similarly, presenting materials visually ('visual aids') may be decided upon as a useful way forward.

- The above point notwithstanding, teachers may feel it appropriate to be aware of the Asperger's students' reading diet. This may show a distinct preference for the non-fiction and the factual. Teachers may feel this is to be permissible and even to be encouraged (it does lead to improved basic reading skills and to the acquisition of more information and knowledge) but that this should not, ideally, make up 100 per cent of that diet. Teachers may want to encourage fiction, but feel that they then have to be careful about the type of fiction. They may feel, for instance, that fantasy books are too far away from reality for the Asperger's, who may not have an appreciation of this gap. When general fiction is read, teachers may want to question their Asperger's students to see how they have understood the story. Discussion of matters around why such and such an event happened, what caused it to happen, what did the characters feel about it happening, may address developmental issues particularly pertinent to Asperger Syndrome students. That said, teachers will never wish to make this too heavy, or turn it into a test or interrogation.

- Teachers of young children may see little point in forcing imaginative play. If it comes to Drama, role-play, etc. teachers may opt to proceed with caution, perhaps by prescribing roles and not looking for spontaneity, for if the Asperger's are not identifying with the scenarios they will not be understanding what is going on, and feel very out of place.

- When it comes to writing, teachers may find that a lack of imagination means that creative writing is limited in scope and quality, and not a very fulfilling activity for Asperger's students. (In an extreme case it may even appear that an Asperger's student has difficulty in understanding what 'fiction' is, or in seeing any point in it.) Therefore teachers may choose to improve writing skills by allowing Asperger's students to write largely about factual things and, comfortable with this, they may write rather well. In due course, in an effort to move on from this nonetheless limited canvas, teachers might decide to ask their Asperger's students to write about a similar situation to one already dealt with, but one in which the teacher has changed the scenario just a little. For instance, if an Asperger's student as interested in cycling, he might well be asked to write a piece clearly explaining how to mend a puncture. This done, probably very satisfactorily, the teacher might contemplate asking him/her to research and then write about how to change the wheel of a car. Or perhaps a two-stage approach could be adopted: if the class as a whole have been asked to write about an exciting/frightening/surprising event that happened on a day trip to the seaside, the Asperger's students might be asked just to do a well-constructed imaginary diary of a day at the seaside. Having done this, they might then be asked to adapt it, and insert at some point a description of an exciting/frightening/surprising event. In fact, teachers might even decide not to give a choice here, and to nominate one of the three events that has to be written about or, at least, to make sure that the Asperger's students have each quickly made up their mind about which it is to be.

- In some classrooms, teachers may have a policy and practice of, while ensuring that the required work is done, students having a choice of activities or a choice in the order in which they do their work. When it comes to their students with Asperger's, teachers may, however, consider being more directive, and of limiting choice; in fact, they may feel it more profitable to limit choice drastically, starting with no more than two options.

- Whatever the activity (unless it is one of those which virtually preoccupies the student) teachers may find their Asperger's students lose concentration, or perhaps a more accurate way of putting it would be, lose focus. In these circumstances, teachers may choose to be very explicit, possibly in writing, about what has to be done. As is mentioned elsewhere, this may be another instance of where teachers think it appropriate to set out any stages there are within the whole task, and the order in which they are to be done.

- Teachers may find that repetitive questioning, which does not really carry the accomplishment of a task forward, may be a feature of their Asperger's students' modus operandi. A strategy which is then open to teachers is to make it clear that the number of questions asked in quick succession will be counted, and that there is a limit as to how many will be permitted (three might be the number). The Asperger's students may learn to ration themselves, and thus improve the quality of their questioning, which may, in turn, lead to something actually being learned through the questioning. Even if this does not happen, at least the teachers and the classes can have some legitimate peace.

- Teachers may come to feel that their Asperger's students have difficulty in looking at a situation from different points of view, which can inhibit their ability to consider a range of hypotheses. This may reveal itself, for example, in difficulty in constructing different possible explanations of the causes of a phenomenon in Science or possible different motivations that people had for their actions in History: thus, Asperger's students may have some difficulty in seeing that there could be a range of explanations as to why the seed did not germinate, or why Charles I was tried and executed. To support such students here, teachers may choose to set out all the possibilities (e.g. 'Charles was executed because Cromwell objected to the King's religious beliefs; Charles was executed because the Parliamentarians considered him to be undemocratic; the seed did not germinate because it lacked light/water/warmth.') Each possibility is considered initially as a separate entity, one at a time.

- Bearing in mind the typical Asperger difficulty with organising how to go about a task of any complexity, and also their likely literal interpretation of language (including teacher instructions), teachers may wish to choose to employ great clarity in setting any task. This includes trying to ensure they understand what is to be done, possibly how it is to be done, and when it is to be done by. Leaving too much to the students' imagination, expecting them to be innovative in deciding how they go about the task, and having a rather vague time-line for how the work should progress and be completed by are approaches likely to be unprofitable with many Asperger's students, and even stressful to them because they are unsure about how to respond.

- The above implies that Asperger's students are likely to perform better on closed tasks rather than open-ended ones. This being the case, teachers may choose to differentiate tasks in order that their Asperger's students can work comfortably. As an example, perhaps the students have been given the brief to 'Design the perfect school playground', but the Asperger's students could be asked to 'Design a playground for an Infants' school, incorporating swings, a slide, see-saw, and sandpit. Your notes must include your reasons for positioning these items in the areas you have chosen.' In English, the class as a whole might be asked to write a piece of dialogue in which two people have an argument, but the Asperger's students might be asked to write a piece of dialogue in which two neighbours argue because one of them parks his car outside the other's house and never outside his own. (This might well still be a difficult task for some Asperger's students because of their lack of imagination, but at least it does give them something of a context and framework within which to think.)

- Teachers' classroom organisation, and the way they deliver the curriculum, might include a good deal of group work. Group membership and cooperative working may pose considerable problems for many Asperger's students; this could well be to the degree that the teacher decides not to insist upon it, and allows the Asperger's students to work individually. If they can, nonetheless, work as adjacent to a group as seems feasible, teachers might well feel this to be a good thing. If and when the Asperger's students can begin to integrate into a group it is entirely possible that teachers will wish to think about the nature and composition of the group particularly carefully. They may well decide that a small group is the starting point, and that the personalities of the other group members are especially important. It may be felt that whereas group dynamics, in effect, generally sort out satisfactorily roles within the group, and each student fairly naturally assumes an appropriate place and task, this just will not happen for the Asperger's students, who just do not pick up the right vibes. If this is the case, teachers will probably want to consider whether it is satisfactory to leave the Asperger's students floating (or sinking) rather aimlessly in the group or if it is better, in these particular instances, to ascribe a task. Assuming the latter, teachers will then want to choose the particular task, perhaps feeling that a real but relatively minor one is called for in the early days, and one that is definitely within the competence of the Asperger's students. Failure within the group might be seen as potentially very detrimental to the Asperger's sense of feeling that they can actually get along with people (students).

- Teachers may come to the conclusion that, because they tend to lack imagination, and do not think laterally, Asperger's students are likely to place themselves in some degree of danger, not foreseeing possible consequences and outcomes of actions or situations. Examples of this could certainly be in the lab or in Science experiments, in the gym or hall, and on excursions and field trips. Fortunately, the type of thinking they do tend to have means they are likely to obey rules to the letter (certainly while they are on an even keel). Therefore, teachers may choose to utilise this, and minimise the risk of harm coming to the Asperger's students by having rules which cover all likely eventualities, and which are spelt out (probably in writing) in totally unambiguous language. A further precaution might well be to question the Asperger's students about the rules, just to make assurance doubly sure that the rules have been correctly interpreted, bearing in mind a certain propensity in Asperger's students to misconstrue.

- Teachers may note in their Asperger's students particular interests which, if not obsessive, can certainly be described as extreme and virtually to preoccupy the students. The interests might also be distinctly minority ones and not shared by peers, or the sort of interests that peers have now outgrown. Such interests will quite likely involve a lot of minutiae. Knowledge of the name of every football player in every team to have won the FA Cup for the last 40 years becomes uninteresting to even the keenest fan if the Asperger's student insists on recounting the list on every possible occasion. Teachers may find this sort of learning (for learning, at a certain level, has taken place) gets in the way of the learning they are much more interested in fostering, but they may find that just occasionally, at least, they can utilise it, if they choose to do so. An Asperger's extreme interest in dinosaurs might be utilised perhaps in early History, or in Science and evolution, or Geography and climatic changes over the epochs; perhaps an excessive interest in car number plates can be used to some extent in teaching something of the regions when number plates are related to their localities, or in Maths, where data related to number plates, their issue, and their distribution can be displayed in different ways and through, perhaps, a range of graphs. It may even be that such preoccupational interests can be the basis of teaching proper research, recording, and data handling skills in due course. (Teachers may, however, wish to prepare themselves for some resistance on this latter point; Asperger's students will quite possibly be only too pleased to deal with their interest as part of their school work, but they may not take well to being asked to deal with it differently.)

- In instances where obsessive behaviour is extreme and gets in the way of the students' proper functioning, teachers may have to bite the bullet and accept that it may not be possible to eliminate it completely, and that it may even make for more difficulties to try to do so. It then becomes a matter of managing the obsessive behaviour, and teachers may want to employ strategies such as limiting it to certain times, perhaps even allowing it as a reward for a task completed.

- As with all disabilities, teachers will want to think about their Asperger's students, and then consider how the individual difficulties may particularly manifest themselves within particular subjects, or subject areas. For instance, the language difficulties and also stereotypical thinking that Asperger's may experience could reveal themselves in Maths by the students really finding it difficult to realise that one concept can have several terminologies that identify it. An obvious example of this is that *subtract, minus, take away* all have, essentially, the same meaning, and might be used almost interchangeably. Such students will need a good deal of exposure to all of the terms, preferably within identical examples, with sometimes one being used, and sometimes another. In CDT, it is particularly true of Asperger's students that they will be most interested in making things which they can use personally, rather than in more esoteric items. These are just a couple of basic examples of how flexible teachers, working from a little knowledge of a disability and good observations of their students (they are not fazed by what they observe because they can place it within the context of the disability) can 'go with the flow' and place work in front of their students with which they are comfortable, in which they can be successful, and from which they can learn.

- On a slightly broader front, homework can be a problem for Asperger's students. Perhaps they cannot get organised, perhaps they cannot get started, perhaps they get stuck and don't know what to do about it, perhaps they have to use some initiative and find some things out for themselves, perhaps they cannot realise what is an acceptable amount, perhaps they answer questions very accurately and briefly but without insight into fleshing out answers or, equally, do not appreciate when to round off the work and bring it to a conclusion when there is no one there to tell them. Homework may appear to be (and sometimes really is) a good working environment for Asperger's students because issues such as group work, turn-taking, being teased, changes of routine, and whereabouts of materials and resources should not be potential pitfalls but, equally, the sort of problems just referred to can rear their heads. All teachers will want to consider if they need to make it abundantly clear to their Asperger's students what the task is, what it will 'look like' when it is finished, quite possibly approximately how long it should take (although approximately can be a difficult notion for Asperger's students to get their heads round), what materials and books they will need, and when they must hand it in. If the version of the homework that the Asperger's students are set is a shade mechanical and routine, teachers may consider that, on some occasions for some students, this is entirely acceptable.

- Most teachers accept that when all is said and done, straightforward praise is still the greatest motivator and, also, the greatest contributor to students' feelings of self-worth. That said, they may find that Asperger's students do not seem to respond much to praise, or to show the usual signs of pleasure at receiving it. If this is the case, teachers will still want to consider giving praise in much the usual manner. Apart from the fact that this is all part of the normal teacher-student relationship in human terms, learning benefits greatly from feedback, and it seems reasonable to persevere in this vein in the hope that it may be reinforcing learning, even if the students' reactions are less obvious than is usual.

- Lastly, teachers will want to consider involving the parents. Parents are the ones with the experience; Asperger's students are students with Asperger Syndrome at home as well as at school, and they are at home a great deal more than they are at school. Parents may be able to advise teachers, they may have strategies of their own; at the very least, they have got to be worth listening to. If it should be that it emerges that they are actually seriously not coping at home, then they may appreciate sharing this with teachers, and it may be possible to support them in the seeking of further help. Less dramatically, it is quite likely that home and school will be able to work together (remembering particularly that Asperger's students are likely to respond well to a consistent approach).

A La Carte of instructions and questions

Virtually all aspects of teaching involve giving instructions to students about how to do a task, how to present it and in what form, and also when to do it, and quite possibly which resources and materials to use. Then, of course, there are the instructions which are to do with behaviour, what the rules are, how they are possibly different in different locations and circumstances, and what happens if instructions are not followed (disobeyed). Similarly, virtually all teachers make use of questions and questioning for a variety of purposes: to check understanding of what is to be done and how it is to be done and, most crucially, to check understanding, and that learning has taken place. The manner in which instructions are given and the techniques employed in insightful questioning are part of every good teacher's armoury, but when teaching students within the Asperger Syndrome, they become even more important. Because of the way they perceive the world, interpret language, fail to make inferences, possibly have difficulty in making the links and cross-references, Asperger's students benefit greatly from absolute clarity about what they are being asked to do when they receive an instruction, and what is required of them by way of appropriate answers to questions (except perhaps the totally closed question which does only require a monosyllabic or extremely factual answer). This being the case, a menu is now provided of points teachers may wish to consider and choose from when instructing and asking questions of their Asperger's students.

Instructions

- As a first consideration, teachers may wish to bear in mind the desirability of always addressing the Asperger's student by name when giving an instruction, even though they are addressing the whole class or a group. (Like a good deal of quality SEN practice, it just sounds like good common sense; that's precisely why it can be valuable to write these things down!) But why is this perhaps particularly worth bearing in mind for Asperger's students? It is because the notion of being a member of a group and a part of a bigger whole may not be fully appreciated by Asperger's students. So, an Asperger's student may not automatically realise that when teachers talk to the class, they are talking to every individual in that class. Besides using the student's name, teachers may choose to add very small bits of identifying language, such as, 'That includes you, please, Simon.' In any event, Asperger's students need to know they are included, and that teachers do mean them. Teachers may, additionally, wish to make sure they use the student's name before they give the instruction, as making sure the students are involved as the instruction is finishing may be too late.

- While thinking about their Asperger's student as group (class) members, teachers may want to consider a further possible reason for making sure that the Asperger's students are directly associating themselves with the instructions. This is to safeguard against assuming that because the rest of the class has understood what is, for instance, to be done next, that the Asperger's students will have done so; or that because students who are slightly unclear will probably realise from classmates what is to be done, that the Asperger's students will do this.

- When giving instructions, teachers may see it as appropriate, while ensuring that sufficient information is given, to keep them simple and minimalist. Also, they may feel instructions are best absorbed if they are explicit and straightforward. Supplementary information and illustrative exemplars, so useful for some students, may be thought to be superfluous, given the thinking processes and working practices of many Asperger's students.

- If teachers do feel that the previous point is of relevance to their particular students, they may wish to consider the precision of their instructions. For example, teachers may choose not to say, 'I'd like you to write a little bit more now, please' (meaning, 'You jolly well haven't done enough yet; this is nothing like finished') because 'a little bit more' may be all that the teachers will get, as language is interpreted literally. (This is, of course, an instance of where trouble may be brewing, if teachers see the production of that very small amount of extra work as being disobedience or laziness.)

- While appreciating that merely repeating an instruction does not necessarily prove that it has been understood (any more than just speaking louder in a foreign language makes it more likely that the locals will understand us), teachers may feel it useful to repeat instructions so that Asperger's students have the time to interpret them, and understand what they really mean. However, they may also feel it desirable to use as nearly as possible exactly the same words and to repeat the instruction verbatim, if possible. Slightly different wording possibly allows for a slightly different understanding on the part of the Asperger's student. (This also underlines the desirability of utterly unambiguous language – if such a thing is possible.)

- In fact, particularly bearing in mind that Asperger's students tend to learn better from what they see than what they hear, teachers may decide that instructions should generally be written down. In effect, the students are then given a framework within which they can operate – although, as ever, the clarity of the instructions will have to be absolute.

- From their knowledge of their Asperger's students, teachers may well wish to choose not only to explain with utter clarity what has to be done, but when it has to be done by. This may be achieved particularly by explaining not only how a task should be started, but what the students will have to show when they reach the end of the task. This may be very helpful in enabling the Asperger's students to appreciate the nature of the task and to engage with it.

- More complex tasks, of course, have stages and steps along the way. Teachers may choose to list and explain these also, rather than expect Asperger's students naturally to move through them in a sequence.

- However, here teachers may feel they have to do a delicate balancing act because they may also feel that instructions are best given to Asperger's students one at a time, not in a sequence. It may be that they find this is true if the sequence of instructions have little or nothing to do with each other, perhaps involving separate activities, different times of day, different lessons or locations, whereas within the same task the explanation of how the steps follow each other in order to complete the task means that the Asperger's students have a better chance of making the links and getting their heads around the wholeness of the task.

- If a sequence of instructions does have to be given, it may be considered a good idea to preface each new step by 'Then' or 'Next'. This is hardly rocket science, but such little clarifying points do anchor the Asperger's students in the task. It is so easy, in the 'business' of a classroom making multiple demands, either not to realise the significance of such apparently inconsequential support mechanisms, or simply to forget.

- Teachers may feel that their Asperger's students are not using the context of a situation to give meaning to information they are receiving in order to comprehend the significance of that information. Teachers may come to feel that just giving information and instructions, assuming that Asperger's students will make elementary inferences from it without further explanation, will not be sufficient. For instance, in an extreme case, a teacher may give a perfectly adequate explanation of the task the class is now to embark on, but find an Asperger's student not getting going because the teacher has forgotten to add, 'So, please take the books you will need out of your desk and start straight away.'

- Teachers may find that instructions relating to rules need to be explained very clearly. The rule, 'At the end of the lesson we pack up our things and put everything away' does sound clear, but teachers may opt to demonstrate it amply to Asperger's students. (However, once Asperger's students have got the rules, they are inclined, generally, to be extremely observant of them, so that can be a great relief to the teacher. Even here, though, problems can arise because they might go to exorbitant lengths to keep the rules; another possibility is that, because of their lack of understanding of the subtleties of social norms, they unabashedly tell the teacher of any student who has erred by even a small margin.)

- Instructions can, of course, like other types of communication, sometimes be give non-verbally. Almost instinctively, many teachers give signals to students without speaking to them at all. Typical and commonplace examples of this are the frown, or the finger to the lips. These are so useful in modifying students' behaviour in non-confrontational, non-escalating ways. Unfortunately, teachers may find these to be virtually lost on the Asperger's students. Teachers may decide, however, not to abandon this style of communication completely with such students, but specifically to teach a few of these signals.

• A last thought about the giving of instructions: teachers may find or feel that shouting is not helpful when Asperger's students have not or will not follow an instruction, whether in a learning situation or with regard to a school or classroom rule. It may be that the students have failed to understand or interpret the instruction, rather than wilfully disobeyed or ignored it. If this is the case, teachers may feel that shouting does not clarify the situation, but may confuse or upset the students, who do not fully appreciate why they are being shouted at or why the teacher is becoming angry.

Questions

Whether by training or by intuition, skilled teachers are skilled questioners. This is true of the questions they set as written exercises, and even more so of the questions they ask by way of a 'teaching dialogue' with groups or individuals. Although there is a place for 'closed' questions, generally speaking, the most important, valuable, and profound questions are 'open' questions; they are not amenable to one-word answers, but require thought and a depth of understanding if the answers are to be full, and a series of probing questions provides a scaffolding infrastructure which supports learning.

Although it does have a degree of importance, the most important question may not be 'When did William the Conqueror invade England?' but 'Why did he invade England?' This can run on into other questions such as 'Why did he invade England when he did?' (thus bringing in the date question, anyway); 'What were the short-term effects of the invasion?' 'What have been the long-term results?'

All of the above is true for the majority of students; unfortunately, it may not be true for Asperger's students! Initially, Asperger's students generally prefer to live in the world of concrete thinking, and are uneasy when asked to move into the less tangible world of the hypothetical, the imaginative, or the speculative. This is not to say that no effort should ever be made to move them onto those areas, which are so rich for so many people, but it is to say that teachers may wish to temper their questioning techniques with an appreciation that Asperger's students may enter those worlds much later and more slowly than many of their peers and, in fact, may well never do so fully. This, of course, does not mean that Asperger's do not have banks of knowledge which are not only useful and worthwhile (as well as, perhaps, banks of knowledge which are of interest largely only to themselves!) but which are amenable to questioning – of the right sort.

Here, then, is a short menu of considerations teacher may wish to choose from when dealing with their particular Asperger's students in question and answer situations.

- First and foremost, and as has been indicated above, in the teaching situation teachers may choose to confine their questions to those which are direct and literal, and to avoid open-ended ones. With caution, and with the passage of time, teachers may wish to develop their questions, to take their students beyond closed questions – at the rate their students can accept them, and can respond in a meaningful way. If this stage is never reached, teachers may decide, in as positive and not as negative way as possible, not to make an 'issue' out of this state of affairs.

- Similarly, teachers may feel it appropriate to be rather directive with their Asperger's students, rather than ask them questions of the 'Do you want to...?' 'Shall we...?' type. Teachers may feel this because such questions can be answered with a 'Yes' or a 'No'; this does not mean that the students have actually understood the question (bearing in mind particularly the Asperger's students' propensity for getting hold of the wrong end of the stick) or that they have necessarily appreciated what will flow from their 'Yes/No' response.

- Teachers may come to the conclusion that it is better to avoid one of their favourite forms of probing question, namely the 'Why...?' questions. This may be because Asperger's students are likely to have difficulty with the notion of 'Why?' To get around this difficulty constructively, while still getting at the essential point or piece of understanding they are trying to engender, teachers may wish to rephrase the question (something many teachers are intuitively past masters at). For instance, instead of, 'Why did the seed not germinate?' teachers may adopt the slightly different yet essentially the same, 'The seed did not germinate because...'

Asperger's students may actually *ask* rather a lot of questions. One reason for this can be a social one in that, in a class or group situation they typically have not absorbed the social norms, and feel that they can ask questions regardless of other members of the group and regardless of the time and place; it is quite likely that these questions will be called out without thought to any 'Put your hand up and wait until you are asked before you speak' type of rule. The disruption to the class can be significant. The other relatively common type of questioning teachers may have to deal with from their Asperger's students is questions which are far too numerous and, more than likely, repetitive. That they are, to a degree, being disruptive will not really have entered the Asperger's student's head.

- Teachers may wish to consider having exceptionally clear ground rules for the conduct of their Asperger's students in the classroom. The classroom rules may have to be dissected so that they are crystal clear; most other students can be left to make common-sense interpretations of rather generalised rules, but the clearest of limits, and sanctions, may have to be spelt out for the Asperger's students.

- In the case of questioning which is not so much disruptive as pointless because it is going over the same ground again and again, an individual rule may have to be devised of, say, no more than three questions in a given time limit is permitted. Teachers may feel that just to make the students aware of how many questions they have already asked will be sufficient to ensure that they do not go over their limit. In fact, teachers may even think it useful to ask the students to log the numbers of their own questions themselves (but take care in case they log the actual wording of the questions, not just how numerous they are).

A La Carte of the school environment and classroom management

How all students respond may, of course, be affected by the environment in which they find themselves, and by their immediate surroundings. Teachers may feel that this is particularly true of their Asperger's students. Perhaps teachers will wish to be aware of the potentially, and seemingly disproportionate, effect on Asperger's students if they have to have a lesson as a one-off in a different room, or if the teacher, for perfectly good reasons, has reorganised how the classroom resources and materials are housed, or if the room is unusually noisy, or even if there is a visitor (an Ofsted Inspector, heaven forbid?).

Against this backdrop, teachers are invited to select from the following menu when considering their classrooms, and also places in the school which students inevitably have to go to, cope with, and function in.

- Teachers may choose to keep a particularly orderly classroom on behalf of their Asperger's students, and to maintain and sustain a calm environment. They may judge that the classroom or the lesson needs a structure to it which is clearly laid out so that the Asperger's students understand this environment and can operate within its clearly defined parameters. Teachers may choose to put these parameters in place by virtue of having a regular classroom routine which soon becomes known and is, therefore, predictable.

- An important part of students' environment is the very immediate one of where they sit in class, and who they sit next to or near. So far as Asperger's students are concerned, teachers may wish to allocate set places and seats, and not to change them without very good reason. If adjustments to seating arrangements do have to be made, as is quite likely as students enter or leave the school, or it becomes clear that certain students need, for instance, to be separated from certain of their peers, or need to be moved nearer the front because of eyesight or hearing difficulties, teachers may choose to arrange it so that as little moving as possible has to be done by the Asperger's students, and that changes affecting other students leave the Asperger's students as undisturbed and unaffected as possible.

- Further, if it has been decided that to exercise the option of very definitely designating to the Asperger's students specific seats, teachers may want to consider how this decision is conveyed to the students. Teachers may decide that the best approach is simply to get on and do it, that is they may choose not to act in the following sort of way: 'Because you make such a fuss about where to sit, and take so long to settle down, I think I'm going to have to say you'd better sit in the front row from now on.' Teachers might instead opt to say, for example, 'Josh, this is your seat. Sit here in every Geography/History/French lesson from now on. Thank you.'

- That said, when allocating the Asperger's students their regular seats, teachers may choose to place them in positions where they can be monitored fairly closely and, perhaps particularly, kept on task. (But again, this is not to say that they would choose to do this in any punitive way, or in any way to suggest that they were expecting trouble. They would do it in a pragmatic, matter-of-fact way.)

- It may be that teachers will choose not to run 'open-plan' classrooms, or classrooms with strong elements of the open-plan type of approach, so far as Asperger's students are concerned.

- If it is felt that the Asperger's students perform better, and feel more at ease, in a classroom with set routines and a relatively firm structure, teachers may decide that that is what they will provide for them. This may involve rejigging for the Asperger's students how some tasks are carried out. For instance, if students are asked to use the library or classroom reference books or the Internet to research a project, and are fairly free to look into or follow any aspect of the project which interests them, the Asperger's students might be directed to specific books, chapters or pages, on the basis that if they know exactly what they have to study and where they have to look, they will be happy to see this as a finite task, and get on and do it, knowing exactly what is expected of them.

- Most teachers would strongly agree that obtaining and keeping students' attention was a crucial part of the job. That said, they may also find that with some Asperger's students the difficulty is not so much gaining and keeping attention but making sure they are attending to the aspect or point the teacher really wants them to focus on. Because Asperger's students tend not to see the big picture, but rather follow personal (but, in this context, irrelevant) interests, what is actually required of them may be missed. For instance, an Asperger's student who is fascinated by combine harvesters (their make, manufacturer, model number, tyre size, etc.) may have difficulty in focusing on the economic and ecological importance of sustainable farming as exemplified by the current state of the Great Plains of USA and Canada. Teachers may decide that, besides always calling in the work of Asperger's students while it is still in the preliminary stage, so that they are not sailing along in their own channels, very clear task-setting is an answer, whereby tasks are so worded or structured that they allow no room for irrelevancies.

- It may be found that even a change of activity within a classroom is unsettling to Asperger's students. In this case, teachers may decide always to try to say how long is going to be allowed for a task, as precisely as possible at what time it will finish, and to let the students know a few minutes before that time has elapsed, and that they will be moving on to something else shortly.

- It may be thought that this is particularly important if the new activity is one with which the Asperger's students are not particularly happy, perhaps because it involves moving into a fluid situation, such as the sports hall or swimming baths. If this is causing some stress, or deterioration in behaviour at these times, teachers may opt to be particularly careful to forewarn the students, and to see if, by so doing, the students can acclimatise to the idea, rather than to feel they have been suddenly landed in a new situation.

- Teachers may feel that not only will the students have their set places in the room, but that they will also ensure that the resources which students can draw upon as they need or wish are also always to be found in the same, set locations. In short, they may feel that Asperger's students perform better in a well-organised classroom run along consistent lines, which the Asperger's students can rely on.

- Teachers may conclude that this consistency which they are seeking should also include where Asperger's students keep their personal possessions (they may have noticed an Asperger's student who is upset because his coat was on a different hook at the end of the day from where he left it in the morning). So rules about lockers, storage trays, safekeeping of PE kit, etc. may be thought to be important, and need to be worked out and explained.

- Teachers may wish to pause and think particularly about the type of organisation and the methods by which students go about their work, for example lots of group work, collaborative work, moving around the room, going from task to task. If these sorts of approaches are the norm, teachers may wish to question the extent to which their Asperger's students can join in with their peers and these ways of operating, or whether some adjustments are going to be helpful. If it is decided that this is the case, perhaps they will consider that somehow they have to manufacture some individual space which is just for the Asperger's students, individual bits of space belonging to each Asperger's student (although it is unlikely that there will be large numbers of Asperger's students in any one class). Teachers may consider achieving this by simple means, such as a desk close to a group table, but with just a small but recognisable gap, perhaps angled away from the group. While teachers may opt not to force membership of a group on an Asperger's student, he or she could still be contributing a piece of work that the group wanted if they were working collaboratively; it would just be that the Asperger's students contribution was an individual one. To achieve this, though, teachers may again feel that direct organisation and intervention on their part was necessary, and that the group dynamics that might otherwise apply would exclude the Asperger's student.

- In fact, teachers may wish to consider the whole issue of personal space, and its boundaries. They may feel that their Asperger's students are made uneasy if other students are too close to them (that is, too close according to the sensitivities of the student). On the other hand, they may feel that the Asperger's students, in their efforts to communicate and socialise, are in the habit of encroaching on the space of other students, of being too much 'in their face', or of almost pursuing them in order to talk about something which is greatly interesting them, regardless of whether or not this is reciprocated. Classroom arrangements, and appropriate ground rules, may be seen as an option teachers wish to adopt if they find either of these scenarios is present.

- If teachers feel that their classrooms are fluid places, and that the Asperger's students seem unaware of the way the tide is flowing, teachers may decide that making expectations crystal clear will help these students survive. These expectations may relate to how tasks are to be done, and when they are to be completed by, or be in relation to behaviour, what is acceptable, what is not, and what the sanctions are.

- Teachers may choose to give Asperger's students a firm base from which to work by not giving them a plethora of choices. These may be appropriate for other students, for whom the developing of individual learning and being responsible for one's own learning is a feasible and worthwhile aim, but it may be decided that this is just too much for some Asperger's students to cope with, and that they will achieve more highly and happily if their range of choices and options is distinctly limited.

- Although teachers may wish to be aware of a degree of emotional distance between the Asperger's students and their classmates, teachers may feel that this can, perhaps, be bridged by getting certain of the rest of the class to support the Asperger's students. This is a delicate matter: teachers will not wish to patronise their Asperger's students, and they will not wish to place too much of a burden on classmates, or place them in difficult situations. But they may, also, feel that gradually they can encourage classmates to include and incorporate the Asperger's students into activities and, even more importantly, to accept that sometimes the Asperger's students will not feel able to respond, or may sometimes respond inappropriately. Teachers may feel that this is a very worthwhile angle, although one that may require a softly-softly approach.

- Teachers may feel that their Asperger's students are particularly unsettled by having to work with or interact with too many different people. Secondary school teachers may particularly find this, where being taught by a number of subject specialists is virtually inevitable. Clear timetables, which are run through by tutors at the beginning of the day, may be options teachers opt for to ease the situation (Asperger's students tend to react better if they are prepared for a situation, but will probably not prepare themselves). Having all staff aware of the presence (and needs) of Asperger's students may be thought to be another aid, and it may be decided that there is a real role for the SENCo in this regard. This may be another way in which peers can be primed to help. In the Primary School, there is likely to be less of a problem, but even here teachers may decide to exercise options such as, if blessed with more than one classroom assistant, delegating only one to work regularly with any one particular Asperger's student. Supply teachers may, unwittingly, present a problem to Asperger's students. If it is known that a supply teacher is going to be coming in, then teachers may again feel that preparing the Asperger's students in advance will help a lot. Preparing the supply teacher, too, may be thought to be advisable, with some classroom tips, even if given at the last minute (including naming the students in question!). For example, 'If the Asperger's student(s) do react badly, don't worry – it's the student(s), not you; don't over-react yourself, keep calm; be patient – things will probably improve as the day goes along and they get a little used to you, especially if they are not feeling "threatened".'

• Given that Asperger's students do not read the prevailing, 'local' social norms well, teachers may decide that they have to remind them often, and in advance of transgressions, what the classroom protocols are, and that they need to do so in a very basic fashion. For example, 'If you want to say something to me, put up your hand, and do not speak until I ask you; Don't talk to other people in the room; Stay in your seat unless you have asked permission to leave it.' In fact, teachers may feel that these rules are best written out, the Asperger's students having personal copies, which teachers can remind them at appropriate times to read. This all sounds, perhaps, a shade draconian but, as with so much in teaching, it is not only what is done but how it is done that makes all the difference. Certainly, teachers may, reluctantly, conclude that the friendly, almost narrative-style of some classroom rules nowadays may be rather lost on the Asperger's students. For example, 'In this room, we are always polite and courteous, and do not speak before we have put our hand up, and been invited to do so by the teacher – and only by the teacher.'

- Despite its being a much-quoted technique, easy to write but harder to do, teachers may think that the Asperger's students are another group of students for whom it is better to eliminate bad behaviours by praising the good behaviours before the bad ones appear. Timing is everything!

- Underpinning the school day in many schools, especially secondary schools, are the students' individual, personal timetables, which can vary considerably from student to student, depending on subjects taken and options exercised. It may be felt that the Asperger's students can be particularly well-anchored by their timetables which tell them precisely where they have to be, when, and what for; the converse may be true, with unclear timetables causing very great uncertainty in students who really do appreciate knowing where they stand. Teachers may opt to check the clarity of the Asperger's timetables, and whether they are proof against becoming prematurely dog-eared and illegible. Teachers may think it a good idea if the timetables are as 'visual' as possible, with helpful colour codings or symbols (while safeguarding against these themselves leading to confusion).

- If teachers have decided that consistency is important to their Asperger's students, by definition, they may go on to conclude that this consistency should be there for the students in all lessons and in all situations. Cooperation and discussion with colleagues, possibly in a formal setting, is something which teachers may feel they need to achieve, more than likely with the very active support of the SENCo.

- Simplistically, it may be decided that it is very important to ask all colleagues to distinguish between behaviour that is consciously disruptive and that which is an Asperger Syndrome characteristic. In so doing, it may be a good idea to acknowledge that the Wisdom of Solomon is sometimes difficult to acquire.

- Teachers will not only be very aware that students do not spend all their time in lessons and classrooms, but that they have to go to other places, such as assembly, dining halls, and playgrounds; not only that, they will know that, for some students, these are the places where troubles and difficulties are most likely to arise.

Therefore, they may wish to give these situations some particular thought, and exercise some options that may head off difficulties, if they think their Asperger's students are liable not to cope.

- In the playground, they may choose to prime a particular playground assistant to keep a watchful eye, and ensure that the students know who this is so they can readily go to this person. They may advise the students that they stay within one particular area or play space, for example if they find the open playground and high-spirited games rather daunting. Again, they may contemplate enlisting the support of some carefully selected classmates. And, if things really are not working (or likely to work) in the playground, they may consider, at least for a time, special indoor arrangements, such as the library. The object of the exercise would not be total and permanent removal from the playground, but an easing of the situation; perhaps 20 minutes inside, 20 minutes outside would be helpful, with the outside period gradually increasing and the inside period, obviously, diminishing.

- In the dining hall and assembly, teachers may want to think about the Asperger's students going in first (or last), and of having special places to sit (even though this is probably not the usual practice). Considerations here might be the end of a row or table, near a door, etc. Dinner ladies and supervisory assistants may again be primed, especially where Asperger's students have very distinct likes and dislikes over which foods they do or do not want, or have difficulty making up their mind if there is a wide choice. It may be felt that teachers taking assembly need to know of the Asperger's students, and not to be surprised if there is possibly some inappropriate calling out, or some slightly offbeat questioning if there is a participation element to the assembly. If visitors are taking an assembly, as often happens at Harvest Festival or Christmas, or when a representative of a charity is in school, perhaps the teacher will opt to sit close to the Asperger's students.

- Occasionally, from time to time, it may be that the Asperger's students are not able to cope with the classroom situation. Teachers may decide that if such circumstances do arise, they will try to avoid making a song and dance about it. They may choose to operate a form of 'time-out', which they operate in as neutral a way as possible, as opposed to making it a punishment. In fact, they may choose some positive terminology for the time-out area; 'Personal Study Area' is one possibility. It may be felt that such an area need not be outside the classroom, and that it could just be one particular desk in a quieter, peripheral area, which is for the sole use of the Asperger's student (it would not be facing the wall or a corner, but it may be angled obliquely in relation to the class). It may be possible to arrange with a colleague a brief sojourn in another classroom or in the headteacher's office. In any event, it may be decided that the purpose of the personal study area (or place) is to lower the temperature, not to ratchet it upwards, and that when the set time has elapsed, the expectation is that things will return to normal. (This is not to say that teachers will choose no follow-up at all, but that is another matter of judgement as to how and when, but they may choose not to link excessively the Personal Study Area with sanctions.) Time-out is more fully discussed in Chapter 4.

- Teachers may wish to give special consideration to the thorny issue of exams and the likely reaction of their Asperger's students, especially if the exams are of a formal nature, as would be the case with GCSEs. Teachers may anticipate problems if they feel that their Asperger's students are particularly affected by change of routine, location, etc. (over and above the worries that many students experience in the face of exams, anyway). Preparation and practice may be thought to be the answer. In fact, teachers may opt to talk up the exam situation; once you know what is involved and what to expect, the exam situation is largely predictable, the routine is pretty much always the same, there is a clear task ahead, and the whole situation is quiet and controlled – the sort of environment many students with Asperger's rather like. So, teachers may well decide that particular preparation for this new situation is necessary, but may feel it appropriate to go about this in a manner which conveys confidence and optimism.

- For the Asperger's students, as with others with a degree of disability, teachers will also need to consider the possibility of extra time in public exams, and whether this should be applied for. If the application clearly makes the case that the student has Asperger

Syndrome, then it is quite likely that the award of extra time would follow. Nonetheless, teachers may wish to pause and consider whether this is a route they wish to go down. They may wish to consider primarily the student's academic abilities and working practice before deciding that the extra time would be of any particular advantage. Indeed, they may wish to consider whether to be one of a small minority either starting an exam paper early or remaining in a room when everyone else or the majority have left is something the Asperger's student is comfortable with. This will, as with all menu choices, depend upon the individual student, but teachers may decide that to go along with the general routine rather than to have a different one is easier for the Asperger's student.

A La Carte of communication

Teaching, of course, is all about communication – preferably two-way communication, student to teacher, as well as vice versa.

Communication is about communicating to someone and enabling them to understand what you say, and it is about both receiving and understanding what is said to you. It is about language. Measured in a relatively narrow sense, Asperger's Syndrome students may well have language skills in the average or above average range, but Asperger's students do not learn language incidentally, as most children do. Thus, their social use of language can often be inappropriate, and they do not understand the nuances of what is said to them. In fact, the real problem is probably one of communication per se, rather than of oral language skills.

Furthermore, communication is, clearly, much more than just words. It is tone of voice, pitch, speed of speech, animation, hesitation, pauses, whispering, shouting. It is also about body language: shrugging shoulders, gesticulating, hurting, welcoming. It is about facial expression: smiling, frowning, crying; showing fear, disappointment, despair, amusement, anger, pleasure.

And it is about eye contact. Many teachers hold their students as if by an invisible thread, eye to eye, as many threads as there are students. The slightest tweak by the teacher on any single thread conveys something to the individual student (usually about paying attention, but not necessarily); sometimes even, a student can send a message to the teacher by pulling this same thread.

Arguably, many of the best, most vivid, most popular teachers are great exponents of the art of non-verbal communication. They may have little impact on Asperger's students, who tend to read, speak, and hear language literally, without picking up on implications, and without drawing inferences. Body language they may not notice, or if they do, its significance escapes them. There are, therefore, considerable ramifications here as teachers ply their prime art of communicating.

- The first thing teachers may decide to do is to be even more aware than usual of the language they are using. They may decide that they have to avoid complex language, especially language that requires insight and interpretation.

- They may decide to be even more careful than usual not to use sarcasm, or even irony.

- They may decide to adopt a kind of parallel language. For instance, in using a metaphor, almost in the same breath they may provide its interpretation: 'Come on, look slippy, and hurry up.' Most students will not need the hurry up which is by way of explanation, but 'look slippy' on its own might be very puzzling to the Asperger's students; so, 'I want to see this room shipshape and Bristol fashion – you've got just five minutes to clear up; keep your hair on, and just calm down.' Teachers are endlessly inventive in this way, and thus need not deny the rest of the class experience of the richness of language, while still communicating with the Asperger's students.

- Teachers may come to feel that their language has to be very explicit. 'Your homework looks as if the cat has walked all over it' may elicit agreement from the Asperger's student but not necessarily a consequent understanding that the teacher is clearly implying this is unsatisfactory, and it should be better presented next time; the teacher may feel advised to add, 'Please hand in much neater, tidier work next time.'

- Teachers may feel they need to be sensitive to the way they react to the language used by the Asperger's students, and not to misinterpret. They may feel they must certainly point out to the Asperger's student that they cannot simply say to someone 'You're very fat' (realising that the social use of language, and its nuances, are things which tend to pass the Asperger's students by) but not to castigate them for rudeness, which was never intended. However, teachers may well feel it appropriate to tell the Asperger's students what they may not say – and, in due course, what they may.

- Teachers may be aware that small talk does not feature highly for their Asperger's students. They may notice that these students talk at people rather than to them; or that conversation is all one-way, that is, their way; and that dialogue does not feature highly. Teachers may see this as quite a bar to enhanced social integration for the Asperger's students, and gently – but not too overtly – coax them into groups, and shape their language and responses in those groups. Teachers may appreciate that this is a slow and long-term process, but still regard it as an area they are not prepared to ignore.

- Hard though it is to do, teachers may want to tutor their Asperger's students with regard to their speech. There may be an issue over the students' volume when they are talking (often too loud); the tone of their speech (often monotonous) may benefit from their attention being drawn to it, and much the same can be true of the pace of their speech. Practice and modelling can be useful if these can be fitted in. Formal and informal input from a Speech Therapist will often not be out of place, if it can be obtained.

- Many teachers very effectively employ humour and jokes. Such teachers may feel that Asperger's students do not see jokes, and even do not have a sense of humour or, if they do, it is a rather unusual one. Such teachers may well decide that they are not going to deny the rest of the class the benefit of their wit, but be prepared to explain the joke (even though this is a tortuous process) if the Asperger's students show any interest in it or, indeed, are unduly puzzled by not understanding it.

- Teachers may find eye contact presents a problem with Asperger's students; quite possibly they avoid it, possibly they engage it to excess, but in an expressionless, rather blank way. In other words, its significance is not realised, and it is a social skill they do not fully have. Again, teachers may feel that it is something well worth encouraging, but that it cannot be forced, and should not be 'trained'. In the course of normal teacher–student conversation, teachers may feel that 'Please look at me' or 'Please don't stare' said matter-of-factly would be appropriate, along with, of course, good modelling on the teacher's part.

A La Carte of social integration

On first acquaintance, especially in a one-to-one situation, an unsuspecting teacher (or anyone else) would not think that students with Asperger Syndrome had difficulties in their social relationships. In fact, initial impressions are often very favourable. In appearance, they are generally neat and tidy, clean and well-groomed. Their language skills may appear to be perfect, and so it is thought that their communication skills (a different matter altogether) are good. It is only later that it becomes apparent that there may be a degree of over-fussiness about appearance, and what may be worn and what may not, or a reluctance to dress differently for different occasions, or a failure to realise what is appropriate for a particular occasion. So far as language is concerned, the formal language used, and rather liked by teachers despairing of sloppy speech, may come to be seen (or heard) as rather pedantic and inflexible, and perhaps inappropriate to the particular setting.

Closer acquaintance, and good teacher observation skills, may reveal that the Asperger's students are frequently making 'mistakes' in social situations or, at least, appear rather gauche, or make gestures which are unusual (exacerbated if they happen to have the coordination difficulties which tend to be associated with Asperger's). The impression strengthens over time that, although perhaps academically relatively able, and perhaps time is ticking by and the students are growing up, they remain socially inept.

It may be observed that they are becoming the butt of teasing because of the way they behave in groups; even worse, they may be being bullied, perhaps just because of the way they are different, perhaps because of the way they behaved or something they said out of place caused offence. In the classroom, they may come to be seen as uncooperative because they do not necessarily fall into line and go with the flow. Indeed, perhaps it is felt that they have behaviour problems.

Consequently, for some Asperger's students, all manner of upsets with peers or staff can result, often when the other party or parties are riled. Such upsets are often not satisfactorily resolved, probably because those other parties do not recognise or acknowledge Asperger Syndrome (but then, in some cases, how could they?).

Perceptive teachers will question why this unhappy state of affairs, with students not integrating with their peers and scarcely being accepted, and thought of as being quite a nuisance and strain in the classroom, has come about. What is it about these students that seems often to produce tetchy and fractious situations, which the Asperger's students may or may not be aware of personally?

Teachers may see that their Asperger's students lack imagination, and this includes social situations. Thus, they do not 'read' situations, and are almost oblivious to different, or changing, situations. Thus, it is inevitable that in some situations they will react inappropriately. Not only do they not always react appropriately to situations, teachers may notice that Asperger's students do not appreciate that others will react to their behaviour, and that in social situations we tailor our behaviour to allow for this; the Asperger's student may be inclined just to do or say what he wants, regardless. This is not a recipe for popularity.

It may come to be appreciated that Asperger's students are not seeing the emotions, feelings, and reactions of others, or if they do note reactions they may misinterpret them, and not wholly realise what the other person is conveying, for example, anxiety or surprise.

In some cases, it may be noted that the Asperger's students are almost oblivious of whatever social situation they are in; they carry on blithely doing their own thing, irrespective and regardless.

Longer-term, if the Asperger's students learn that they are not learning how to predict and interpret other people's reactions, as well as being upset by any teasing and made fearful by any bullying, they may opt for solitary activities which are physically and emotionally independent of other people. This may be seen as a good, practical remedy which suits everybody, or it may be seen as papering over the cracks, and not really dealing with the problem. At the same time, the Asperger's students could be feeling anxious because they may have an awareness of their social difficulties, but no real idea of from where they originate or how to improve matters. If this is the case, low self-esteem may be a consequence.

So, having come to an appreciation of all these factors at play, how does the good-hearted teacher proceed with efforts to improve the Asperger's students' unfortunate social lot? It should fairly be acknowledged that it may be hard for the sociable and gregarious teacher to see the world from the Asperger's students' point of view. It is possible to set oneself exercises which, for instance, help one appreciate how a dyslexic student with visual discrimination problems 'sees' things when he looks at the black or whiteboard. It is much harder to 'see' relationships as Asperger's students may do. However, there follows a menu of strategies which are helpful. As always, choices are made from it appropriate to the particular needs of the students in question, and the circumstances they are moving in.

- It may be decided that one of the very first things that needs to happen is that the whole staff and all adults in the school have some awareness of the social deficits of Asperger's students. Otherwise, it is likely that they will rub people up the wrong way, and there is bound to be conflict. Probably this task will fall to the SENCo but, whoever leads, it may be advisable to expect some resistance from a few people, who cannot see that 'bad manners' can be attributable to anything other than wilful rudeness.

- Then it may be thought that a general, straightforward policy-decision can be made just to tell the Asperger's students what is acceptable, and what is not. Illustrations, examples, and going over situations when things have gone wrong may be thought all to be very desirable while, at the same time, not going into elaborate explanations. These may not be fully understood, so it may be decided just to get on and tell them the way it is, but not in critical tones.

- It may be thought that all manner of social skills and social interaction do have to be shown and demonstrated repeatedly as they arise, which they probably will frequently, with every opportunity being seized upon. Sharing, turn-taking, queuing, listening, not interrupting are examples of activities which may need to be dealt with, in as neutral a fashion as possible, time and time again. Learning these apparently obvious attributes may be surprisingly demanding for the Asperger's students.

- Making appropriate approaches to others is another area where teachers may wish to try to find time to tutor their Asperger's students. The social skills of meeting another person with a smile, while looking them in the eye, of making a conventional opening remark ('I like your new glasses'; 'You played the piano really well in assembly'; 'Did you find last night's homework hard?'; 'Did you watch the football on the telly?') may well not come naturally to Asperger's students.

- Being neat and clean is not, generally speaking, a particular problem, but being appropriately dressed for the occasion in question, sorting out what to wear when, certainly can be. Is a teacher's work never finished?

- If the Asperger's students commit something of a social faux pas, the choice of action may be just quietly to put them right. (They probably will not mind.) But it may also have been decided not to make a big thing of it, on the grounds that this would do no particular good and might do some harm by provoking a scene.

- It may be decided to ask the Asperger's students to tell you about social contacts that have made them unhappy, or where they knew there was something not quite right, even if they are not fully aware of in what way or why it was not right. Teachers may then have to take appropriate action against bullies or students who tease, but they may also decide that they need to work with the Asperger's students to try to explain, hard though this is, how they may be bringing difficulties upon themselves, such as by constantly interrupting and wanting their say.

- It may be decided to nominate particular members of staff to whom the Asperger's students can go if they are in bother. It is likely that the Asperger's students would be consulted in some measure on this; they are unlikely to be willing to go to just any member of staff, and, of course, it is then likely that the staff 'selected' would have to be well-primed.

- It may be decided to choose a form of 'buddy system'. If it is felt that this puts too big a burden on the buddy (for it can be a difficult task) teachers might ask if there is something the Asperger's student can do for the buddy in return. For instance, does the Asperger's student have some educational skills in a curriculum area (or leisure pursuit or hobby) with which he can help the buddy?

- Appreciating that it is outside the classroom (the classroom having supportive structures, routines, and clear expectations) that the Asperger's students may run into difficulties (e.g. dining hall, assembly, breaktimes), teachers may choose to see if the Asperger's students can say what it is they don't like about these situations, and what it is that gives them problems (e.g. the mêlée of students, the movement, the noise, the physical contact, no one to talk to amongst so many students, nothing to do amongst so many activities of other students).

- Thus, at breaktimes it might be decided to encourage cooperation and participation on the Asperger's student's part, but not to force it – and to allow solitary play and activities, without comment.

- Simple games might be organised, and the Asperger's students included in a matter-of-fact sort of way. It may, further, be decided that staff will not go on about, 'Now, are you going to join in with the rest of the children today for me?'

- Accepting that Asperger's students may very possibly have difficulty in being a full member of a team, certainly in appreciating the *esprit de corps*, it might be decided to find out what they actually would like to join in with. (No child wants to play every game.)

- With regard to moving around the school, especially a large one, if this is presenting difficulties, it might be decided to allow the Asperger's students to go first or last so there is less 'traffic' to contend with.

- It could be decided that it would be useful to arrange for someone to provide individual support and to be a mentor to each Asperger's student, particularly with regard to the handling of social situations and social interaction. There may be practical difficulties in arranging this within the school's timetable and the school day, and 'turning around' Asperger's students quickly may be an ambition that needs to be tempered with a little pragmatism, but it is another menu choice teachers can, at least, consider, particularly if they are willing to give it time to work.

- Involvement in groups is likely to be a desirable aim for anybody and everybody (hobby/enthusiast clubs, sports clubs, Scouts, Guides, etc.) but can prove to be a problem for Asperger Syndrome students. Although they may want to join, difficulties with positive social integration can arise, and can lead to problems which seem to make membership of the group counter-productive (as well as difficult for the other members, an aspect which really should not be overlooked). Relatively individual activities within a group setting may be the best, particularly initially, for example, weightlifting, art, etc., moving on to ten-pin bowling, snooker and pool, for example.

Asperger Syndrome students may (come to) have an awareness that they are not understanding the school, its dynamics, its expectations, its norms, the other students – and that conflict results. If they have this degree of awareness, they will experience stress. Stress makes everything worse, more difficult: behaviour; learning; social interaction. To help Asperger Syndrome students avoid becoming stressed is very worthwhile, and makes life so much easier for them (and for those around them).

In conclusion

As ever, teachers will choose items from the above menus which fit the particular bill at the particular time. They will aim to put in support, while keeping well in view the ultimate aim of independence, but crutches are necessary when they are necessary. Over time they may become more lightweight. They may be removed.

Choices from the menus will be made in a spirit of optimism. Teachers will bear in mind that Asperger Syndrome students and people have many virtues. We have only to think of how their love of routine can mean they are very punctual and reliable; of how their special interests, even if idiosyncratic, appropriately channelled, can mean they are highly dedicated.

Teachers will feel that they can improve the surface behaviours by choosing from the above menus. In doing so, they will not be claiming to have 'cured' Asperger Syndrome, and will not be denying that deeper clinical intervention may not be highly desirable in at least some instances. But they may claim that they have made school life somewhat better for the Asperger's students, probably also for their classmates – and that that is better than doing nothing.

Chapter 6

~

Marking, Spelling Correction and Readability

Marking and students with learning disabilities
Theory and practice

> Schools could usefully review their marking and assessment policies for accessibility. (Department for Education and Skills 2006)

> 'Please sir, I can't read what you've written in the margin.'

> 'It says, "Take more care with your handwriting."'

This is a classic. It happens; believe me.
Here's another:

> 'Watch your spelling!'

Did any teacher ever meet any student who deliberately spelt a word wrongly? If not, what is the point of the comment? What does it actually mean? When doing the work, how does the student know which words to 'watch' (especially the SEN student)?

Why do we mark students' work?

As always, let's take a step back, and pause for reflection:

- What is the point of marking?

- Is it to point out mistakes? Is it to point out *every* mistake? Is it *only* to point out mistakes?

- Is it to check learning (that learning has taken place)? Is it to enhance learning? Is it to help in the avoidance of the repetition of mistakes?

- Is it to discourage or encourage?

- Is it to deface a student's page by large and ugly red ink scrawling, or is it discreetly to indicate areas and items where improvement is desirable?

- Is it to let the student know how he has done, and how he is getting on?

Working through a series of questions such as this brings us to the conclusion that marking is to help a student with his learning, and performance. In other words, the only really worthwhile marking is marking that is highly likely to lead to student improvement. Except in very rare circumstances, there is no point in any other marking.

Is our marking useful?

There are two main reasons why marking, in fact, is generally not marking for improvement. The first is the style of marking used, and the second is that the student pays scant attention to the marking. Let's deal with the latter first.

The typical scene is that a class does a piece of work, quite possibly for homework, which they all hand in (or most of them do). The teacher takes all the books or scripts away, and marks them in some other place and time, expending long and conscientious effort doing so, gives a mark out of 10 or 20 (which is entered in a markbook), writes a comment, hands all the books back to the students after variable periods of time, and gives them about two minutes to open their books to see what they have got. The students look at the mark, either breathe a sigh of relief because the mark is satisfactory, or feel a pang of disappointment because it is less than hoped for, or grimace in some horror at the lowliness of the mark, and look to see if some purgatory such as 'Repeat' or 'See me' is an added postscript. Having ascertained into which category they fall, they snap their books shut or file away their scripts, and forget about the marking completely, and largely forget about the exercise, too.

All right, the above is a bit of a caricature, but, if it was distilled, the essence would largely remain in many classrooms in all sorts of schools. So, how do we encourage the students to take any notice of the marking, and place some value on it? Partly this depends on the quality of the marking, which we will come to, but initially it depends on giving them time to look at their marking. It's no good saying that they should study the teacher's comments (even if they are helpful ones) for homework before they start their next piece of work in that exercise book or file. Experience tells us that far too many won't do that, but study those comments they must. There is only one way they will do this, and that is if the teacher makes class time available for them to do so. By far and away the most effective time to do this is as soon as the books or scripts are given back. It needs to become the set pattern of working that up to ten minutes is allowed for this. Students can then ask the teacher to clarify any number of points about the comments they have made, or how marks have been allocated; the teacher can be going round the room elucidating with individuals and checking they appreciate the comments; and discussion through the class can ensue as points of common relevance arise. Teachers protest that they have not time to do this. I sympathise. But lessons have to be geared not just to allow for this, but to highlight it. Marking is feedback. Feedback is a powerful tool in enabling learning to occur, and the more immediate the feedback, the better the learning. Without it, all that teacher effort in doing the marking is virtually wasted if we see marking as an aid to learning, and not just a way of attributing marks and placing students in rank order.

That is the first principle and practice, but all will be to no avail if the marking is not meaningful to the student. The only person we should mark for is the individual student, not for the class, not the head of department when he does his annual audit, not the Ofsted inspector, and not really for the parent (although we might well want to have told parents of our approach to marking). When marking, have an image of that particular student in mind, and 'speak' to him in a way he will respond to (which is what we would do if we were really speaking to him).

School policy

That said, this should happen within a school framework, and not at the whim or idiosyncrasy of the particular teacher (not that there is no room for such characteristics in the profession, but they must, in marking, be tempered by sound practice).

This leads to the conclusion that there must be a Marking Policy within the school. Ideally, it should be arrived at after staff involvement and discussion, with all participating. Total agreement will not be possible and, as ever, the discussion will need shaping and enlightened leadership, but a consensus (as opposed to a compromise) should be achievable. At any rate, a common Marking Policy is essential, and thereafter all staff must adhere to it. This is where heads of department or faculty have a very real monitoring role. Students must know what the guidelines are, and must expect them to be operated in every subject and by every teacher. Parents should be made aware of them, too.

What are we looking for?

The Policy must clearly indicate what is acceptable and, indeed, what is not. Very much included will be the principle of making it clear to students beforehand what the teacher is going to be particularly looking for in the exercise at the same time as the exercise is set. (There may be some personal targets for individual students to aim at as well, as we shall see.) In many cases, it is perfectly true that what is asked for is completely obvious, as in a Maths exercise which is really a practice exercise and the working of some examples to follow up new work introduced in the day's lesson, although even there advice about, for example, clearer setting out, more use of the space on the page can also enter into grading criteria, not, obviously, with regard to ticks and crosses but with regard to the chances of an additional merit being awarded (see p.200). In the case of other work, the teacher may wish to be very clear about particular aspects he is looking for, for example, in a Science subject, asking students to make sure that they consider all the possible variables, and not just some they happen to select; in the 'Compare and contrast...' type of exercise, making sure that each of these receives its fair share of attention; in a piece of writing in, say, French, Spanish, etc. students can be asked to demonstrate that they can use vocabulary learned some time ago as well as that learnt recently, or to make some use of particular tenses. This kind of preliminary request and guidance not only helps the students' learning through engendering a constructive approach to the exercise, but enables the teacher to make clear why a mark may be lower than the student was expecting, even if the exercise is adequate in other respects. All of this does presuppose that the teacher will actually apply these criteria when he comes to do the marking. This is not a remark designed to imply criticism; it is an acknowledgement that marking does, of necessity, often have to be done in something of a hurry, and it is only human to be in danger of not remembering what you had so carefully told the class when you were setting the exercise. Not to apply these rather informal but nonetheless helpful criteria is, clearly, very bad for the teacher's long-term credibility, and may induce a casual attitude from at least some of the students.

Schools should arrive at their own detailed Policy, but one of the first things they should consider is the desirability of marking on at least two fronts simultaneously yet separately, namely those two factors to which much lip service is often paid but seldom seriously addressed, 'Effort' and 'Achievement'. The latter refers to the level of achievement and the quality of the work produced and will be a pretty objective measure, especially if the exercise was within an examination framework or course. The former is much more subjective, and credit will be awarded with the individual student much more in mind, with full regard being given to his ability and aptitude in that particular subject or task. Great tact is needed when, despite best efforts, quality does not match up to the 'required' standard, and is a real problem on occasions when a syllabus demands a certain level of achievement. Giving a numerical mark for the level of 'Achievement' and a letter ('A' for a really excellent attempt (whatever the actual outcome) through to 'E' for, 'You really haven't bothered at all with this exercise') is a scheme which works well. This sort of dual system is very common on end-of-term school reports, but seldom used systematically in the marking of exercises. Perhaps not all exercises require this amount of attention, but anything resembling a major piece of work does. However, a real word of warning: make absolutely clear to the students, and be sure they know, that the number is for 'Achievement' and the letter for 'Effort', and what the difference is between them. They can get this confused, and thus take away completely the wrong message from your zealous marking.

Timing is everything

Your constructive and insightful comments will also be worth *nil points* so far as the students are concerned if by the time they get their scripts back they can scarcely remember doing the exercise. This is particularly true for the students who had some real difficulties with the exercise, whereas some prompt and helpful advice, suggestions, or illustrations which they could absorb as they recollected what they experienced as they did the exercise can certainly help carry them forward. Also, marking is a message to the student. If any message is very late arriving, it tends to be almost disregarded. If a reply is received well after the expected date, at some level, the recipient assumes that the sender does not attach much importance to the reply, so the recipient (the student) does not value the reply.

Getting marked exercises back to the students really promptly is, then, vitally important but, understandably, teachers may well exclaim that, with their workloads, they cannot turn round marking any quicker. Undeniably, they have a point and a genuine problem. The crux of the answer to this dilemma lies in looking at priorities, and time management. As soon as the prompt return of marked scripts is seen as being very high indeed on the priority list, the perspective alters a little, prime time is allocated to it, and other items on the 'to do' list have to take their place. Perhaps hard decisions have to be made and one or two things have to fall off that list completely, or perhaps others can be delayed (whereas marking and returning exercises quickly cannot). Perhaps some of the actual marking can take less time than certainly some teachers spend on it, but we shall come on to that in due course.

The moment of truth

What the student actually sees the moment he opens his returned exercise book or script, those first impressions, make a real, and probably lasting, impact upon the student, and how he reacts to the marking. Does he see a page which has, in effect, been defaced, by heavily ringed words and sentences, with explosive exclamation marks heavily dominant; has his script become submerged by the teacher's marking?

Or does he see a page where the marking is discreet, where (if it is an essay) there are ticks indicating good points well made throughout as well as crosses, and where comments are neatly written in a legible hand in proper sentences? Of course, there may be occasions where thunderous marking full of teacher expletives about effort and content may be justifiable but, generally speaking, if he were able to articulate in this form, would the student say that he felt, from just looking at the marking, that his exercise had been respected?

What shall we write?

That said, what is it that the teacher should actually be writing on the student's page? First, as we have already said, it is not, in fact, what 'the teacher' should be writing, but what all teachers in the school should be writing in the same style and to the same code.

The colour of ink or pencil used rears its head as a matter of debate from time to time, particularly by those who advocate avoiding the traditional red ink, which they claim is threatening or confrontational. In the whole-staff discussions which should precede the drawing up of a school's Marking Policy, it is a point well worth discussing but beware, because it is one of those arguments which can generate a lot of heat and not much light, and waste a lot of time. Come to a conclusion reasonably quickly, even if there is a minority who are 'outvoted'. The really important thing is to make sure that any who do not agree with the decision (particularly if the decision was the slightly controversial one not to use red ink) do abide by it in practice.

Does using a colour coding system sound too complicated and time consuming? Probably it does, but is it really? How about, again in exercises where it is appropriate (such as a History essay) marking the history aspects of the essay (facts, discussion of people's motivations, analysis of consequences of actions, etc.) in green, and points with regard to the construction of the essay (e.g. order of paragraphs) in red. Just having two pens to hand is perhaps not so difficult for the teacher and may, indeed, help the teacher see the merits and demerits of the exercise as the student has completed it, and help the teacher better see how the student can, through the marking, be best advised.

Is it pushing it too far to ask that the use of even a third coloured pen might be considered? This could be one for the marking of spelling (see Chapter 6), grammar, punctuation, etc. Enabling students to think of their work in an itemised way is to give them a very functional tool, whereas their tendency is to review a piece of work, if they do so at all, in a very muddled, mish-mash sort of way.

There are several dimensions to marking. Marking for 'Effort' and 'Achievement' is one, as we have seen, perhaps with the award of numerical marks for 'Achievement' (e.g. 7/10) and grading letters for 'Effort'; written comments at the end of the script is another; and what and how teachers write within the body of the student's script is yet another, which we now turn to.

Highlighting items within the actual script is absolutely fine; it should indicate a close reading of the script by the teacher, but back to those first impressions, it should not be visually the dominant thing the student sees as soon as he looks at the returned script. Also, he must understand why the teacher has marked certain points, and what he means by those marks; in fact, he must understand what every teacher means by the hieroglyphics he sees peppered across his page.

This leads to the conclusion that a common approach must be agreed and adhered to, and schools can work this approach out for themselves with everyone having their say, once the principle of a communal system has been accepted. Simple, but effective examples are: places where punctuation errors occur are underlined and 'P' written in the margin; an ungrammatical term is underlined and 'Gr' written in the margin. Hardly rocket science, but there are discussion points here: for instance, with reference to what has been said previously, are mistakes of punctuation and grammar to be indicated in one particular colour of ink? These details, which may sound pedantic, are well worth some preliminary discussion and can then, with goodwill, be quickly absorbed into every teacher's modus operandi, with the result that every student will, in every subject, be able to grasp quickly what every teacher is telling him.

This leaves us with the vexed question of what teachers write at the end of a student's exercise. Sometimes, of course, it is necessary to write very little. At the end of a Maths exercise, in which a student has done well there may be a point in writing very little indeed. It's clear to the student he has done well by the number of ticks and the numerical mark, but never underestimate the value of the positive written comment, or even just the addition of that magic word 'Good'.

On the other hand, if another student has done poorly and clearly is not understanding, if the teacher can only find time to do a couple of illustrative examples on the student's page with helpful explanatory comments (rather than only crosses), when he gets the exercise back the student has a positive element to think about rather than just having it reinforced that he can't do this Maths, which he quite possibly realised anyway. If the practice is adopted of always allowing students time to peruse their returned work, the student has time to study the teacher's examples and, ideally, the teacher and student can grab a minute or two together in this review slot.

In the more discursive subjects, such as History, Geography, English, etc., the written comments at the end are of even more importance. They should provide the student with a summary of the teacher's overall impression of the quality of the work and the teacher's opinion of the amount of effort the student has put in. All this really can be encapsulated in, say, three sentences, but remember that there is no point in writing anything if you do not give the students a prescribed amount of time to read it, with you present.

Why a low mark has been awarded should be explained; perhaps the student already knows this, but perhaps he does not, and feels he made a good effort and, indeed, did what was required. Generally, there is no need to make this comment critical; it is likely to be more productive just to be objective. Sometimes criticism is certainly called for, but there is a danger that critical comments can seem to become personal or personalised, whereas objective comments just emphasise what is expected and acceptable across the board.

Where negative comments are used, it is a good idea to separate them from positive ones; there is a danger that the negatives detract from the positives, and so avoid, 'This is very good, but...' State exactly what is good and state separately what is not.

Do avoid vague, rather meaningless comments, or at least, do not allow all your comments to fall into this category. Comments need not be and, indeed, should not be numerous, but each must be truly meaningful. Critical comments are certainly allowed but, for most students, positive suggestions about ways to improve should very much be in the majority.

Where the task lends itself to it (many do), generally speaking, asking a supplementary question within your comments is a good way of getting students to think further about their work (and a good, non-critical way for the teacher to drop a broad hint) for example, 'Do you think you should have given more details about why people came to be dissatisfied with Charles I as monarch?'

Making the connection

Marking may have, to some extent, to be geared to external criteria, but marking is also very personal, and should be. The teacher is marking a particular student's individual piece of work. It is generally good practice to recognise this by using the student's name within your written comments. Without overdoing it, this is particularly useful in sugaring the pill when you have to point out major weaknesses in the way the exercise has been done.

A couple of words of warning: students with learning disabilities do need encouraging, and they seldom need to be 'put down'. It is right that teachers always look for the positive in the exercises completed by the SEN student. In doing this, there can be a danger of patronising the student. We are treading on eggshells here, but do not underestimate the student's perception. He probably has some awareness of what his classmates are achieving, and he will not be helped if his own very modest efforts are over-praised. Just as we do not over-emphasise all his shortcomings, we must be very sensitive, especially perhaps where the older student is concerned, about how we look for and acknowledge what is good in his exercise.

In the beginning

Marking is about feedback on a particular exercise but, as we have said, marking is for improvement. For some students, it is good practice and motivating to tell them specifically which aspects of improvement in their work in this type of exercise you are looking for (e.g. wider range of adjectives used; less waffle and more attention to historical detail in History essays; shorter/longer sentences; more cause/effect type reasoning when writing about climatic conditions or weather in Geography). Not only that, this can be made into a longer-term goal; for instance, you can say that you will be particularly looking for this over the next three similar exercises. Marking is about what has been done, but what's done is done, and good marking looks to the future, also.

Storage and retrieval

Marks awarded should be recorded and kept, unless the exercise is a very slight one. Does the practice still exist of the teacher going around the class and down the register with students calling out the marks for the teacher to enter in his markbook? One hopes not; it's great for the students who achieved high marks, not so hot for those who have achieved low marks, especially as they are likely to be the students who almost always achieve low marks. Publicising one's shortcomings does not do much for the ego, and probably does nothing to empower you to do better next time. So, teachers have to record the marks as they mark (and thus have more teaching time in lessons). But markbooks, or however the marks are recorded and filed, especially in this technological age, are important and, as the term progresses, the line of marks against a student's name should be regularly scanned. It is useful if particular marks, as they are entered, are noted if there is anything exceptional about them. Really good marks can be ringed, perhaps, and disappointing marks underlined. Thus, both strong and struggling students can be identified but, even more, changing trends within a student's performance over time emerge at a glance; for instance, the student who was having his mark regularly ringed for its excellence at the beginning of term but for whom this has not now happened for several weeks (or vice versa!). If marks and letters for 'Achievement' and 'Effort' are being awarded, both should be recorded, and if the teacher can bear to use two colours of ink to do this corresponding to the two colours he has used in the student's script, the more vivid is the picture the teacher can then quickly notice when the student is reviewed. Some teachers will say they can carry all this in their heads and that they know their students well enough not to need these procedures, but the veracity of what they claim is difficult to prove; it is only impressionistic.

To mark or not to mark

Should each and every exercise be marked; if so, should each one be marked to the same scale for example, a mark out of 10 given for every piece of work? There is very little that the teacher does not need to see; this demonstrable interest in virtually everything the student produces benefits the student. But does that mean a mark has always to be given, or the same marking scale used? There may not be too many occasions but there will be some where the work expected is relatively slight and undemanding; this does not mean it was not worth setting or doing, but it may occasionally be enough for the teacher to skim/scan mark the work, and tell the student he has done so by a single tick and, possibly, a brief comment; in such cases, no mark or, probably, letter need be awarded. When marks are awarded, which will be on the considerable majority of occasions, it is possible to decide that some pieces will be marked out of 10, and bigger pieces marked out of, say, 20. If the maximum available is always the same, it is tantamount to saying that all exercises are equally demanding and equally time consuming, which cannot be strictly true. There can be debate about whether a class should be told in advance how many marks are available for an exercise, the concern being that some students will only put in maximum effort where higher marks are possible. This may be true in a minority of cases but if students are not told they will soon learn to ask, and is the teacher really going to say to them in effect, 'Wait and see'? However, there is a positive aspect of telling the class beforehand how many marks an exercise is to be worth because it gives them a good indication of the amount of effort and depth of thought they are expected to put in. Anyway, all these are whole-staff debating points, and the conclusions should figure in the Marking Policy.

What's it worth?

Over and above the marks for a particular exercise, there is a lot to be said for linking into a wider reward system that runs through the school. The work ethic, said to be lacking in many schools nowadays, particularly with regard to boys, may be improved if there is a system of additional reward being given for an exercise which deserves it. Thus, if, for instance, the school is divided into 'Houses', a merit earned by the student can be added to a House running total in a termly competition between the Houses. Linking a student to a corporate body via potentially virtually every exercise he does can lead to an *esprit de corps* (which does not have to be confined to the traditional games field) and be a source of external motivation. Then, perhaps, for every ten merits, a further reward is earned, such as a certificate for the student and bonus merits for the House. This sort of system only works well if staff actively and positively implement it on a regular basis. The positions of the Houses in the merit league table needs to be publicised and drawn attention to on notice boards and in assemblies. Those who have earned merits may well need similar publicity. Great thought should be given before deciding to put on a notice board the whole school roll and the number of merits earned by each student week by week. This may well be great for the student who gains lots of merits, but what about the student who, for whatever reason, gains none; is he really likely to be spurred to gain a merit, or merely deflated or, even worse, begin to kick against a system he cannot seem to join?

Cooking the books

However, it is vitally important that the staff as a whole do know the students who, across the board, are gaining very few merits, and there needs to be a system for identifying them. This, then, needs to be a regular staff meeting agenda item, and there needs to be discussion as to why this is the case.

As a result, the student can be advised by the class teacher or subject teacher what it is that he needs to do to figure on the merit board. And teachers should certainly not be shy in stretching a point by giving the deserving student a merit which might not be given to another student; this type of strategy can be part of the Marking Policy. It will cause some colleagues to react against it on the grounds that it is not 'fair'. This is so, but we are after something greater even than fairness; we are after boosting the output, the attainments, and self-esteem of every member of our school. Of course, those colleagues who oppose this would have a point if artificially rewarding students was taken to extremes or if the relative positions of the Houses was drastically altered by such a policy, so that is something to watch out for, but unlikely to arise if common sense is applied.

Of course, if a two-tier marking system is being employed (illustrated here earlier was the 'Achievement' and 'Effort' model) then merits can be given under either, or both, headings, with each carrying the same weight. This is where it is possible to reward some SEN students particularly, but try not to give them only 'Effort' merits. It was said above, that they will probably know if the teacher is making an artificial exception for them. On the other hand, even that does show that regard is being paid to their work and efforts, and that is very important.

Particularly where the SEN student is concerned, there is the difficulty not only of awarding a merit for the quality of the work, but of even giving a good mark for the work. If the student is studying for an external exam (typically GCSE) or the exercise is specifically geared to SATs criteria, this is a real dilemma. If the standard of attainment has not been reached, then marks cannot be manufactured for the student. This is where the concept of 'Effort' criteria can be so useful. Perhaps not all exercises are controlled by such external factors. In these, the teacher should feel free to mark for 'Achievement' less mechanistically and, to a degree, mark against what they believe the student's capabilities to be, and a student who struggles with a particular subject but has produced a reasonable piece of work may be rewarded by a slightly higher mark than might seem justifiable if only strictly objective criteria were employed. Again, the cry will go up from some colleagues, 'It's not fair to other students' and, strictly speaking, they are right, but this is outweighed by the encouragement that may be imparted to the student to whom we have shown a little (only a little) discreet 'favouritism'.

Variations upon a theme

Whether the same merit system should run throughout the whole school is another point staff should decide upon. It may well be that what is appropriate in Year 7 is not appropriate in Year 10, but do not underestimate the possible advantages of some sort of system for even the older students. Feedback is a powerful tool for nearly everyone, and if that feedback is further bolstered by additional recognition, even quite sophisticated students may respond even better.

Credit crunch

The value of the currency that a merit represents is very important. It would be farcical for one teacher to be giving merits by the dozen, and another to be Scrooge-like, and give a merit as if it was a piece of gold dust. There cannot be total consistency, but it must be decided in advance by the staff if it would be typical to give, within a class, say two merits per set of homeworks marked, or two merits per week, or two per half-term. But just as a £1 is worth a £1 wherever the student goes in town, so he should have confidence that a merit from one teacher is broadly worth the same as a merit from another teacher, and that he has an equal chance (whether the school has decided that that chance is great or small) of winning a merit from whichever teacher he is with.

The last resort

Earlier, emphasis was placed upon the desirability of schools having a School Policy with regard to marking, preferably one that every teacher had the chance to debate at its inception, and one to which everyone has to subscribe and implement. If that happy state of affairs should not exist, the individual teacher must do the next best thing, which is to have an individual, personal policy. In this case, it is even more important that it is conveyed to every class or classes that that teacher teaches. If students find other teachers' marking erratic, indecipherable, opaque, and idiosyncratic, they will come to appreciate your consistency and clarity. You never know, it might even get noted by colleagues!

Marking spelling

We generally refer to 'spelling'; what we actually mean is spelling mistakes, but we will mostly use here the trade term of 'spelling'.

Structured staff debate about marking spelling is highly desirable; when it occurs, it is likely that it will prove to be a hot potato to the extent that it warrants a separate sub-section all of its own within the Marking Policy.

- Who should mark spelling (every teacher, only the English teacher)?

- How should it be marked (words crossed through, underlined, correct spellings written in by teacher)?

- Should every spelling mistake be marked? Should no spelling mistakes be marked?

- Should students do spelling corrections? If so, how many words and how many times?

All these points, and others, are likely to emerge once a debate gets going, and it is more than possible that every point will have its protagonists and detractors. Before the Marking Policy can be finalised and subscribed to, there is likely to be a tangled web of differing opinions to unpick.

So, let's start at the beginning with getting back to first principles by asking a couple of questions:

First: is it not eminently reasonable to work on the basis and sound assumption that no student deliberately misspells a word, and that the vast majority of spelling mistakes are, at that moment, inherent? Although it may well be true that the student has the occasional feeling that a word is probably/possibly not correct, and he could perhaps check this for himself, generally speaking, don't students make the assumption when they write a word that they are spelling it correctly?

Second: is there any point in indicating a spelling mistake, if nothing else happens and the student is no nearer being able to spell that word correctly? Does just pointing out that a word is wrongly spelt much help to the student next time he wants to use that word? Those are good starting points for getting that staff discussion going.

We hope that the conclusion will be reached that the marking of spelling is only useful if a system is adopted which will positively influence and improve students' spelling. This means that *some* spelling mistakes do have to be learnt by the student (and 'corrections' done), and that there is limited value in marking spelling mistakes which you do not expect to be learnt.

Every spelling mistake?

But why not mark and expect every single mistake to be learnt? There are, at least, two parts to the answer to this question: a student may make many mistakes in one exercise, and it would be unreasonable to expect him to correct and learn all of them; and even a student making relatively few spelling mistakes within one exercise may, cumulatively, make a large number within the totality of his output, and it would, again, be impracticable for him to be expected to learn them all. So, is there any point marking those mistakes which you do not expect to be learnt?

Which spelling mistakes?

How many errors do you point out, and how do you decide which ones? To a large extent, this will depend upon the ability of the student to learn them, since some students clearly do have much more difficulty in this area than others. If the words are to be *thoroughly* learnt, rather fewer as opposed to rather more is the watchword.

However, one still has to decide which particular words you should identify, and expect to be learnt. A helpful way to resolve this tricky issue is to think of words in three categories.

- Subject-specific words: these are words that it really is desirable that, within the context of a subject, module, or topic the student should be able to spell. It is quite hard to justify, in the vast majority of cases, doing a Biology project on 'Photosynthesis' if the student repeatedly misspells that word, hard though it may be for some students to learn it.

- Everyday, commonplace words: it is not doing the students any favours to allow them not to be able to spell, for instance, the days of the week, months of the year, although some will undoubtedly need time to accomplish this.

- Any words (but not too many at one time) which the student has misspelled which you sense he would be able to learn with a little focus upon those particular words. These words especially will vary from student to student.

'Corrections'

We have now reached the situation where, when he gets an exercise back from any teacher in any subject, the student will see a small number of spelling mistakes indicated, and the whole ethos is that he is expected to try to learn them. This should be done immediately. We saw earlier the desirability of giving the class several minutes to absorb the teacher's comments and note the marks he has been given as soon as exercise books or scripts are returned; the learning of these spellings has to commence within this same small block of time. *How* the student learns them is another matter, but now is the time to do this, although the teacher needs to try to guard against the students spending all this precious time on the spellings to the detriment of considering the wider issues raised by the teacher's marking. It is suggested that how these spellings are learnt, and what procedure a student goes through in learning them, is also indicated in the Marking Policy.

Are 'corrections' effective?

With spellings, in particular, there is not much point in expecting students to learn them if they are not to be checked ('tested'). The subject teacher cannot possibly do this in a comprehensive manner, but what he can do is do spot checks, and if these are also included during this brief piece of time we have set aside it should persuade students to try to learn their spellings. This task will have been eased because not too many misspelt words will have confronted them, and the words will clearly be personally relevant. If the superhuman teacher can possibly then keep a weather eye to see that words learnt on this occasion are not misspelt on subsequent ones, so very much the better.

A helping hand

Once the student has his script back, and knows which spellings he has to learn, there are various methods he can use, and probably no one method is best suited to all students, but the school should have a policy of how it wants students to go about this learning. But, no matter what the method, it is axiomatic that the starting point has to be that the student has access to the correct spelling. Expecting the student to look up the word in a dictionary is not as straightforward as it may sound. Desirable though it is that students should be quick and familiar users of dictionaries, these can be mysterious places for poor spellers, which are not all that helpful. Many students will be rather slow in their use of dictionaries, and even electronic spellers and dictionaries, and spellcheckers can pose problems; they may very well all have a place in the specific teaching of spelling and within a spelling programme, but this is not what we are talking about here. We want the students to learn a small number of words that we have identified for each student in a limited amount of time, and the best and quickest way to get them started is to give them the correct spelling. This may be varied for particular students occasionally, or perhaps with particular vocabulary, but the aim is to get the student learning the words as soon as possible.

Therefore, in the students' scripts when they are returned, they will notice that a small number of words have been neatly underlined and the correctly spelt version of it either written immediately above or, if better clarity can be achieved, in the margin. Teachers do need to take great care with the legibility of their writing; many children do have difficulty reading adults' handwriting and it is, of course, hopeless if they misinterpret a word and learn that!

Patience

The above is a long-term strategy. It will not produce overnight miracles; a little longer is needed. It is a drip-by-drip approach that takes time to show its results. This is where patience is needed; it is needed by the student but it is much more needed by the teacher, who must gently but consistently remind himself of the need to give this structured, relevant practice – as part of and through his marking – virtually day in, day out, exercise in, exercise out.

Spelling corrections and students with learning disabilities

Prologue

This is a true and recent tale.

Dramatis personae (in order of appearance):

Waitress A

Waitress B

Customer X

Customer Y

The scene is set in the dining room of a three-star hotel at 7.30 pm. Customers X and Y are seated at a table together, about to order their dinner. They leave their table to look more closely at the 'specials' board on the wall. They have just started reading this chalkboard, when Waitress A bustles up.

Waitress A: Please excuse me, ladies, I've just noticed a spelling mistake.

Customer X: (in a shocked voice) Have you? I really should have seen that; I'm a teacher.

They are joined by Waitress B, who has been attracted by this slight commotion.

Waitress B: I can't see anything wrong.

Waitress A: Yes, look! 'Fillett'.

Waitress B: I can't see anything wrong with that. But, I can't spell, and never could.

Customer Y: No, I can't see anything wrong. But I can't spell either.

Waitress A makes the correction, with much energetic rubbing out of the superfluous 't' with a damp cloth.

The waitresses resume their normal duties, and the customers go back to their table.

Customer Y: I never could spell as a child.

Customer X: Well, I've got this little girl in my class. She's a bright little thing but she can't spell. Yet she nearly always gets ten out of ten on our spelling lists. But in her ordinary writing, her spelling's terrible. And I've had her for nearly two years now. She gets upset, but I said to her the other day, 'Time to stop worrying about it, dear, and just get on with your writing.' She was pleased, I think, because she had said to me a while back, 'I've got such wonderful words in my head, but I'm scared to use them.'

Why include this true and recent tale? Because it epitomises so many of the issues that surround 'spelling.'

Spelling is clearly still thought by many people to be important: the general public (both waitresses), and the educated section of the population (the teacher).

Students think that spelling is important; they are conscious of poor spelling, and this can be a source of anxiety to them.

A considerable percentage of the adult population feel themselves not to be good spellers, which is a matter of some regret to them; their attitude to this situation is pretty fatalistic. Teachers feel their own spelling should be good.

Teachers encounter in mainstream classrooms students with marked spelling problems. Teachers do not ignore this fact, but they feel rather perplexed as to what to do about it. Suggesting that the little girl just get on and enjoy her writing has much to commend it (encouraging her creativity and self-expression, avoiding making a drama out of a crisis and not sowing the seeds of inhibitions and complexes) but there was, evidently, no consideration of a method to address the problem of the spelling itself, or of giving the girl a strategy that would help her avoid mistakes or learn from them.

Yes, the above little scenario represents a much broader picture.

The following short section follows particularly on the heels of the previous one on Marking. It provides particularly a method whereby students of any age can learn those spelling mistakes which have been delineated by the teacher's marking (the fact that they have been particularly noted by the teacher meaning that the teacher does expect the student to try to learn them).

It does, however, have a wider application than just the learning of spelling 'corrections'. It can be used as a method for learning any spellings, and in the acquisition of new spellings, perhaps of words that a student has only just recently learned to read.

However, it is not a spelling diagnostic tool; it does not, of itself, tell a teacher why a student has spelt a word wrongly, or if there are specific difficulties with spelling or, if there are, what the nature of those difficulties is. (If the teacher can observe the student as this method is put into practice, then the teacher might, in fact, gain a degree of insight into the nature of any particular difficulties, but that is not why some space is here donated to this method.)

It is included because there is limited value in a teacher highlighting spellings which are to be learnt, and then just telling the student to learn them, or practise them, or work on them. Students need a method. This is but one such method. It is not comprehensive, in that the teaching and learning of spelling should, ideally, be embedded within the whole programme of acquiring all the skills of literacy. What is presented here is a method with limited aims and limited application. But it is a method with certain virtues: it is simple; it can be implemented by the student working alone; it can be implemented by any subject teacher; and if adopted, it can easily become part of the Marking Policy across the whole school.

It is, in fact, a well-known method in some schools and by a good many (although by no means all) teachers. Here, however, it is presented with one or two slight variations, and the contention is that these additions are important to poor spellers. It is important that students learn the method and really put it into practice. As stated in the previous section, for almost all students learning to spell correctly words that you have previously spelt wrong (this being a somewhat different process and a distinctly different matter from spelling a new word) is likely to be a laborious business for many students, and not too many words should be practised/learnt at any one time.

Anyway, the method detailed below is a variation on *Look – Cover – Write – Check*:

1. *The student makes sure he can read the word.*
   If it is a word taken from his own work, he will, of course, know it, but if it is, for example, copied from the board, this may not always be the case. So, teacher input, or perhaps another student, may be needed before the student proceeds.

2. *He copies the word reasonably neatly onto a decent piece of paper.*
   Spellings, on the whole, are not best learnt on scraps of paper.

   Lower case letter should be used.

   Preferably, the handwriting is cursive, but that's really another topic.

   If the word is a spelling correction from a piece of work already marked by the teacher, the teacher will have written the word into that piece of work, or noted it in the margin or at the end. If it is not, it is still generally best if the teacher writes the word. Dictionaries are certainly valuable things, but if the student looks up the word for himself, can we be sure that he copies down the right word, and not one with a similar but different spelling?

3. *The student checks that he has copied the word correctly.*
    This sounds blindingly obvious. In fact, students often do not check.

    The frustration of a student who has leant to spell a word that he copied wrongly in the first place is something to behold. It is not unusual.

    But this checking is also something that is one of the things that it is most difficult to get a student to do.

4. *The student studies the word visually.*

5. *If he wishes, he accompanies the visual studying of the word by writing it out whilst also looking at it.*
    This *can* be done on a scrap of paper! It can be done on the opposite page of the exercise book, if that is what is being used.

    It must not be done on the same piece of paper as the word itself, as this is being kept pristine for the actual practising and learning of the spelling.

6. *While doing both the above, he also says the word.*
    This can be done very quietly indeed, but with the lips nonetheless moving (subvocalisation). In older students, it can be done 'in the head', but the student really should be focusing on the word by saying it (one way or another) as he envisages it and quite possibly as he writes it.

7. *When the student feels himself to be reasonably certain of success he (a) covers the word and (b) writes it immediately underneath the original.*
    The word is best covered by a solid ruler. A suitably opaque piece of paper is all right, although an appropriately cut piece of card kept for the purpose is better than paper.

    Writing underneath the original, rather than alongside, is preferable.

---

*   See p.213.

8. *The student checks his spelling.*

   Mostly, this is done visually, and writing his newly attempted spelling immediately underneath the original makes this easier.

   It is a stage where students can be quite 'careless' and fail to see that they have not spelt it correctly. Checking is not necessarily something that is of great intrinsic interest, but it is very important.

9. *If correct, the student ticks the word.*

10. *10 (a) If incorrect, he repeats all the above. (b) If correct, he repeats (7) and (8). If correct again, he repeats (7) and (8) one more time.*

11. *The whole aim of the exercise is to get three ticks in a consecutive row – and then move on to the next spelling. But until the three ticks are consecutive, steps (7) and (8) have to be repeated.*

   A cross among any sequence of three ticks means the word has to be considered 'not learnt'. But three ticks in a row mean that the word is (probably) learnt, and the student can go on to the next word. With regard to the student who just cannot get those three ticks in a row, there is obviously a limit as to how many attempts he should be expected to make in one session, and an 'issue' should not be made of the difficulty; however, in practice, students almost always quite quickly achieve their three ticks in a row.

The above description has taken quite a long time to write; it has taken a few minutes for you to read; a student who is familiar with and confident with the method will probably take about 90 seconds to put it into practice, and learn a spelling.

This is not to say that three ticks in a row prove for certain that a word is totally learnt, and if revision and further practice can possibly be built in subsequently, that is a good thing, but three ticks in a row – achieved by following the above process precisely – do give the exercise meaning, and something definite to aim at for the student. They do not prove that the student will never misspell the word again (although we certainly hope they make that much more unlikely) but they do provide a real focus as he does the task, and give him a success criterion which is almost always attainable, and very reasonable in terms of the amount of time required. Put like this, the student works in a way which is probably very much more productive than just being told, 'Learn your spellings.'

So, a student's piece of paper might look like this:

expedition	The student, having spelt the word wrong, has copied it down, having checked that he can read it, and checked that he has copied it down correctly. As detailed in **4, 5 & 6**, he now 'studies' the word.
expedishion **✗**	The student has covered the word at the top of his column, attempted the word by writing it immediately underneath, and marked it – that is he has done **7 & 8**.
expedition **✓**	Obviously the student has had another go, checked it, and marked it.
expedation **✗**	Another attempt, which has been checked, and marked. As it was wrong, **4, 5 & 6** are done again. The above tick will have to be discounted.
expedition **✓** expedition **✓** expedition **✓**	Three attempts, each checked and marked; three ticks in a row, no crosses in the sequence. Job done. Time taken: 90 seconds approximately.
(Note how each word written by the student has formed a neat column.)	
*Steps 4, 5 and 6:	
4: Visual analysis of the word, looking at it, envisaging it. **5: Practising the word by writing it.** **6: Backing up these by simultaneously saying the word.**	

In the process of learning to spell a word, getting a visual image of the word can be very important. It is not the only thing that counts. Writing the word can be important (this gives kinaesthetic feedback and builds up a physical pattern, or motor memory), and saying the word can be important (to gain auditory and aural feedback). In other words, a multi-sensory approach is likely to be beneficial, and the above method draws on such an approach.

As is often the case, though, students – especially students who are struggling somewhat – can be helped by being given a method of working. In truth, this consists of no more than tricks of the trade, or common sense. But these may not be so apparent and obvious to the student. Do we always point these things out to them?

The most common strategy is *syllabification*, which can perhaps be expressed to the student as *chunking*. It consists simply of looking for ways to chop words up into sections – preferably sections which hang together cohesively – and learning each section, and then putting them back together for the whole word, for example:

> *ex – ped – i – tion*
>
> *in – form – a – tion.*

Students may need to be taught to see words in this way, and have opportunities to practise this kind of analysis. There may be students who persist in trying to remember longish words as a whole and, understandably, find this difficult.

While it is definitely preferable that their *chunks* are nice neat syllables (as in the two examples above) it is not essential, and too much emphasis need not be placed on syllabification, if the student is *chunking* in their own way, for example:

> *e – qui – la – teral* (instead of *equi – lat – er – al*)
>
> *ant – ipo – des* (instead of *an – tip – o – des*)
>
> *miss – pel – ling* (a classic, instead of *mis – spell – ing*).

This section of this book does not give a complete guide to the teaching of spelling, but it does give a useful approach to learning how to spell, most particularly those words which are proving difficult and/or have been wrongly spelt. It is useful for words the student has tried to use. It is useful for subject-specific words (e.g. respiration, triangulation). It is useful for those commonplace, awkward words (e.g. Wednesday, February).

Also, it gives students and teachers a practical way of working; a way of doing something positive rather than doing nothing constructive.

Postscript (with regard to computers/word processing)

Incidentally, it is possible for the student to put this version of *Look – Cover – Write – Check* into practice using the computer, and some students may prefer to do this.

This possibly has certain advantages, not the least of which is the added interest and motivation some students may feel just by virtue of using the computer. Other plus factors may be that students can choose the colour of their print, the style and size of the font (all of these may conceivably make a difference) and they can automatically keep their spelling attempts in the neatest of columns. Most importantly, with the spellchecker switched on, they get instant and accurate feedback at every stage.

This just leaves the problem of them typing their efforts without being able to see (copy) a correct version. This is achieved by holding down the Return key at the end of the newly typed word, so that this correct version is scrolled up and out of sight.

If he then types it correctly on the now blank screen, the spellchecker will indicate (or, rather, not indicate anything, thereby 'accepting' the word). If the spellchecker does indicate a mistake, usually by that all too familiar wavy red underlining, this give the student instant feedback. However, if the teacher wishes for the student firstly to ascertain for himself whether the spelling is correct, he can be operating with the spellchecker switched off, and have to use his own judgement and decide; he could then double-check by turning the spellchecker on.

Either way, he has to bring in close proximity, one under the other, the known correct version of the word (which has been scrolled up and out of sight) and the word he has just typed. This is either to check for himself by comparison whether his latest spelling is right or wrong or, even if the spellchecker has been switched on so he knows already if it's wrong, by comparison to check in which way and where it is wrong.

Bringing the two words into close vertical alignment is simply done by positioning the cursor at the beginning of the newly typed word, and then holding the delete key.

The three tick rule still applies so, of course, this is just repeated as necessary.

Teachers will have to decide, depending on the individual, the student's liking for the computer, and the amount which he word processes his work as to whether to make the computer the vehicle for implementing the above approach to spelling. Or perhaps, it might be decided that, even if only to introduce variety, both methods can be used in turn by the same student.

Epilogue

This is another true and recent tale, witnessed a day or two after the Prologue. Seen on another chalkboard, this time in a sea-side café at a Sunday lunchtime:

DISH OF THE DAY

**Roast Lion with Sage
and Onion Stuffing**

Readability and students with learning disabilities
Read a what?

How do we know that what we ask students to read is not too difficult for them? Are we sure that the poorer readers are able to manage the books we expect them to read; that they are not barred from performing well on the worksheets we prepare for them because we have written the instructions and asked the questions in words and language that are too difficult for them to read; or that the fact and information sheets we provide are written in such a way that the reading level required is not so much above them that the task of decoding the writing gets in the way of their accessing and comprehending the information?

Similarly, are we sure that the reverse of all these is not true and that, quite possibly because we have bent over backwards not to put unnecessary obstacles in the students' way, the written materials we put before them are not too easy, even patronising or 'babyish', from the reading point of view?

Of course, we have our common sense to guide us; we have our professional experience; we have our knowledge of the student(s); and we have our gut feeling. None of these is in any way to be underrated, but are they enough to guarantee that the reading difficulties within the material are pitched so that, although they might slightly tax the student's reading skills and competence, these difficulties do not debar him from reading the material? Or (less likely but possible) that he is not undermined in terms of self-esteem, nor plain bored, because he regards the material as being too simple from the reading point of view? These considerations, of course, apply across the whole curriculum; in fact rather more so than in 'literacy' or English where, arguably, this consideration is likely to be more to the forefront of the teacher's mind.

So, readability is about matching material to be read to the level of the reading skills of the person who is to read it. And there are ways of analysing written material to check what level of reading skills are required to read that material. The suggestion is that, from time to time (not on every occasion, which would be totally unrealistic) teachers check this readability level of the material they are wishing their students to read so that they confirm that all is well in this regard, or can then make modifications to written materials to be presented to the students if there are signs of a mismatch.

Readability can be viewed in two – complementary – ways. One concerns how the material is presented to the student on the page (or screen), so that it looks as 'attractive' as possible and certainly not off-putting; key features of this are summarised later in this section. The other way is actually to calculate a readability score or level by a systematic analysis of the reading matter in question. Typically, this involves simple enough techniques along the lines of sampling a given number of sentences, probably from different sections of the passage, counting the number of polysyllabic words, doing a bit of maths on this data, coming up with a score, and then interpreting this result by reference to norms, which may be encapsulated on a conversion scale or in a graph. All of this is straightforward enough, but does consume time, and most people do not find the mechanics of doing this chore very interesting, although they may find the final result very enlightening.

Fortunately, as we live in a technological age, it is possible to have the computer do most of the boring tasks very quickly, just leaving us to consider the results, confirm our beliefs or modify our practice.

Readability courtesy of Information Technology
FLESCH-KINCAID
For many people the easiest and quickest way to obtain a measure of Readability will be to use the 'Flesch-Kincaid' formulae. The reason why

this will be the easiest method for many people is that many people use Microsoft Word. If this is the case, it is very simple to tell the computer to give you readability scores for everything you type into it (not, of course, that you need this information for everything). This is achieved by going, in turn, to *Tools, Options, Spelling* and *Grammar*. Many users will go this far in any case in order to utilise the spellchecker. However, following the sequence through, you can finally then click, on *Show readability statistics*.

This will instantly display for you fascinating information about how many words, paragraphs and sentences, including sentences using passive verbs (which are generally best avoided) have been used; and about the length of the sentences and the paragraphs. All this is well worth looking at and noting, and, over a period of time, a feel for the appropriateness and 'rightness' of a piece can be developed as you become familiar with this sort of basic data.

However, what is even more useful, is that the Flesch-Kincaid method of calculating Readability levels will have been activated, and the results of this are also instantly displayed.

Hence, a *Reading Ease* score is shown as a number on a 100-point scale. The lower the number, the harder it is to read the text in question. The scale is calibrated:

0–29	Very difficult
30–49	Difficult
50–59	Fairly difficult
60–69	Standard
70–79	Fairly easy
80–89	Easy
90–100	Very easy

This would be of some use, but not a great deal. Difficult *for whom?* Easy for *which* students? would be questions that would immediately arise. Fortunately, the Flesch-Kincaid method also puts the text under consideration into context. Slightly unfortunately, though, the context is a US one in that a Grade Level is also given. So, if a Grade Level of 9.0

is shown, it means that an average student in the Ninth Grade should be able to understand this text. So, we need to convert US Grades into chronological ages. These are:

Grade	Chronological age (years)
1	6
2	7
3	8
4	9
5	10
6	11
7	12
8	13
9	14
10	15
11	16
12	17/18

Of course, many of the students (although not necessarily quite all) that we are thinking about in this book do not read at the level of their chronological age so, in matching text to student, we need to think about the student's reading age. Therefore, if we know a student has a reading age of 8.5 years, we would want the texts we present him with to show up on the Flesch-Kincaid as Grade Level 3; a student with a reading age of 12.02 years 'should' be reading and working with texts which, having gone through the Flesch-Kincaid process, come out with a Grade Level of 7. A reading age of 10.5 suggests that suitable texts for that student would have a Grade Level of 5.

No one is in any way claiming that the link between reading age and Grade Level is absolutely perfect:

- The same student will more than likely obtain somewhat different reading ages on different reading tests.

- A student with a reading age which is well above the half-way mark within the 'year' (e.g. 6.7, 6.8, 6.9; 10.7, 10.8, 10.9) may well be able to read some material at the next Grade Level up (i.e.

Grade Level 2 and Grade Level 6 respectively in the examples just given).

- The same applies in reverse. Students whose reading ages only just creep into the 'year' (e.g. 8.0, 8.1, 8.2; 11.0, 11.1, 11.2) may be more successful for at least part of their time reading texts which show on Flesch-Kincaid as being at one Grade Level lower (i.e. in the examples just given, perhaps some of their reading should be at Grade Level 2 and Grade Level 5 respectively).

- The student's level of motivation and interest in any reading task will influence his capacity to cope with or persevere with that task.

- The student's emotional state (e.g. anxious or confident) will have a bearing.

- Likewise, the time available actually to do the reading will be relevant.

All the above factors can contribute in practice to students reading above or below the Grade Level which is theoretically the most apt for their reading age.

In other words, as is almost always the case, common sense is important, and teacher judgement is required in interpreting the information, and in relating it to an individual student.

However, this Flesch-Kincaid Readability information is information the teacher would not otherwise have; it is another string to the teacher's bow; it is easily available, and it makes us think about just what it is that we are putting in front of our students.

Besides Microsoft Word, at least one other way of accessing some information through the Flesch-Kincaid formulae is to go to *Readability Index Calculator* on www.standards-schmandards.com.

SMOG

SMOG is the delightful acronym for the equally delightfully named *Simplified Measure Of Gobbledygook* (although it emphatically does not apply to Gobbledygook, but to all reading matter). And it is a simplified measure, the full and original maths behind the calculations of this Readability level being quite sophisticated. Fortunately, the simplified version was entirely accurate enough for the busy, practising teacher, but the mechanics were a little laborious, involving counting sentences, counting polysyllabic words, doing some multiplication, finding a square root, and more.

Fortunately, all that is a thing of the past; computers can do it for us. Go to www.niace.org.uk/misc/SMOG-calculator.

There you will find admirably clear instructions and an entirely simple process which will immediately tell you, with regard to the text you have chosen and entered, the total number of words, the number of words with three or more syllables, and the number of sentences. Most important of all, it will give the SMOG Readability score, and this is basically the reading age required to read that text which you put in.

THE FRY READABILITY PROGRAM

This is another electronic method for calculating Readability, and speeds up the manual method considerably. It is available through www.educational-psychologist.co.uk. Click on *SEN Information*, then scroll down to *The Fry Readability Program*, click again, and you are ready for action (Long 2000).

A merit of this program is that it has the potential to work particularly quickly because the text does not even need to be typed into the computer. Instead, you read the text and, in effect, analyse it as you go along by typing *n* for each syllable, *m* at the end of each word, and ". at the end of each sentence. Note particularly how to record the end of the sentence (i.e. ".) which is not quite clear in the on-screen instructions.

This typing of *n*, *m*, etc. is not initially quite so straightforward as might be thought because it is something one is not used to, but is soon picked up. Also, this really makes one look at the text oneself.

One further very interesting point about operating this program is that it can give a Readability level for every single sentence, rather than just an average for a text viewed as a whole. Isolated, quite small areas of particular difficulty within a text can render the comprehension of the whole disproportionately difficult, particularly if the area of difficulty carries vital information.

In fact, what this program is doing is replacing Fry's graph which is what one refers to if the manual method is used, and which is not the easiest thing in the world to read off quickly.

MISCELLANEOUS

In fact, there is a way of running one passage through several Readability measures simultaneously (Automated Readability *et al.* 2008). This can be done by going to www.addedbytes.com/tools/readabilityscore.

Besides the Flesch-Kincaid and the SMOG, you will also immediately receive Readability levels as calculated by the Gunning-Fog, the Coleman-Liam, and the Automated Readability Index procedures.

All this information is given in US Grade Levels.

You may want to watch out for variations in scores between the measures (even though, as already pointed out, the same piece of text is being scrutinised by each method).

Readability 'scores': final thoughts

Claims are not being made that calculating Readability levels is an absolutely exact science, or that the levels are absolutely spot-on, but they do provide a starting point in making us think objectively about what we are expecting our students to read, and respond to, appropriately. This is especially true when a Readability level is produced which surprises us, or with which we disagree! They make us look at the texts in perhaps a different light.

Readability levels can certainly be used to compare the levels of different texts. (Use the same method on different texts to assess their relative levels of difficulty.)

But, principally, they can be used to make sure that students are reading material that is, broadly speaking, commensurate with their reading age.

If the Readability level calculated is greatly different from what we believe the student's reading age to be, then it behoves us to have a think about why this might be. One angle here, of course, to be explored, could be whether the reading age is accurate (when was it last assessed? Is it out of date? Has the student made a lot, or only a little, progress since?) and are we regarding this student's reading ability accurately, or are we making certain assumptions (which the Readability level might call into question)?

If the reading age/ability of the student is as we thought it to be, then – with reference to the Readability level that has been generated – we have to look at the material we are putting before him to read, and ask ourselves if it really is appropriate.

We do not need to do this all the time (which would be impossible, anyway) but it is a monitoring exercise that we do periodically throughout the school year by sampling a range of materials currently being read. This includes reading material of every type from across the curriculum: text books in every subject; worksheets prepared by teachers; PowerPoint discs; novels to be studied, etc.

However, a word of warning at this point. Readability assessments are designed to operate on more or less normal running prose. They are not really suitable for charts, tables, etc., nor even for poetry.

Supplying reading material at different levels for different members of the class (i.e. within the general curriculum and over and above the basic reading books in a reading or literacy scheme) is a difficult management task but, if it can be achieved, it is one of the best methods of 'differentiation', and of demonstrating that 'reasonable adjustments' are being made in respect of students with disabilities. Using Readability levels helps us achieve these ends, and provides, to a degree, an evidence-based justification to back up our professional decisions.

Reflections

The SMOG Readability score (see www.niace.org.uk), when applied to the following national institutions, produced these results:

	Reading age (years)
The Sun	under 14
The Daily Express	under 16
The Telegraph	over 17
The Guardian	over 17

A similar exercise (see Johnson 1998) but using the average scores produced by the Fry, Gunning, and Flescher-Kincaid indicated the following:

	Reading age (years)
The Times Educational Supplement	17
The Financial Times	17.5

This latter source also quotes:

	Reading age (years)
A Tale of Two Cities	13
To Kill a Mockingbird	11.5
Lord of the Flies	11
Kes: A Kestrel for a Knave	10.5

As is remarked on the web page, it is surprising that *Lord of the Flies* and *Kes*, which are GCSE English type books, seem to require such modest reading ages.

Would we have predicted this? Or, indeed, that a true classic such as *A Tale of Two Cities* evidently requires a reading age that is not high!

Page layout and presentation

As already mentioned, Readability scores certainly do give an indication of how readable a text is, but there is another aspect to the notion of 'readability'. This is page layout; the way that the text is presented – on the page, worksheet, text book, the computer screen, the whiteboard, the PowerPoint, etc.

Is the reader faced by an impregnable block of solid print in small type, which immediately suggests that a boring and arduous task lies ahead, or is the text (and any other material) so arranged on the page to suggest that engaging with it may be fully manageable?

References about presenting to students material that is not immediately off-putting have been made in other parts of this book (e.g. Chapter 2), so just a summary of the main ones from this readability perspective is now given.

- Make sure that the text is broken up into chunks. Avoid over-long paragraphs.

- Use sub-headings to facilitate this. Sub-headings can be 'manufactured' just to break up bulky blocks of text, but it is, of course, even better if they actually give an indication of the text that is to follow. Phrasing them as questions can be very helpful, and is often quite easy to do at many points in a text.

- Avoid fully-justified text (even though it does look very neat). The reason for this avoidance is that fully-justified text probably leads to slightly irregular spacing between words in the body of the text (as words are slightly jostled into positions that enable that neat right edge to be achieved). The result of this can be off-putting to some readers, particularly as they see 'rivers' of white paper running down the page through the text.

- Allow ample space between the lines. Double spacing, or more, between paragraphs makes for clarity.

- 12-point font is likely to be the minimum; larger may be appropriate.

- It is not too difficult to print off worksheets in different sized fonts to suit individual students (although they must not become too pernickety, because the world is not like that).

- Similarly, worksheets can be printed off in colours other than white. This can help some students, but the same comment as above applies about over-fussiness creeping in.

- Plain fonts (e.g. Times New Roman) are likely to be more accessible than more ornate ones. *Sans serif* are generally preferred.

- Different colour, graphics, judicious use of capitals, bold, underlining, framing/boxing in words all break up text, and can be used to link teaching/learning points.

- Use the paper itself (space out the material) to break up text, and thus display it more prominently, and memorably.

- On worksheets, etc., number the pages. Quite possibly, number the paragraphs, for example, 1.1, 1.2, 1.3; 2.1, 2.2, 2.3.

- Avoid passive verbs, and use concise instructions. 'Shade the sea in blue and shade the land in green' is better than 'The sea can be shaded in blue while the land may be shaded in green.'

- Finding ways for the students to interact with the text (e.g. worksheet) as the students work through it can aid readability, that is, instead of just reading the sheet and/or answering questions at the end, answering questions at intermediate points through the text can aid understanding of what is to follow – and doing tasks other than just answering questions can help engagement, for example, highlighting what they think to be the key sentence in a paragraph just read, noting on the worksheet in a space provided what they think the three most important points that have been covered so far.

- Despite conservation considerations, do not produce worksheets on both sides of the page. Clarity of both sides can be lost as the print on one side interferes with the print on the other, and organising the material can be physically and mentally more trying for the student.

And one or two final points:

- If text books do not meet these sort of criteria, try to find ones that do.

- Novels may offer less options, but even here different editions do immediately look and 'feel' different.

- In your buying policy, try to consider these aspects of Readability when you choose, rather than price (difficult thought this is, especially when Heads of Departments are keen to point out the cheaper options!).

- In choosing materials and in preparing them, do not go overboard in implementing the above points. Moderation in all things: text and written materials that are too colourful, too much broken up, and generally too 'fancy' can, also be off-putting.

- Very importantly, in preparing your own materials, remember that writing for a group of people (i.e. students) who constitute a group of readers that is different from the group to which you belong, is not easy, and is very different from writing for your own group. This is one of the arts of teaching. And teachers may have several groups within one class!

But, as with utilising actual Readability formulae, going that extra step and considering and, if necessary, re-jigging materials in the above ways, does show a willingness to make reasonable adjustments, and to make differentiation a reality. It is also a way of going towards meeting a wide range of needs within that one class.

Chapter 7

ॐ

So What Have Special Needs Got to do With Me?

Introduction

Is the above remark by classroom teachers or subject specialists still heard across the schools of the country? Let us hope not, but may we visit one or two scenarios and possible further remarks of someone who might open up with the above question:

> I teach English/History/PE/Maths [or any subject you wish to nominate] and get on and teach my classes.

> I teach my subject and I do it to the best of my ability. I make what allowances I can but, if they still can't learn, there's no more I can do about it.

> I teach my subject, and if I realise students are not learning, I refer them to the SENCo.

These are not entirely unreasonable remarks; one must understand where these teachers are coming from, but, in effect, they are saying that students with SENs are not their problem; they are the responsibility of someone else. They are probably also saying that they do not have the understanding of SENs which they believe they need in order to cope, and certainly they believe they do not have the teaching skills. Of course, it is entirely true that students with extreme difficulties may well have complex needs that can be met only by highly specialised teaching, for which their teachers have probably obtained further qualifications. But by no means all students fall into the category of having such specialised needs (and the Special Educational Needs Code of Practice (Department for Education and Skills 2001) makes clear there is a continuum of SENs). This is not to diminish the needs such students do have; on the contrary, this book is about trying to ensure that at least a sensible, realistic, and practical attempt is made to meet all levels of need wherever they are found. Many of the students in our classrooms have a level of needs which teachers can at least begin to address, and for which they do have the skills, if only they will realise it, or can obtain these teaching skills, not least by working and thinking in the ways suggested in this book.

One thing such teachers will have to do, though, is show an open mind, and be prepared to try to meet the SENs they will almost certainly encounter; a change of attitude may well be necessary, and this can be a major problem. Bringing about a new and positive outlook in certain colleagues is one of the greatest ways a SENCo can serve the school, or an individual teacher serve numbers of students. Intransigence is as likely to be the result of a lack of confidence as it is a lack of compassion. Once a teacher has a choice of a few strategies to try, watch the confidence rise, and the 'expertise' flourish.

Professional peer expectation is important here, too. Perhaps meeting the needs of the student in question is not a straightforward business. But teachers are not expected to work miracles; we should not expect instant success of ourselves or colleagues. Success (i.e. student progress) may take time to arrive. Perhaps it may not arrive at all, using the chosen strategies. This is disappointing, but there are always other strategies to try, and where there are strategies, there is hope.

This is one of the greatest gifts we can give teachers – hope. If the quotes at the top of this section were really from teachers, those teachers would be hopeless, namely, without hope. They have no hope of bringing about any worthwhile improvement for some of their students. This is, professionally and spiritually, moribund. On the coattails of hopelessness cling despair and even cynicism, those two deadly enemies to enhancing the learning and lives of SEN students. What teachers need to do is realise that there are certain things that any teacher can, at least, systematically try. Reference to this book will help them come to this belief, and suggest ways in which they may make this attempt. Just by trying, the teachers will feel much better about their work, and their SEN students will seem less of a burden, and there is a good likelihood that their SEN students will benefit.

It's a fair cop: legal implications

When teachers think about what, indeed, SENs do have to do with them, there is, nowadays, also another way in which they must think. Consider the following:

> At the end of the lesson, the teacher writes the homework on the board. A student with dyslexia is unable to copy it all down in time, and so does not do all the homework. As a consequence, he or she is given a detention. The fact that the student could not write down the homework is, in this case, related to the disability, and no 'reasonable adjustment' (a term we shall return to) was made, for example, allowing the student extra time to write it down, or to come back later to write it, or the teacher writing the task down for the student. This detention is likely to amount to unlawful discrimination.

Here's another perfectly feasible scenario:

> A student with Asperger's goes straight to the front of the queue waiting at the teacher's desk for work to be marked (this may not be the greatest of teaching models, but surely it still happens). He or she is told not to barge in. The student shows signs of anxiety, but does not actually move. The teacher insists strongly that the student must not jump the queue. The student now becomes most agitated, and is highly abusive to the teacher, thus causing great disruption to the lesson The teacher reports the matter, which has escalated into an 'incident', to a senior colleague, and the student is temporarily excluded. The reason for the exclusion, though, is related to the nature of the student's disability (students with Asperger's quite typically have difficulty in managing social situations, might well be unappreciative of the 'rights' of the others already in the queue, and might not understand, or even be further confused by, figurative language such as, 'Don't jump the queue'). The justification given for

the exclusion may be that the behaviour had contravened the good order and discipline of the school. On the face of it, this does not sound unreasonable and one is always sympathetic to the school's dilemma in such circumstances – but were there further steps that could have been taken to prevent the incident happening in the first place? Have staff had sufficient training in Asperger Syndrome, and been advised of strategies to manage such students, and is the student being appropriately educated in the light of the disability? If reasonable adjustments of this type could have been made but were not, it may not be possible for the school to justify the exclusion. Recommendations 12 and 42 of the Lamb Inquiry (Department for Children, Schools and Families 2009b) both talk about reducing SEN exclusions and the Headteacher's regard for the guidance on SEN and disability. On the other hand, if appropriate steps were taken but the incident still happened, the school is likely to be able to justify the exclusion.

In the sequel to the potentially unhappy circumstances described above, a claim of discrimination – for that is what we are talking about – cannot be made against the individual teacher. A claim might well be brought against the responsible body (which is responsible for the actions of the teachers, and of all employees of all types, and volunteers and helpers). The responsible body is generally either the governing body, or the 'proprietor' of an independent school.

However, the *Special Educational Needs Code of Practice* (Department for Education and Skills 2001) states that every teacher is a teacher of students with SEN (although the individual teacher is expected to be supported by a whole-school approach). Within the Education Act (1996), not only do all pupils have a right to access the National Curriculum, but a (qualified) duty is placed upon Local Education Authorities to place pupils with special educational needs in mainstream schools, and the Ofsted Inspection Framework (Ofsted 2000) encompasses educational inclusion. Recommendations 34, 35 and 36 of the Lamb Inquiry recommend that Ofsted and inspection providers ensure that their inspectors have the skills and capacity to inspect special provision effectively and that the progress of disabled students and students with SEN is reported on as part of school inspection.

Additional duties added to the original Disability Discrimination Act (DDA 1995) in, for instance, the Special Educational Needs and Disability Act (2001) and the Disability Discrimination Act (2005), now affect teachers and, in fact, all staff, namely, teaching and non-teaching, permanent and supply teachers' responsibilities. Lamb, in Recommendation 51, recommends further strengthening of the DDA with regard to schools' responsibility. It is clear that the statutory duties set a clear framework for the development of inclusive practice.

If a case of unlawful discrimination is brought against a school, it will be heard by the Special Education Needs Disability Tribunal (SENDIST); generally such actions are brought by the parents. If SENDIST finds in favour of the parents, that is, that unlawful discrimination did occur, it can insist on various measures being carried out, including disability training for the staff and a formal written apology to the student.

An individual teacher cannot personally be charged and be personally accountable to SENDIST, but if the teacher will not follow the school's anti-discrimination policies, he or she may well be liable to the school's formal complaints procedure and disciplinary policy.

The Special Educational Needs and Disability Act (2001) covers every school (private, publicly funded, mainstream, special, nursery, primary, secondary, Sixth Form, community, voluntary, foundation, academy) and schools' duties include education and associated services. This is a broad umbrella to cover all aspects of school life (including sports days, class trips and extra-curricular activities), but of particular interest to classroom/subject teachers are their obligations with regard to: teaching and learning; classroom organisation; grouping of students; homework; and discipline and sanctions.

So, apart from their own ethical, professional, and personal feelings and reasons, teachers do have to be very aware that it is unlawful for a student to be treated less favourably for a reason related to the student's disability. It is important to add that 'disability' does not necessarily mean the existence of a very severe or serious condition. In any event, a student must not be placed at substantial disadvantage, including loss of opportunity and/or diminished progress.

The term disability is something that teachers need to get used to, and to understand how it is used and, of course, to which students it refers. The first point here is that it does include learning difficulties, and it does include dyslexia, dyspraxia, ADHD, and Asperger Syndrome

(DDA 2005). The Equality Act (2010) definition applies to someone who has 'a physical or mental impairment which has a substantial and long-term adverse effect on his or her ability to carry out normal day-to-day activities.' Thus, it covers a much larger group of students than is, probably, generally thought: a Cabinet Office document (Prime Minister's Strategy Unit 2005) spoke of 777,000 children in the UK having a disability, which was about 7 per cent of all children. Clearly, one begins to see that the definition does not apply only to those with physical or sensory impairment (e.g. sight, hearing, mobility), and that the DDA definition of disability is broad and the thresholds are quite low, and it is really important to get one's head around this much wider spectrum of students who legally come under the disability banner. Going on from this, teachers need to appreciate that many students who have a statement of SEN will be included in the definition of disability under the DDA, but it is also likely that many of those at School Action Plus or Early Years Action Plus will count as disabled, and it is certainly not inconceivable that students who do not come within these categories could also be considered disabled.

In fact, a disabled child does not actually need to be assessed as having a special educational need in order to be protected from discrimination under Part 4 of the Disability Discrimination Act (1995) and Special Educational Needs and Disability Act (2010). An official diagnosis is not the issue; it is considered that a condition exists whether or not it has been officially diagnosed. If the child cannot carry out normal day-to-day activities and this is long-term (more than 12 months) and substantial (more than trivial), the child must not be discriminated against. The Code of Practice (CoP) (Department for Education and Skills 2001) expects that teachers will be informed of a student who has special educational needs, but also that teachers will identify special educational needs, and provide for them (in Community Voluntary, and Foundation schools). CoP also points out that an individual's needs may change over time.

In fact, CoP encapsulates the duties due to individual children with special educational needs as originally spelt out in the Education Act (1996). A child has such needs if he or she has a learning difficulty which calls for special education provision, and defines a child as having a learning difficulty if he or she has (a) significantly greater difficulty in learning than the majority of children of the same age, (b) a disability which prevents or hinders him/her from making use of educational facilities of a kind generally provided for children of the same age in schools within the area of the local education authority (LEA), or (c) he or she is under five and falls within the definitions at (a) or (b), or would do so if SEN provision was not made for the child. Special education is (i) for a child of two or over, educational provision which is additional to, or otherwise different from, the educational provision made generally for children of the child's age in maintained schools (*other than special schools*) (my italics) in the area, or (ii) for a child under two, educational provision of any kind. If CoP beefs up requirements including inclusion and avoiding discrimination, it is only reflecting several other documents. One can think of: the amendments to Section 316 of the Education Act (1996) as detailed in the Special Educational Needs and Disability Act (2001), which strengthens the general duty to provide a mainstream place for a child with special educational needs when the parents want it; the National Curriculum Inclusion Statement (Qualifications and Curriculum Authority 1999); and the inspection of educational inclusion by Ofsted (2000). Then there are the expectations of the Department for Education and Skills, clearly expressed in their Removing Barriers to Achievement (2004), that it hoped that all teachers will have the skills and *confidence* (my italics) – and access to specialist advice where necessary – to help children with SENs to reach their potential (p.17, para 3.2). This follows, though, on concerns expressed in their preceding paragraph about how effectively some schools are able to respond to the wide range of student needs in today's classrooms and how far children with SENs are helped to achieve to the full. All this is on the back of a firm commitment to the principle of inclusion (p.12, para 2.1) and to an increasing proportion of children with SENs attending mainstream schools. Then this document makes a crucial point about inclusion being about much more than the type of school children attend, but being about the quality of the experience, and how far they are helped to learn, achieve and participate fully in the life of the school. Tellingly, the document immediately acknowledges that reality does not always match this.

So, where does all this leave the school as an institution, and the teacher as an individual? We will deal with each in turn, starting with schools.

In England and Wales, the Special Educational Needs and Disability Act (2001) has covered school education since 2002. The Disability Equality Duty came into force in 2006 as a result of the Disability Discrimination (Amendment) Act (2005), and applies to all publicly funded schools. It is generally referred to as 'the Duty', and that is what is done here. Schools are required to be proactive in promoting disability equality and in eliminating discrimination. The Duty applies to the school in its main function of providing education to students, and in other ways, although what the school does is *only* (my italics) expected to be reasonable and practical. More on this general point anon. Moreover, schools are required to publish their disability equality scheme, and to report on it annually. The possibility of substantial disadvantage has to be anticipated and prevented, or the Duty is breached, which could, of course, lead to a claim of disability discrimination being presented to SENDIST. The National Curriculum Inclusion Statement (Qualifications and Curriculum Authority 1999) emphasises the importance of providing effective learning opportunities for all students, and offers three key principles for inclusion: setting suitable challenges; responding to students' diverse needs; and overcoming potential barriers to learning and assessment for individuals and groups of students. Primary schools should consider the kinds of options and the variety of activities available within the class setting to enable children to access the National Curriculum, while in secondary schools the provision for a student with special educational needs should match the nature of those needs, and there should be regular recording of a student's needs, the action taken, and the outcomes.

The Equality Act (2010) covers many fronts, including Education, and 'tidies up' and brings together much of the legislation which is currently spread about the statute books. Although it is not yet fully implemented – it is being phased in – this Act is now in being and it should prove easier for us to access information largely within the one document.

It is worth pointing out here that there is one piece of legislation that schools might wish to enquire about of their LEA. The Education and Skills Act (2008) gives LEAs the power to arrange assessments for people with learning difficulties who have no Statement but who are in their last year of compulsory schooling and likely to receive post-16 education or training. All does not depend on the Statement. Is your school's LEA responding to requests for such assessments? Would such assessments be useful to any of the school's students? It is a 'needs' assessment, and is colloquially referred to as a Section 140 assessment. As it should highlight what support will be needed in Higher or Further Education, it is something that should potentially be of use to students, their families, and schools as they work for these young people's futures.

Turning now to teachers, how are they to meet the requirements of the law and not be culpable of disability discrimination? The really significant answer to this question, and the truly professional and committed teacher's answer, lies in other sections of this book, where guidance about how to choose and implement strategies for individual students is given. Such a teacher will not want to stand outside of and apart from this. In any case, can any teacher now remain isolated from all that has been said here? Can any teacher just say, even if they wanted to, 'I will not have any "disabled" students in any of my classes'? Such students are bound to be met, and teachers are bound to provide for them. But there is a legal dimension which it would be unfair to ignore, and the answers given in this section are couched in such a way as to indicate how the law can be honourably satisfied.

The key words here are 'reasonable adjustment', and these are words teachers should permanently have in the forefront of their minds, and have a good understanding of what they mean, and what their implications are. In order that less favourable treatment is not handed out to a student with a disability (which would be unlawful) reasonable adjustments must be made (DDA 2005). Less favourable treatment that can be justified is not unlawful discrimination, but can be difficult to justify; the real emphasis is on making reasonable adjustments in order not to treat a disabled child less favourably, and this should be regarded as a duty. The Inclusion Statement (Qualifications and Curriculum Authority 1999), referred to previously, refers to teaching and learning, and all teachers must have regard to it. Strictly speaking, even with reasonable adjustments, the teacher is not the responsible body, but such adjustments may well include classroom organisation, interaction with peers, and other fundamentally classroom-based considerations.

The duty to make reasonable adjustments is a fairly heavy one; for instance, starting right at the Foundation Stage, such adjustments are expected to be made, if necessary, in all six Foundation curriculum areas. But at no stage is either a school or a teacher expected to move heaven and earth in every conceivable circumstance; to do so would not be 'reasonable'. Factors such as the maintenance of overall or general standards where this is important can legitimately be considered, as in an inter-schools' sports competition; the cost of an adjustment can be weighed against the financial resources available at the time; Health and Safety regulations and considerations are not overruled by reasonable adjustments; and that the interests of other students warrant consideration is recognised.

What does all this mean for the busy teacher?

The heart of this book, the *A La Carte* approach, is, in fact, entirely about 'reasonable adjustments' – but not at all because they are a legal requirement, and a requirement which very few teachers would be able to evade even if they wanted to, but because teachers wish to make a reasonable attempt to meet the needs of all children, because that is what good teachers want to do for their students. However, what they perceive as the possibility of legal sanctions does weigh on the minds of some teachers, particularly as there is a perception that we live in an increasingly litigious society, so here are a few examples of quite small modifications which it is likely would be regarded as legitimate reasonable adjustments. It will be seen that they are not very daunting, they are what many a teacher would be doing almost as a matter of course, and are well within the scope of any conscientious teacher.

Asperger Syndrome

- In Literature studies, use tasks more akin to close procedure rather than deep analysis of characters.

- Make sure that activities have a clear beginning and end, that is, a clear target. Limit choices; give some, but not too many.

- Give student(s) regular seats in the classroom, and have well structured tasks for them.

- They may benefit from having information and material given to them in writing, rather than just listening to it; despite superficial appearances to the contrary, visual skills are often stronger than auditory ones.

- Try to double check the quality of their learning; their understanding may lack depth and breadth, again despite superficial appearances suggesting otherwise.

Dyspraxia

- To avoid the exhaustion of handwriting, provide worksheets that require little handwriting by way of response.

- Provide mini-whiteboards instead of paper initially, so that frequent wiping clean can take place until the student is satisfied (although, of course, this is of limited use in that a permanent record is often required – or is it?). Provide sloped writing boards.

- In Science, when dissecting flowers, provide alstroemeria, or possibly eustoma (lisianthus); they should be easier to manage.

- In PE, allow your student(s) with dyspraxia to choose the size of bat they can best manage. Similarly, in catching activities, allow the dyspraxic students to choose the size of the balls they are able to catch. (Over time, teachers will adjust the size if they think the students can manage something a little more demanding. This gentle restructuring of activities is an important theme which can and should be applied to virtually all adjustments.) Adapt games to accommodate such students, for example, in rounders, allow the dyspraxic students extra time to try to complete their rounders by not allowing the fielder to move towards the ball until a certain number of seconds have elapsed.

- Back in the classroom, have available pens, pencils, and crayons in a range of sizes; and have large building blocks available (including for Maths if blocks are used in Maths activities).

Dyslexia

- Have an able student either read a worksheet to a student with dyslexia, or have the able student check the dyslexic student's reading before work on the sheet is started. Or have worksheets on which the information you give is in simplified language (readability is very important), possibly making use of pictures and symbols.

- If the students' timetables are complex, involving many room changes, help the students rework them using colour codes, symbols, etc.

- Be generally wary of asking students with dyslexia to read aloud in front of the class.

- Accept briefer pieces of written work (without compromising on quality of content). Expect minimal copying from boards and books, but try to provide the information in other ways, for example appropriate handouts, hard copies of PowerPoint slides. Instead of copying, students may find it helpful if they are able to develop personal idiosyncratic methods of notetaking.

ADHD

- Review the previous lesson at the beginning of the next (but make this interesting and/or fun). Going on from this, let them know the outline of the lesson at the outset, and what the objective of the lesson is. Tell them what they will be able to do at the end of the lesson, or what they will have learnt.

- Provide a personal or personalised workspace, probably to one side or to the back of the room, which they can use if necessary, not, of course, as a punishment but as a helpful way of working.

- Have a spare set of pens, etc. handy which they can draw on in a 'no-fuss' way, as they may often lose theirs.

- Check their work frequently to see they are still on task.

- Be prepared, on occasion, to allow them to move onto another task, and have that alternative task ready.

- Think very carefully before not allowing a student to go on a school trip or field trip; really try to make reasonable adjustments so that he or she can go.

All the above are relatively random examples, some of which, of course, may be useful as ways of working with more than one kind of student with a disability. But, applied thoughtfully and consistently, they do give a flavour of what sorts of things are encompassed within 'reasonable adjustments'.

So, teachers need not worry about 'reasonable adjustments'. The strategies in this book, chosen and applied as the book suggests, mean that teachers should certainly be meeting the requirements to make reasonable adjustments. In that sense, teachers can forget about the terminology and fears of prosecution, and just go back to thinking about how they work out how best to attempt to meet students' special needs; that is, just get on with the job in sensitive and thoughtful ways. Certainly, teachers should be very aware of the legislation, but they need not allow all their focus to be on it; instead, they should focus on the students and their needs, and then on their own professional pride and satisfaction, within the legislative and advisory framework.

Chapter 8

≈

What is a Special Need? And is a Disability a Handicap?

Something to digest

Special needs, disability, and handicap: three words or expressions; is each a synonym for the other two?

> He's got special needs.

> He's a special needs child.

> He's disabled.

> He's got a disability.

> He's handicapped.

> He's got a handicap.

These are, in essence, probably common enough sentences and descriptions. Do they all mean the same? Thinking of a student, if one description applies, do they all, therefore, apply? Does it matter which is used?

A relative of mine, as a young man, had a leg blown off in World War II. Immediately after that happened, he was clearly disabled, and also handicapped. In due time, with the aid of an artificial limb, he learnt to walk pretty well. He could walk for miles, so was he still handicapped? He had been a keen and talented athlete but he could never manage to run again, the point of amputation was far too high for that. So, was he handicapped? He quite soon learnt to drive, and to drive very well, a modified car. Was he handicapped? Just before the war, he had been on the point of joining the police force. After the war, and with his physical disability, he was ineligible. Was he handicapped? Can a man with only one leg ever not be described as having a disability? Must he, as a consequence, always be said to have a handicap?

A friend of mine decided to learn to drive rather late in life. He took a course of lessons, which went well, and was quite soon entered for the test. The first thing he had to do at the commencement of the test was the eye-sight check. He failed. He never even got in the car. He was sent home and told not to even contemplate presenting himself again for the test until he had some proper glasses. In terms of eyesight, was he to be regarded as disabled? Was he to be regarded as handicapped? Was he only handicapped after the attempt to take the test? Was that when his disability became a handicap? Did the disability become a handicap only when it prevented him doing something he really wanted to do? Once he had the glasses, was he still disabled? Was he still handicapped?

Harry was definitely dyslexic. Harry couldn't read much, but he didn't seem to mind not being able to read; he was quite intelligent, had worked out several strategies for compensating for his dyslexia, was well-balanced, had lots of friends, and managed to do all right in exams. Was his dyslexia a disability; was he handicapped? The same Harry was not very good at Maths. He did not have dyscalculia, but the dyslexia probably made itself felt in his Maths as well as his reading. His Maths marks were not disastrous, but they were always pretty mediocre. Harry wanted to be a pilot. His level of Maths proficiency prevented him achieving this long-held ambition. Harry was bitterly disappointed, it was a shattering blow to all his life-plans. Was Harry disabled? Was he handicapped? Did he have special educational needs?

Tamwar was fairly severely dyslexic and, as a consequence struggled all through school up to and including Year 11. Although regarded by most members of staff as being quite a bright boy, his dyslexia meant that he had difficulties in many subjects. He was certainly regarded as having a special educational need, and to have a disability which was definitely proving to be a handicap. He scraped a few GCSEs and, partly as a result of a reasonably enlightened school approach, was admitted to the Sixth Form, even though his academic success judged by GCSE grades and passes barely warranted it, if taken at face value. Again, the school was rather wise and, with his full cooperation, directed Tamwar towards A-level subjects which made much fewer, rather than more, demands on his formal literacy skills. For the first time in his school career, Tamwar positively thrived. What happened to his disability, what happened to his handicap? Does he still have special educational needs?

Definitions

1. Children have special educational needs if they have a learning difficulty which calls for special educational provision to be made for them.

   Children have a learning difficulty if they:

   (a) have a significantly greater difficulty in learning than the majority of children of the same age

   (b) have a disability which prevents or hinders them from making use of educational facilities of a kind generally provided for children of the same age in schools within the area of the local education authority

   (c) are under compulsory school age and fall within the definition at (a) or (b) above or would do so if special educational provision was not made for them.

   Special educational provision means:

   (a) for children of two or over, educational provision which is additional to, or otherwise different from, the educational provision made generally for children of their age in schools maintained by the LEA, other than special schools, in the area

   (b) for children under two, educational provision of any kind.

   (Education Act 1996)

2. (i) Disability – a condition, such as a physical or mental handicap, that results in partial or complete loss of a person's ability to perform social, occupational or other everyday tasks.

(i)   Handicap – a physical or mental disability that results in partial or total inability to perform social, occupational or other normal everyday tasks.

(Chambers 21st Century Dictionary 1996)

3.   A person has a disability for the purpose of this Act if he has a physical or mental impairment which has a substantial and long-term adverse effect on his ability to carry out normal day-to-day activities.

(Disability Discrimination Act 1995)

Note: Dyslexia, dyspraxia, Asperger Syndrome, and ADHD are all recognised within the Disability Discrimination Act (1995).

Commentary

Consideration particularly of point 1(a) above shows that a 'learning difficulty' is fairly loosely defined – or, to put it another way, is a broad definition – and therefore, and importantly, has a wide application. This has implications for schools, which they have surely taken on board during the several years since this legal definition came into being.

Notice also that here no reference is made as to why the student is having 'a significantly greater difficulty.' Conditions are not itemised, disabilities are not described, and labels are not attached. Although open to interpretation (what, how much is *significant?*) all that matters is the extent of the difficulties.

The immediate reaction to the definitions of disability and handicap (2(i), 2(ii)) might be that a cigarette paper could not be slid between them? Clearly, they are linked but, in fact, they are essentially different. The disability is the condition (dyslexia, dyspraxia, Asperger's, ADD, ADHD); the handicap is the degree to which the condition prevents someone doing what they wish and want to do.

Thus, it is not really permissible to talk about 'disability' and 'handicap' as one and the same. In everyday conversation, perhaps we all do it. But equally, perhaps when we are seriously considering a student, reviewing his needs, choosing our strategies, and helping plan his future we should be precise, so that the two are kept separate in our language and in our thinking.

It is, then, the role of education to seek to prevent the disability manifesting itself as a handicap. It is the role of the teacher to minimise the extent to which the student's disability, which it might not be possible to eradicate, continues to be a handicap to him. It is the role of the school to do its utmost to ensure that a student with a disability is not automatically also a student with a handicap.

Labels

If we are to think of disability and handicap in the sort of context outlined above, what then do we make of 'labels' (such as those used in this book; dyslexia, Asperger Syndrome, etc.)? And there are many more, as Woliver (2009) points out. What do they tell us; what do they mean; how useful are they? All these questions have, of course, to be predicated on an assumption that the label is accurate.

Often parents like labels, as do some teachers. Labels do provide a measure of an explanation of a child's difficulties. It is helpful to know that a child is dyslexic; it probably tells us that he is not unintelligent, that he is not being deliberately obstinate, and matters of that ilk. But to what extent does it actually inform us? To what degree does it help our teaching? There are many types and shades of dyslexia. In fact, every dyslexic child is different, in personality and in the ways they learn; but that is true of every child. So, what use is the label? A label is not a prescription for guaranteeing progress; a label indicates a teaching approach, but there will be a myriad of individualised details for the teacher to paint into the teaching strategy for that one particular student. Attaching the label may be of some use, but it actually solves and resolves very little.

Better to think along the following sort of lines:

We have been told that Oliver has been diagnosed as dyslexic. 'Therefore', he is a very poor speller. That does take us a little further (although we already knew only too well that he couldn't spell) because we do know something about the foibles and problems that the English spelling system poses for many dyslexic students, but it does not carry us the whole way. Can we be more precise about the nature of his particular spelling difficulties; can we turn to some teaching strategies which will particularly suit Oliver? Thus, if we go on to see that Oliver has very poor phonic skills, and that this seems to be attributable to poor auditory discrimination and an inability at present to distinguish reliably between the sounds for *b* and *p*, between *m* and *n*, and *f* and *th* we are much nearer to understanding his poor spelling, and thus providing some appropriate teaching activities. Oliver's having a dyslexia label does not, of itself, enable us to do that.

An educational model, which focuses on an individual student's disability as you observe it (semi-regardless of what you call it), and your assessment of how that is a handicapping feature in his life and learning, and leads to some specific strategies being employed on that student's behalf, is more fruitful than just attaching a diagnostic label. Students are children and young people first; attached to them they may have some special educational needs. It is useful to have an accurate name for those needs with regard to each student. However, it is not the most important thing. We may not be qualified to make a diagnosis; we may have to wait for a long time for someone to see the child who can carry out an assessment. But we can use our teacher observation skills to learn about how our students function, and our teacher common sense and knowledge to utilise strategies that might enable them to operate more successfully.

Teachers can do more than they often think. Use strategies such as the ones in this book, and see. Teachers who do so will be able to say, 'I did not do the impossible, but I did all that was possible, and that was more than I thought possible.'

Chapter 9

∂

Food for Thought

Views of a *bon viveur*

A gourmet knows how to peruse a menu: how to make choices, how to sample dishes, how to reflect on them, and how to store that knowledge and experience away for next time. Additionally, although acknowledging always his own personal preferences and tastes, he also heeds the wisdom of other connoisseurs.

It is the same with the teacher choosing and using these strategies.

Although teachers certainly must stick to school policies, teaching guidelines, and the National Curriculum, etc. they can also be proactive in choosing their own strategies for individual students, borne out of their knowing the student, having an awareness of the disability, and a belief that relatively small and simple adaptations may be surprisingly beneficial and, therefore, certainly worth trying. Teachers will feel that this is preferable to continuing in a vacuum in which progress is absent or, indeed, putting up with a situation which is really a downward spiral.

While selecting and implementing their appropriate strategies, teachers will always bear in mind:

- Different students find different support 'acceptable'. For instance, the use of a laptop may be distinctly motivating to many students, and even a status symbol, but could be a source of embarrassment to others, who feel they have been singled out in being told to do their written work on a laptop, whereas they would prefer to struggle to do their written work with pen and paper, just like everyone else. Or, in an unfriendly classroom, they could be the victims of ridicule from other members of the class.

- Rather similarly, teachers will recognise that different students learn in different ways. In choosing their strategies, teachers will always look at things from the point of view of the student's preference, as well as their own. If a student with dyspraxia is 'hopeless with his hands', but reasonably ably to express himself in writing (perhaps on a laptop), it is likely that the teacher will allow him to write an account of the Battle of Hastings, rather than make a model of the battlefield. In choosing a dish, many people have to do the 'does not contain nuts' check to make sure their choice does not provoke an unwelcome reaction. Teachers have to do the educational equivalent in making selections with or for their students.

- Teachers will be proactive rather than reactive. They will not go looking for problems, but they will be ever vigilant for them, and ready to take action. They will not wait for trouble to brew as difficulties accumulate; they will try to head it off almost before it arrives.

- Teachers will appreciate that often, to some degree, disabilities tend not to exist as single entities, in splendid and neat isolation. While it is possible that a student with dyslexia might experience only, say, short-term visual memory problems which 'account' for his dyslexia, it is just as likely that the dyslexia has its roots in more than one 'cause'. Not only that, he may exhibit elements of, say, dyspraxia and ADHD. It just depends on the individual student, and no two are identical.

- So, from whichever perspective teachers start, whether at the outset they see a student as dyslexic, or as dyspraxic, etc., they will be alert to the possibility of at least traces of other disabilities also being present, and of disabilities having an overlap or degree of interrelatedness.

- There is a really pragmatic reason for making this point strongly. It means that there can be a real practical value in looking at every menu in this book, no matter how the teachers primarily view the student. It is entirely possible that they will find in another menu an additional strategy that they think will fit this particular student. For instance, there may well be strategies for supporting students over personal organisation described in the dyspraxia menu that will be useful for some students with dyslexia; there may be pointers in the ADHD menu that are also applicable to a student with dyslexia.

- Being wise people, teachers will not use these strategies to try to change everything at once and immediately. Furthermore, the first thing that they do decide to try to change in their students' learning or behaviour may not be the one that is most in need of changing (i.e. it may not be the most important). It will be the one they think they have the most chance of changing. This is for the sake of the student and the teachers. Once teachers are beginning to see real progress over a reasonable period of time, then they will begin working on another area of need.

- Also, within one target area, teachers will often proceed stage-wise, and not go for the ultimate goal in one fell swoop. For instance, the principal aim may be to have the student sitting still in lessons. But what is 'sitting still'? Rocking the chair is unacceptable, but sitting with the chair legs four-square on the ground, but the student squeezing in his hands a small beanbag may well be acceptable as a positive, interim step.

- Although teachers will most certainly not want to be tardy, they will not attempt to bring about changes in or for their students until they have gained some insight into those students, and the ways in which they are disadvantaged.

- While being highly aware of some students' disabilities, teachers will not merely allow these students, as a consequence, necessarily to avoid subjects or activities because they find them difficult. Teachers will look for ways of encouraging students to find their own ways of coping positively or of 'getting round' the obstacles; this is a very different mind-set and process from just avoiding (dodging) activities. For instance, the student with dyspraxia whose handwriting is irredeemably poor and who is not currently greatly helped by a laptop because of poor keyboard skills could be given extra time and tuition on a word processing or typing program in order to bring about at least a certain amount of progress. This is different from just accepting for ever and a day that this student will only ever be able to produce small amounts of poorly presented work.

- Teachers will avoid making unnecessary allowances for a student (which is patronising). They will maintain appropriate expectations; this will be true of work and behaviour.

- Teachers will remember that a student, despite needs, disability, and handicap, may still have strengths that can be built on; teachers are not wanting to build dependency into their students' psyche.

- Teachers will want to be upsides of their students, who may have devised their own strategies to avoid tasks they know or believe that – because of their disability – they will find difficult. On the whole, though, teachers will try not to be too cross with them about this. They will remember where the students are coming from, and how they see the situation (see later on in this chapter, under 'Empathy'). However, this is not the same as saying students can pick and choose what they do.

- Having chosen a strategy (and stuck with it for a worthwhile period of time), teachers will review it. They will possibly consider it to be successful, and just continue with it. More likely, they will build on it, identifying what in particular it is that seems to be working well, and develop it further.

- Very importantly, they will change what is not working. If this means, after due consideration (and that's an important point – decisions are not best made in a moment of frustration) discarding it completely, they will not be afraid to do this. From time to time, this is almost inevitable, and teachers need not be overly discouraged by the experience.

- In this regard, and many others, teachers will see and feel the value of liaison with other teachers, particularly teachers within their own school. It is to be hoped that this is formalised to some extent within the school's policy on inclusion but, in any event, there is always room for conversations with colleagues. However, teachers will want to give these conversations a framework so that, even with the best will in the world not to allow this to happen, such conversations cannot degenerate into a moaning session.

- Remembering the dining analogy (in the Introduction) when talking with colleagues about preferences (i.e. preferred strategies), good headings for fruitful discussions are likely to be: SENCo involvement; planning and differentiating work; student grouping; peer working; outside agency advice and support; and reviewing and evaluating progress and methods.

- Come what may, teachers will not want to work in isolation, marooned within their own classrooms, so if this sort of contact is not happening within a school's formal development of inclusive practices, individual teachers can initiate it semi-formally (or even informally) with responsive colleagues (and then try to expand this group – inclusion means staff as well as students!).

- A particular point, worthy of a note all of its own, is the sharing of things (strategies) which a teacher has found to work. This can save another teacher a lot of legwork, but it must be remembered that probably the strategy a teacher commends was for that particular teacher working with a particular student. So, it cannot necessarily be said that it will work for other teachers in other circumstances (although there is a likelihood that it will).The reason why it works for one teacher may be something to do with the particular situation, or the particular relationship with the student, or because the teacher strongly identifies with the strategy, that is, she thought about it, decided upon it, and implemented it. There is a dynamic process involved, and a strategy is not a mass-produced, one-size-fits-all commodity. That said, there is great value in colleagues exchanging proven strategies.

Further food for thought
Success and praise

We are back to 'teaching Granny to suck eggs'; we are also emphasising the importance of twin eternal truths of teaching.

For all students with disabilities (all students, actually) the art of enabling them to experience success (and not constant failure) is one of the greatest gifts and attributes that teachers can seek. The success has to be success in the eyes of the student (not the teacher). It has to be meaningful to the student (not synthetic, or manufactured by the teacher). The teacher skills-up the student; the teacher creates the environment in which the success can be achieved; the success may be very small; it may well be that the teacher has to point it out to the student (very important); but it is the student who appreciates the success, and *feels* the success for himself. Success is, then, the greatest reward.

Success and praise are inextricably linked. Where there is success, there should be teacher praise (possibly peer and parental praise, too). There is also an art in finding things to praise, because praise must not be gratuitous. Students generally know the 'value' and merits of what they have produced; they tend to know the level at which they are working. They may well appreciate the intrinsic worth of what they have managed to produce, and realise it is not great, or they may judge it in this light when they look around the room and make comparisons with the other students. It can get very debilitating. So, in most circumstances, teachers will seek to find something good to say about the work, and mostly to be positive. However, this is where the art comes in; in acting in this way, teachers will not want to patronise students by trotting out over-hyped and irrelevant praise in an infantile sing-song tone. Finding that certain something to praise, and linking it with advice and suggestions about how they may be able to improve – there's the art.

Empathy

Teachers who merely feel sorry for their students with disabilities are not much good for them; sympathy does not achieve much in these circumstances. Teachers who empathise with their students are great for them.

Let's move out of the classroom for a moment. Let's visit a rugby match. The forwards win the ball quickly from a scrum. The scrum-half picks the ball up cleanly, gets it away, and sets his backs in motion. The ball is transferred swiftly from hand to hand until it reaches the winger. He has pace – and space. His objective is to use both to arc around the outside of his opposite number. He sets off on a slanting, curving run, trying to outdo his opponent. The crowd sees and knows what he is trying to do; as he swings into action, whole sections of the crowd sway with him, suck in air, and grit their teeth – just like him. That's empathy.

Let's take a more static example. A singing teacher has been tutoring, coaching, and training a student for a soloists' singing competition. They have been practising hard together for hours and weeks in preparation for the few brief minutes of the competition. The day arrives and they travel to the venue. On arrival, after a few brief words, they must part; the student backstage to await his turn to perform, the teacher to the auditorium and to a back seat in the audience. The teacher's stomach is full of knots. The curtain goes up and the spotlight is on his student. As the student sings, the teacher mouths every word and every intonation, he breathes to the rhythm of the song, and, although he does not actually do so, every muscle feels as if he is making every gesture along with his student. At the successful conclusion, he exhales deeply, and experiences a great sense of relief. That's empathy.

Try to put yourself in the student's place; try to see the world, the school, his learning, his behaviour as if you were him. That's demanding. Each student is in a different place, and the teacher has got to try to get in each. No wonder teaching is emotionally draining.

This may lead the teacher to seeing that the dyspraxic student who writes all over the page and not on a single line is not really likely to be trying to wind him up; it is because he can do no better. And what does that feel like? Thus, the teacher will not put him down, and further rupture that self-esteem, without which they are not going to have the inner resources to confront their difficulties, and not merely give up. Instead, they can start working together.

Last morsels

- Nowhere in this book is it claimed that strategies and techniques are being invented, or that a revolutionary, rocket-science approach to the education of students with disabilities will follow in its wake. Rather, many good practices have been collated, and made available, so that teachers can choose which are appropriate for a particular student, in a particular circumstance, at a particular time.

- Thus, in choosing their strategies, teachers are asked to remember that labels which categorise students (dyslexic, ADHD, etc.) are useful but of secondary importance when they are actually considering a real student who is known to them, whom they will be teaching again in the near future. All they are interested in is choosing the right strategy – from wherever. They are thinking not about a dyslexic student, but a student with dyslexia, not an Asperger's student, but a student from within the Asperger Syndrome. They will see the student first, the handicap and his consequent needs second, and the disability third.

- Assessment – a 'diagnosis' of a disability is not a solution; it simply marks the beginning in pointing the way to a solution. In actual practice, there may not be a diagnosis of a student's 'condition' – and it is not absolutely necessary to have one before moving forward – or, at least, making a systematic and sensible attempt to do so (rather than do nothing, or just wait for the 'diagnosis').

- The assessment, and the diagnosis, may not necessarily produce resources, or not immediately. For instance, a student with dyspraxia may be assessed as likely to benefit from an occupational therapist, or a physiotherapist, or a speech and language therapist, but these highly valued people can be in short supply, there might be a long wait. Teachers do not claim to replace these people entirely, but what are they to do? Nothing? We think not.

- However, teachers will not think in terms of 'Can it be cured?' It may well be that 'it' cannot be 'cured' (not many students entirely 'outgrow' their difficulties), but to say, 'It can't be cured' sets the wrong tone, and occupies the wrong mind-set. Teachers will think about easing difficulties, even 'getting around' difficulties – and how to achieve this. They will think about what can be done to alleviate problems to make learning and life that much more easy, better, more enjoyable, less stressful, more fulfilling. They will develop strategies that 'sidestep' problems rather than expect to 'cure' them all.

- Thus, they will wisely learn how and when to promote laptop use instead of handwriting; they will appreciate how a student may be well served by being allowed to highlight sentences in a text rather than produce his own written notes, etc.

- Thinking like this, they will find plenty to work on, and they will often see worthwhile, useful improvements.

- Crucially, teachers will appreciate that students with SENs are, in the vast majority of cases in the inclusive classroom, united with other children by more than that which separates them. Becoming comfortable with this fact will mean that teachers can feel confident and competent to work with these students.

- If teachers say they don't have the time, the resources, the expertise to cope with all the students with disabilities they may meet nowadays in their mainstream classes, they are right – but only up to a point. They are forgetting resources such as this book, they are forgetting what they can do, they are seriously underrating their own skills. They are underestimating not only what can be done, but themselves. They are worth so much more than that.

References

Ainscow, M. (2001) *Developing Inclusive Schools: Implications for Leadership.* Paper prepared for the National College for School Leadership, Nottingham. Available at www. nationalcollege.org.uk/media/1D7/F2/developing-inclusive-schools.pdf, accessed on 7 January 2010.

Asperger, H. (1944) 'Die autischen Psychpathen im Kindesalter.' *Archiv fur Psychiatrie und Nervenkrankheiten 117*, 76–136. English translation in U. Frith (ed.) (1991) *Autism and Asperger Syndrome.* Cambridge: Cambridge University Press.

Asher, J. (2009) 'Gary, suicide bids, and inside the mind of a young man with Asperger's.' *Daily Mail*, 4 July 2009.

Autism Act (2009) Norwich: The Stationery Office.

Automated Readability; Coleman-Liau; Flesch-Kincaid; Gunning-Fog; SMOG readability scoring systems (2008) Available at www.addedbytes.com/code/readability-score.

Auyeung, B., Baron-Cohen, S., Ashwin, E., Knickmeyer, R., Taylor, K. and Hackett, G. (2009) 'Fetal testosterone and autistic traits.' *British Journal of Psychology 100*, 1, 1–22.

Campbell, D. (2009) 'Scientists find genetic clues to how autism can develop.' *The Guardian*, 29 April 2009.

Channel 4 (2005) *Dispatches: The Dyslexia Myth.* 8 September 2005. London: Channel 4.

Conners, K.C. (2008) *Parent and Teacher Rating Scales: Conners* (3rd edition). Newbury: MHS.

Department for Children, Schools and Families (2009a) *Identifying and Teaching Children and Young People with Dyslexia and Literacy Difficulties.* Independent Report by Sir Jim Rose to the Secretary of State. Nottingham: DCSF Publications.

Department for Children, Schools and Families (2009b) *The Lamb Inquiry: Review of SEN and Disability Information.* Independent Report by Brian Lamb to the Secretary of State. Nottingham: DCSF Publications.

Department for Education and Skills (2001) *Special Educational Needs Code of Practice.* Nottingham: DfES Publications.

Department for Education and Skills (2004) *Removing Barriers to Achievement.* Nottingham: DfES Publications.

Department for Education and Skills (2006) *Improving Access for Disabled Students: School Plans in Implementing the Disability Discrimination Act in Schools and Early Years Settings.* Nottingham: DfES Publications.

Department of Health (2009) *Adult Autism Strategy.* London: Department of Health.

Disability Discrimination Act (1995) Norwich: The Stationery Office.

Disability Discrimination Act (2005) Norwich: The Stationery Office.

Disability Discrimination (Amendment) Act (2005) Norwich: The Stationery Office.

Education Act, Part 4, Special Educational Needs Framework (1996) Norwich: The Stationery Office. (See also *Special Educational Needs and Disability Act* 2001.)

Ecker, C., Marquand, A., Mourao-Miranda, J., Johnston, P., Daly, E., Brammer, M., Maltezos, S., Murphy, C., Robertson, D., Williams, S. and Murphy, D. (2010) 'Describing the brain in autism in five dimensions – magnetic resonance imaging-assisted diagnosis using a multi-parameter classification approach.' *Journal of Neuroscience 30*, 32, 10612–10623.

Education and Skills Act (2008) Norwich: The Stationery Office.

Equality Act (2010) Norwich: The Stationery Office.

Frith, U. (ed.) (1991) *Autism and Asperger Syndrome.* Cambridge: Cambridge University Press.

Johnson, K. (1998) *Reading Age (Readability): Results of applying the tests.* Available at www.timetabler.com, accessed 3 August 2010.

Long, M. (2000) *Fry Readability Program.* Available at www.educational-psychologist.co.uk/fry_readabilty_program.htm, accessed on 1 August 2010.

Hakonarson, H. (2009) 'Common genetic variants on 5p14.1 associated with autism spectrum disorders.' *Nature 459*, 528–533.

House of Commons Public Accounts Committee (2009) *Skills for Life: Progress on Improving Adult Literacy and Numeracy.* Third Report of Session 2008–2009. Norwich: The Stationery Office.

Irving, B. and Bloxsom, C. (2002) *Predicting Adolescent Delinquent Behaviour and Criminal Conviction by Age 30.* The Bedford Group for Life Courses and Statistical Studies. London: University of London, Institute of Education.

National Audit Office (2009) *Supporting People with Autism through Adulthood.* Norwich: The Stationery Office.

National Institute for Health and Clinical Excellence (2008) *Attention Deficit Hyperactivity Disorder.* Norwich: TSO NICE.

Ofsted (2000) *Evaluating Educational Inclusion: Guidance for Inspectors and Schools.* Manchester: Ofsted Publications.

Prime Minister's Strategy Unit (2005) *Improving the Life Chances of Disabled People.* London: Cabinet Office.

Qualifications and Curriculum Authority (1999) *Inclusion: Providing Effective Learning Opportunities for All Students* (The National Curriculum Inclusion Statement). Norwich: QCA.

Robinson, M. (ed.) (1996) *Chambers 21st Century Dictionary.* Edinburgh: Chambers.

Siddique, H. (2009) 'Pupil with Asperger's rejected by school.' *The Guardian*, 20 April 2009.

Special Educational Needs and Disability Act (2001) Norwich: The Stationery Office.

Stringer, G. (2009) 'Dyslexia is a myth.' *Manchester Confidential.* 12 January 2009. Available at www.manchesterconfidential.co.uk/Health-and-Beauty/Kids-confidential/Dyslexia-is-a-myth_6402.asp, accessed on 6 July 2010.

Wing, L. (1981) 'Asperger's Syndrome: a clinical account.' *Journal of Psychological Medicine 11*, 1, 115–129.

Wing, L. and Gould, J. (1979) 'Severe impairments of social interaction and associated abnormalities in children: epidemiology and classification.' *Journal of Autism and Childhood Schizophrenia 9*, 1, 11–29.

Woliver, R. (2009) *Alphabet Kids: From ADD to Zellweger Syndrome.* London: Jessica Kingsley Publishers.

Resources

Handwriting

BrightMinds
Suppliers of the 'Handwriting Rescue Pack'.

Wellsway Works
Wells Road
Radstock
Bath
BA3 3RZ
Tel: 0844 41 22249 (customer services)
0844 41 22250 (orders)
Fax: 0800 26 6787
e-mail: info@brightminds.co.uk
Website: www.brightminds.co.uk

Pen and pencil grips, special pens and writing slopes can be obtained from the following suppliers:

LDA Ltd
Pintail Close
Victoria Business Park
Nottingham
NG4 2SG
Tel: 0845 120 4776
Fax: 0800 783 8648
e-mail: enquiries@LDAlearning.com
Website: www.LDAlearning.com

Philip and Tacey Ltd
Johnsonbrook Road
Hyde
Cheshire
SK14 4QT
Tel: 0845 123 7760
Fax: 0800 138 0091
e-mail: sales@philipandtacey.co.uk
Website: www.philipandtacey.co.uk

SoHo Express Ltd
Studio 20
The Arches
Hartland Road
London
NW1 8HR
Tel: 0870 350 4664
Fax: 0870 350 4665

Taskmaster Ltd
Morris Road
Leicester
LE2 6BR
Tel: 0116 270 4286
Fax: 0116 270 6992
e-mail: info@taskmasteronline.co.uk
Website: www.taskmasteronline.co.uk

Books

Hull Learning Services (2005) *Supporting Children with Co-ordination Difficulties*. London: David Fulton Publishers. (Includes much information on dyspraxia besides handwriting.)

Sassoon, R. (2003) *Handwriting: The Way To Teach It*. London: Paul Chapman Publishing.

Sassoon, R. (2006) *Handwriting Problems in the Secondary School*. London: Paul Chapman Publishing.

Manual dexterity

Dycem Ltd
Suppliers of non-slip products, such as stabilising sheets of paper and mats.

Units 2–4
Ashley Trading Estate
Bristol
BS2 9BB
Tel: 0117 955 9921
Fax: 0117 954 1194
e-mail: uk@dycem.com
Website: dycem-ns.com

Taskmaster Ltd
Suppliers of various teaching aids, including adapted scissors. See full contact details above.

Maths

BESTiLEARN
Suppliers of structural materials, such as cuisenaire rods.

9 Castleford Close
Higham Ferrers
Northamptonshire
NN10 8FA
Tel: 01933 355931
e-mail: info@bestilearn.com

Maths Extra Ltd
Suppliers of teaching aids and Stern kits.

3 North Street
Mere
Wiltshire
BA12 6HH
Tel: 01747 861503
Fax: 01747 860882
e-mail: orders@mathsextra.com
Website: www.mathsextra.com

Philip and Tacey Ltd
Suppliers of various educational resources, including unfix. See full contact details on p.259.

Mind Mapping

Mindjet (UK) Ltd
Provide computer software to aid visual organisation, such as MindManager.

100 Great West Road
Brentford
TW8 9HH
Tel: 0845 355 5501 (customer services)
0208 261 8240 (sales)
Website: www.mindjet.com

Books

Buzan, T. (2004) *Mind Maps at Work*. London: HarperCollins.

Buzan, T. (2006) *The Ultimate Book of Mind Maps*. London: Harper Thorsons.

There is also a series of Tony Buzan books, *Mind Maps for Kids*. London: HarperCollins.

Spelling

Franklin UK

Supply a range of electronic portable spelling devices.

Seiko UK Ltd
Franklin Division
SC House
Vanwall Road
Maidenhead
SL6 4UW
Tel: 01628 770 988
Fax: 01628 799 107
Website: www.franklin-uk.co.uk

LDA Ltd

Suppliers of various learning aids, including the ACE Spelling Dictionary. See p.258 for full contact details.

Writing skills

Crick Software

Supply educational software, such as writing grids, for all abilities.

Crick House
Boarden Close
Moulton Park
Northamptonshire
NN3 6LF
Tel: 01604 671 691
Fax: 01604 671 692
Website: www.cricksoft.com

UK contacts

ADD/ADHD
ADDISS ADHD Information Services
Premier House
112 Station Road
Edgware
Middlesex
HA8 7BJ
Tel: 0208 952 2800

Fax: 0208 952 2909
e-mail: info@addiss.co.uk
Website: www.addiss.co.uk

ADDers.org
For ADHD support groups and contacts in many countries.

Website: www.adders.org

AUTISM
Autism Education Trust
393 City Road
London
EC1V 1NG
Tel: 07795 667749
e-mail: info@autismeducationtrust.org.uk
Website: www.autismeducationtrust.org.uk

National Autistic Society
393 City Road
London
EC1V 1NG
Tel: 0845 0704 004 (Helpline)
Fax: 020 7833 9666
e-mail: nas@nas.org.uk

DYSLEXIA
British Dyslexia Association (BDA)
Unit 8
Bracknell Beeches
Old Bracknell Lane
Bracknell
RG12 7BW
Tel: 0845 251 9003
0845 355 5500 (Helpline)
Fax: 0845 251 9005
Website: www.bdadyslexia.org.uk

Dyslexia Action
Park House
Wick Road
Egham
TW20 0HH

Tel: 01784 222 300
Fax: 01784 222 333
e-mail: info@dyslexiaaction.org.uk
Website: www.dyslexiaaction.org.uk

The Dyslexia Specific Learning Difficulties (SpLD) Trust

Unit 8
Bracknell Beeches
Bracknell Lane
Bracknell
RG12 7BW
Tel: 01344 381 562
e-mail: info@thedyslexia-spldtrust.org.uk
Website: www.thedyslexia-spldtrust.org.uk

DYSPRAXIA
Dyspraxia Foundation

8 West Alley
Hitchin
Herts
SG5 1EG
Tel: 01462 454 986 (Helpline)
01462 455 016 (Admin)
Fax: 01462 455 052
e-mail: dyspraxia@ dyspraxiafoundatioin.org.uk
Website: www.dyspraxiafoundation.org.uk

Dyscovery Centre

For information and support with regard to a variety of disabilities.

University of Wales Newport
Alit-yr-yn-Campus
Newport
NP20 5DA
Tel: 01633 432 330
Fax: 01633 432 331
e-mail: dyscoverycentre@newport.ac.uk
Website: www.dyscovery.newport.ac.uk

USA contacts

ADD/ADHD
Attention Deficit Disorder Resources
The National ADHD Directory
223 Tacoma Avenue S #100
Tacoma
WA 98402
Tel: 253 759 5085
Fax: 253 572 3700
e-mail: office@addresources.org
Website: www.add.org

National Resource Center on AD/HD
CHADD
8181 Professional Place
Suite 150
Landover
MD 20785
Tel: 1 800 233 4050
Website: www.help4adhd.org

ASPERGER SYNDROME
US Autism and Asperger Association
PO Box 532
Draper
UT 84020 0532
Tel: 801 816 1234
Website: www.usautism.org

Asperger Awareness
For lists of support groups, etc.

Website: www.aspergerawareness.wordpress.com/supportgroups

DYSLEXIA
The International Dyslexia Association
40 York Road
4th Floor
Baltimore
MD 21204
Tel: 410 296 0232

Fax: 410 321 5069
Website: www.interdys.org

Dyslexia USA
Website: www.dyslexia-usa.com

DYSPRAXIA
Learning Disabilities Association of America
4156 Library Road
Pittsburgh
PA 15234–1349
Tel: 412 341 1515
Fax: 412 344 0224
Website: www.ldanatl.org

Parent-Plus
Website: www.parent-plus.org

Canada contacts

ADD/ADHD
e Mental Health
311 McArthur Avenue
Suite 200
Ottawa
ON K1L 8M3
Tel: 613 738 6990
Fax: 613 738 4891
Website: www.esantementale.ca

The Centre for ADHD Advocacy, Canada (CADDAC)
40 Wynford Drive
Suite 304B
Toronto
ON M3C 1J5
Tel: 416 637 8584
Fax: 416 385 3232
e-mail: michelle.beer@caddac.ca

ASPERGER SYNDROME
Autism Society Canada
Box 22017
1670 Heron Road
Ottawa
ON K1V 0C2
Tel: 613 789 8943
e-mail: info@autismsocietycanada.ca
Website: www.autismsocietycanada.ca

Autism Speaks Canada
Suite 504
1243 Islington Avenue
Toronto
ON M8X 1Y9
Tel: 416 362 6227
Fax: 416 362 6228
e-mail: autismspeakscanada@autismspeaks.org
Website: www.autismspeaks.ca

DYSLEXIA
Canada Dyslexia Association
290 Picton Avenue
Ottawa
ON K17 8P8
Tel: 613 722 2699
Fax: 613 722 7881
e-mail: cda@ottawa.com

Canadian Dyslexia Association
57 rue de Couvert
Gatineau
Quebec
J9H 3C8
Tel: 613 853 6539
Fax: 819 684 0672
e-mail: info@dyslexiaassociation.ca
Website: www.dyslexiaassociation.ca

DYSPRAXIA
Dyspraxia Foundation
C.P. 26024
Sherbrooke
Quebec
J1G 4J9
Tel: 01256 763 443
Fax: 01256 764 492
e-mail: dyspraxia@sympatico.ca

Parent-Plus
Website: www.parent-plus.org

Australia contacts

ADD/ADHD
Every Day With ADHD
PO Box 7789
Cairns
QLD 4870
e-mail: info@everydaywithadhd.com.au
Website: www.everydaywithadhd.com.au

Relationships Australia
15 Napier Close
Deakin
ACT 2600
Tel: 02 6285 4466
Fax: 02 6285 4722
Website: www.relationships.com/au

ASPERGER SYNDROME
Asperger Services Australia
PO Box 159
Virginia
QLD 4014
Tel: 07 3865 2911
Fax: 07 3865 2838
e-mail: office@asperger.asn.au
Website: www.asperger.asn.au

Rural Health Education Foundation
PO Box 324
Curtin
ACT 2605
Tel: 02 6232 5480
Fax: 02 6232 5484
e-mail: rhef@rhef.com.au
Website: www.rhef.com.au

DYSLEXIA
Dyslexia Australia
4–B La Senda Court
Springwood
QLD 4127
Tel: 07 3299 3994
Website: www.dyslexia-australia.com/au

Dyslexia Parents
Website: www.dyslexia/parents.com/australia

DYSPRAXIA
Australian Dyspraxia Association Inc
PO Box 5519
South Windsor
NSW 2756
Tel: 0245 776 220
e-mail: information@dyspraxia.com.au
Website: www.dyspraxia.com/au

Listen and Learn Centre
Level 1
62–66 Whitehorse Road
Balwyn
Victoria 3103
Tel: 03 9816 8811
e-mail: team@listenandlearn.com.au
Website: www.listenandlearn.com.au

Index